"An inspiring addition to the ISPS book
childhood experiences, ethnicity, migration,
it becomes clear how 'toxic interpretations o. ....
least as problematic as those states themselves ... a refreshing antidote to the
stigmatising 'medical model' of human distress that has been so dominant."
Professor John Read, author of *'Models of Madness'* and
'A Straight-Talking Introduction to the Causes of Mental Health Problems'.

"A clearly written, evidence-based account of the contemporary state of
knowledge about the most difficult kind of mental ill-health we have, psychosis. This 'social geography' has for too long been a peripheral focus for
research."
Nick Manning, *Professor of Sociology, ESRC Centre for Society
and Mental Health, King's College, London.*

"This book makes an original contribution of high relevance to clinical
practice, and should be read by anyone wanting to understand how relationships and society, including the mental health system, can help or hinder
mental health recovery."
Mike Slade, *Professor of Mental Health Recovery
and Social Inclusion, University of Nottingham.*

"His erudite, balanced and composed writing is a most important addition to
the growing literature on this most serious of contemporary matters for
western society. This book merits very serious attention from policy makers
and providers of mental health services."
Brian Martindale, *Past President of ISPS.*

TOXIC INTERACTIONS AND THE SOCIAL GEOGRAPHY OF PSYCHOSIS

Toxic Interactions is a consideration of quantitative research revealing how urban living, trauma, ethnicity, stress and familial influences contribute to the risk of troubling psychotic experiences.

Each of these is reviewed in search of their social implications, and a constructivist approach identifies their common threads. The contributions of newer psychotherapeutic approaches such as Open Dialogue and Recovery programmes are considered, and a consistent interpretation emerges; that it is not the observable features of disturbed mental states that deserve key attention, but how these are generally understood by others, and in particular the 'client's' close associates.

This book will be welcomed by all who find conventional approaches to mental health difficulties unsatisfactory, whether that is as a practitioner frustrated by the counter-productive expectations of their institutional setting, an academic exploring different perspectives, a 'service user' disappointed by not experiencing the care they feel is needed, or as third party perplexed by the contradictions of contemporary psychiatry.

Hugh Middleton is a retired medical psychiatrist and university lecturer. His experiences of clinical psychiatry, and social sciences research and teaching have combined to provide a singular perspective. Previous works include: *Understanding Treatment Without Consent* (2007), *Psychiatry Reconsidered* (2015) and *Mental Health Uncertainty and Inevitability* (2017).

THE INTERNATIONAL SOCIETY FOR PSYCHOLOGICAL AND SOCIAL APPROACHES TO PSYCHOSIS BOOK SERIES

Series editor: Anna Lavis

Established over 50 years ago, the International Society for Psychological and Social Approaches to Psychosis (ISPS) has members in more than 20 countries. Central to its ethos is that the perspectives of people with lived experience of psychosis, their families and friends, are key to forging more inclusive understandings of, and therapeutic approaches to, psychosis.

Over its history ISPS has pioneered a growing global recognition of the emotional, socio-cultural, environmental, and structural contexts that underpin the development of psychosis. It has recognised this as an embodied psycho-social experience that must be understood in relation to a person's life history and circumstances. Evidencing a need for interventions in which listening and talking are key ingredients, this understanding has distinct therapeutic possibilities. To this end, ISPS embraces a wide spectrum of approaches, from psychodynamic, systemic, cognitive, and arts therapies, to need-adapted and dialogical approaches, family and group therapies and residential therapeutic communities.

A further ambition of ISPS is to draw together diverse viewpoints on psychosis, fostering discussion and debate across the biomedical and social sciences, as well as humanities. This goal underpins international and national conferences and the journal Psychosis, as well as being key to this book series.

The ISPS book series seeks to capture cutting edge developments in scholarship on psychosis, providing a forum in which authors with different lived and professional experiences can share their work. It showcases a variety of empirical focuses as well as experiential and disciplinary perspectives. The books thereby combine intellectual rigour with accessibility for readers across the ISPS community. We aim for the series to be a resource for mental health professionals, academics, policy makers, and for people whose interest in psychosis stems from personal or family experience.

To support its aim of advancing scholarship in an inclusive and interdisciplinary way, the series benefits from the advice of an editorial board:

Katherine Berry; Sandra Bucci; Marc Calmeyn; Caroline Cupitt; Pamela Fuller; Jim Geekie; Olympia Gianfrancesco; Lee Gunn; Kelley Irmen; Sumeet Jain; Nev Jones; David Kennard; Eleanor Longden; Tanya Luhrmann; Brian Martindale; Andrew Moskowitz; Michael O'Loughlin; Jim van Os; David Shiers.

For more information about this book series visit www.routledge.com/The-International-Society-for-Psychological-and-Social-Approaches-to-Psychosis/book-series/SE0734

For more information about ISPS, email isps@isps.org or visit our website, www.isps.org.

For more information about the journal Psychosis visit www.isps.org/index.php/publications/journal

TOXIC INTERACTIONS AND THE SOCIAL GEOGRAPHY OF PSYCHOSIS

Reflections on the Epidemiology of Mental Disorder

Hugh Middleton

Routledge
Taylor & Francis Group

LONDON AND NEW YORK

Designed cover image: © Getty Images

First published 2024
by Routledge
4 Park Square, Milton Park, Abingdon, Oxon OX14 4RN

and by Routledge
605 Third Avenue, New York, NY 10158

Routledge is an imprint of the Taylor & Francis Group, an informa business

© 2024 Hugh Middleton

British Library Cataloguing in Publication Data
A catalogue record for this book is available from the British Library

Library of Congress Cataloging-in-Publication Data
A catalog record has been requested for this book

ISBN: 978-0-367-18012-6 (hbk)
ISBN: 978-0-367-18013-3 (pbk)
ISBN: 978-0-429-05909-4 (ebk)

DOI: 10.4324/9780429059094

Typeset in Times New Roman
by Taylor & Francis Books

CONTENTS

CONTENTS

INTRODUCTION

[John] Perceval [1803–1876] believed that religious terror had brought on his insanity, and that the behaviour of his family had exacerbated it. But the real cause of the appalling severity and prolongation of his condition was the medico-psychiatric treatment he had received. Perceval unambiguously condemned as intrinsically counter-productive the very philosophy of placing mad people in lunatic asylums. It set the lunatic amongst 'strangers' precisely when he needed to be with his fellows in familiar surroundings. It estranged him from his family. It put him in the charge of an unknown doctor, rather than those members of the caring professions he knew well, his regular physician or his clergyman. It set him in the midst of fellow lunatics, who, if truly mad, must surely be those people least capable of sustaining the mind of one who had just been crushed under a terrible blow. Precisely at the moment when a person needed his morale to be boosted, he was thrown into a situation that must 'degrade him in his own estimation.'

(Porter 1990, pp. 180–181)

It is not difficult to feel that things haven't changed much since Perceval offered this account of his experiences. In 1812 his father, then the British Prime Minister, was assassinated. John was nine at the time, and within two years his mother had remarried. After a troubled adolescence John became sufficiently disturbed for family and friends to consider him 'lunatic', and he went on to spend some four years in first one and then another asylum. After recovery and release in 1834 he lived a relatively settled life for another forty years, during which he married, brought up his own family, and bequeathed a rich account of how he had been treated. As Roy Porter emphasises, a central feature of that is John Perceval's sense of having been misunderstood and misused. Many with experiences of 'being mentally ill' who are alive today would empathise with this. 'Being mentally ill' is not just the experience of uncomfortable, sometimes seriously disturbing thoughts and feelings. It is also the experience of being judged unable, incompetent, unwelcome,

DOI: 10.4324/9780429059094-1

and marginalised as a result. Despite some 200 years of considerable medical advance in many directions, and many well-meaning initiatives, this aspect of 'being mentally ill' has changed very little.

Had medical science been able to achieve as much for mental health difficulties as vaccines, antibiotics and a host of other developments have elsewhere in medicine, then perhaps this would be different, but it has not. All sorts of 'treatments' have been used, some quite brutal, but none as cleanly effective as giving penicillin to someone with pneumonia or insulin to someone with juvenile onset diabetes. Previously these were commonly fatal, but with the discovery of insulin, the emergence of antibiotics and other comparable developments, the last 200 years have seen dramatic changes in the course of many illnesses. Mental health difficulties have not yielded to scientific enquiry in anything like the same way. Recent decades have seen an enthusiasm for viewing them as 'abnormalities of brain chemistry', and this has been accompanied by huge increases in the use of antidepressants, antipsychotics and other psychotropic medicines. However, there is now growing concern about their unwanted effects, risks of dependency, limited efficacy, questions about the quality of research underpinning their development and endorsement, and recognition that viewing mental health difficulties in this way is an unwarranted oversimplification.

The literature expressing such concerns is authoritative, considerable and growing (see, for instance Whitaker 2010; Read and Dillon 2013; Moncrieff 2013; Kinderman 2014; Middleton 2015; Johnstone and Boyle 2018; Harrington 2019; Moncrieff 2020; Timimi 2021; Scull 2022 and Moncrieff et al. 2022). What these variously share is: the view that it is unrealistic to attempt a clear distinction between 'mental health difficulties', and the experiences of everyday life. The former might be more intense, confusing or disabling, but distinctions are more of degree than they are of substance; that neurobiology is intrinsically so complex that it is unrealistic to associate relevant psychological phenomena with identifiable neural pathways or 'brain chemicals', and that one of the most powerful influences upon the progress of an episode of mental health difficulty is the 'patient's' relational environment. Perhaps not everyone would fully agree with all of these but many do to some degree or another. Sadly, their implications conflict with prevailing developed-world service configurations, professional training programmes, the bulk of funded research, and popular media portrayals and public debate. Currently these reflect the view that mental health difficulties can be understood and responded to using the same conceptual framework espoused by medicine as a whole; they reflect distinct and separable conditions, they reflect the consequences of abnormal function within the individual, whether that be conceived of as biologically or as psychologically mediated, and they are best 'treated' by addressing such abnormalities. If mental health difficulties are more accurately recognised as indistinguishable from the turmoil of everyday life only by degree, and not by substance, that a full and sufficient neuroscientific understanding of human behaviour remains a castle in the air, and that it is primarily a person's human relationships that determine how they progress through a difficult patch, then an entirely different framework is called for.

This is not the place to rehearse these arguments in any further detail. Here, they function as a starting point. A reader who is not uncomfortable with the widely prevailing framework; essentially, that mental health difficulties are 'illnesses like any other', and reflect little more than the effects of abnormalities within the individual which are best treated by professionals, might be advised to pause for a moment and consider why that approach could be flawed and potentially harmful. As offered above, there is a rich and varied literature to turn to if that is their choice, or they might choose to suspend belief and enjoy what follows.

For those whose journey has passed the point at which they no longer find it helpful to squash mental health difficulties into a box labelled 'illnesses like any other', another difficulty arises. The journey might have been as one with lived experience of mental health difficulties, as a healthcare practitioner, as an investigator, or as a curious bystander, but whichever that is, they are likely to have encountered resistances to other ways of framing them. The expression 'illnesses like any other' glosses over some important mis-understandings and seductive simplifications. Medical thinking was, and continues to be, profoundly influenced by late nineteenth century develop-ments in microbiology. Micro-organisms, in particular certain bacteria, were found to be implicated in many conditions which had previously been understood in a variety of other ways. The success of this enterprise estab-lished the doctrine of specific aetiology (Dubos 1959, p. 102), and it con-tinues to frame medical thinking. Essentially it is that a medical condition is not formally defined as such until or unless it's cause(s) have been identified. Much of medical practice, thinking and research are organised around this principle, and so the expectation is that when a condition is identified as 'an illness', that also means that it is or can be understood as the result of iden-tifiable causes. This is a misleading simplification, especially when applied to mental health difficulties (Ross 2018). Mental health difficulties are barely if at all understood in this way and addressing them constructively depends upon adopting a more eclectic approach to what might influence their pro-gress. As John Perceval so pointedly described, certain forms of distress and attempts to express and deal with them generate frequently toxic responses on the part of others. These make a considerable contribution to that distress in their own right, whatever the initial 'cause' of that distress might have been. Considering this has a respectable history. Scholarly interest in how someone identified as mentally unwell might be responded to dates back at least to the 1960s (Goffman 1961; Scheff 1966). Both argued that the experience of 'being mentally ill' is significantly influenced by the social position a 'patient' is caused to occupy by the opinions and related practices

3

of those around them. This has been taken up more recently by Ian Hacking (2007).

One of the most, if not *the* most disabling consequences of this process is damaging discrimination. Chapter 1 considers that in more detail, and specifically focuses upon the part played by how 'madness' is generally understood and responded to. There is no shortage of evidence that powerfully toxic practices are at work, resulting in unjustified and defamatory prejudices and stereotyping. Chapter 2 offers some reflections upon how differing opinions concerning the nature and consequences of mental illness may be generated, both from a 'scientific' perspective and more widely. Goffman (1961); Scheff (1966) and Hacking (2007) all focus upon live human interactions as the stage upon which meanings, opinions and related practices are generated and consolidated; broad use of what might otherwise be considered a symbolic interactionist (Blumer 1969) perspective. This is used alongside Bernice Pescosolido's (2011) structured model of healthcare activities to offer a way of understanding how opinions and practices in relation to 'mental illness' might be propagated. There is emphasis here upon the identity and roles of those shaping such opinions and practices.

Recent years have seen the accumulation of considerable, robust, reliable and broadly unquestioned epidemiological research findings concerning mental illness, and in particular, troublesome psychotic experiences. Developing information technology has enabled the collection and analysis of increasingly large and complex sets of data. As a result, there is now little doubt that troublesome psychotic experiences are more likely among those who have suffered adversities in childhood, among those with a family history of troublesome psychotic experiences, among those living in difficult circumstances, among migrants and others living as an ethnic minority, and among those from an urban background. Their effects overlap and different research enterprises have defined them in different ways, but there is little disagreement in the established research community that a variety of socially defined circumstances are associated with an increased risk of troubling psychotic experiences. In several instances; adverse childhood experiences, family history and difficult life circumstances for instance, contemporary research simply confirms historical prejudices such as 'madness runs in families', and 'stressful circumstances can drive you mad'. What is new and can drive future research is that these can no longer be dismissed as mere folklore. Chapters 3–7 summarise this research.

What might it be about a person's background and social circumstances, that influences the risk of being troubled in this way? How might someone's background and social circumstances influence how mental health difficulties are understood and responded to? Chapter 8 considers this through the lens of symbolic interactions that was introduced in Chapter 2, and offers some testable hypotheses with which to explore this perspective. The thesis is that mental health problems are hugely amplified by ways in which they are habitually understood and responded to. Relevant psychiatric epidemiology can be interpreted as offering signals of this. Socially determined variations in risk may reflect differing, socially determined patterns of human interaction, that themselves reflect differing constituencies of understanding and response. Psychotherapeutic approaches all share the aim of influencing how psychological experiences are understood. Thus, the success or otherwise of differing psychotherapeutic approaches offers one, albeit indirect way of evaluating this perspective. Their relative merits are considered in Chapter 9, and appear to argue that addressing how mental health difficulties are understood could be as helpful as attempting to address them directly.

Some reflections on terminology

As a contribution to the *International Society for Psychological and Social Approaches to Psychosis Book Series*, the focus here is mainly upon psychosis, though parallels can be drawn with other forms of mental health difficulty. Psychosis is a broad term that refers to circumstances in which an individual suffers confusing experiences; commonly hearing voices or seeing things that others are not aware of (hallucinations), understanding or interpreting things in ways that others cannot agree with (delusions), or feeling persecuted or misunderstood by others. It is often referred to as an abnormal condition of the mind that results in difficulties determining what is real and what is not, but that definition runs into all sorts of difficulties with defining 'mind', 'difficulties' and 'real', and so it is not uncontested. Nevertheless, what is generally understood as 'psychosis' roughly equates to what in earlier times might have been identified as 'madness' or 'insanity'.

Confusing experiences, hallucinations, misunderstandings or feeling threatened can all occur quite clearly as a result of certain forms of drug intoxication, in the course of a delirium associated with acute physical illness, as a result of brain damage and as a result of certain metabolic disturbances. When it is clear that none of these are present, then the convention is to refer to the disturbance as an instance of functional psychosis. The hallmark experiences of confusion, hallucinations and a sense of being under threat can each take a variety of forms, and can last for between a few days and indefinitely. They may also be accompanied by other disturbing psychological experiences such as despair and despondency, on the one hand, or elation and excitement on the other. The disturbing experiences may focus upon specific individuals or situations, or they may be more generalised. Finally, persistent psychotic experiences can become associated with social withdrawal, poor motivation and related difficulties with self-care and everyday competencies. Thus, functional psychosis can take a variety of forms. In the course of attempting to identify particular forms of functional psychosis that might qualify as discrete 'illnesses', much has been invested in developing diagnostic criteria that allow them to be categorised in agreed ways.

5

These diagnostic criteria are the substance of the American Psychiatric Association's Diagnostic and Statistical Manual, DSM (American Psychiatric Association 2013) and the World Health Organisation's International Classification of Diseases, ICD (World Health Organisation 2022) of which Chapter V refers to Mental and Behavioural Disorders. Frequent references are made to research which has used one or other of these classifications, which have been modified over the years. DSM-III was introduced in 1980, superseded by DSM-IV in 1994 and again by DSM-5, which remains current, in 2013. ICD-8 was introduced in 1968, superseded by ICD-9 in 1979, by ICD-10 in 1994 and by ICD-11 in early 2022.

These systems of classifying functional psychosis distinguish between Schizophrenia, Schizotypal Disorder, Delusional Disorders, Acute or Transient Psychosis and Schizoaffective Disorder. They do this on the basis of 'diagnostic criteria', in other words, exactly which forms of psychotic experience are present, how long they have been present, whether or not they are accompanied by other significant psychological disturbances such as elation or low mood, and how socially disabled the person has become. These classifications by established criteria have become known as 'diagnoses'. It is debatable whether or not this is an appropriate use of that term but that has become common practice, and so when research where that approach has been used is mentioned, reference is made to a 'diagnosis' of Schizophrenia, or another so-defined condition, and to the criteria that research used to arrive at such a 'diagnosis'.

In recent decades it has become clear that less disturbing psychotic experiences are a very common phenomenon, even if they do not fulfil DSM or ICD criteria for one of the defined conditions. In one study, one or another form of psychotic experience was present in more than one in six of the sampled population (Van Os et al. 2001). Thus, the critical question is not necessarily, 'Why does Schizophrenia (or any other psychotic disorder) happen?', but 'Why do one person's psychotic experiences become troublesome and/or disabling, and another's do not?'. For these reasons it seems appropriate to use the more general terms; 'troubling psychotic experiences', or 'psychosis', unless reference is being made to research which has used one of the formal systems of classification. Effectively the two terminologies overlap. In what follows, where 'diagnoses' have been used, this is largely because reference is being made to research based upon hospital records or other sources which have used them. The formal criteria for one or other of the functional psychotic disorders imply, whatever else, 'troubled by confusing experiences, hallucinations, misunderstandings, and/or feeling persecuted or under threat.' Where the expressions 'troubling psychotic experiences' or 'the experience of troublesome psychosis' have been used without reference to formal 'diagnosis', these too refer to being 'troubled by confusing experiences, hallucinations, misunderstandings, and/or feeling persecuted or under threat.'

Literature concerning discriminatory behaviour uses a number of overlapping terms which also deserve clarification. Besides 'discrimination',

6

scholarly approaches variously use the terms 'stigma', 'label', 'stereotype' and 'prejudice'. Strictly speaking, 'stigma' refers to the recognisable feature that marks someone out as distinct from others, a 'label' is the category a person might be assigned to within an agreed set of classifications, 'stereotype' refers to a set of generalisations commonly applied to a particular grouping of people and 'prejudice' refers to a (usually derogatory) judgement against others based upon superficially evaluated characteristics. 'Discrimination' is what happens if any of these are in play, and their practical implications are so overlapping that these finer distinctions are frequently overlooked. In particular, in relation to mental health difficulties 'stigma' seems to have drifted away from its original use in relation to an identifying mark or feature towards equivalence with 'stereotype' and 'prejudice' (Mental Health Foundation 2022), perhaps because these already have established places in social science, and the languages of marketing and race relations respectively. For these reasons 'stigma', 'stereotype' and 'prejudice' have been used somewhat interchangeably in Chapter 1, and wherever else the concepts are discussed. In relation to mental health difficulties 'label' tends to refer to the application of a 'diagnosis' or some other explicit and externally applied classification, and that has been respected where possible. 'Discrimination' is held to its general use as a reference to what happens when any of these influence others' behaviour.

References

American Psychiatric Association (2013) *Diagnostic and Statistical Manual of Mental Disorders*. Fifth Edition. Arlington, VA: American Psychiatric Publishing.

Blumer, H. (1969) *Symbolic Interactionism. Perspective and Method*. Berkeley and Los Angeles: University of California Press.

Dubos, R. (1959) *Mirage of health: utopias, progress, and biological change*. New Brunswick: Rutgers University Press.

Goffman, E. (1961) *Asylums: Essays on the Condition of the Social Situation of Mental Patients and Other Inmates*. Garden City, NY: Anchor Books.

Hacking, I. (2007) 'Kinds of People: Moving Targets', *Proceedings of the British Academy*, Vol. 151, pp. 285–318.

Harrington, A. (2019) *Mind Fixers. Psychiatry's Troubled Search for the Biology of Mental Illness*. London: Norton and Company.

Johnstone, L., Boyle, M. with Cromby, J., Dillon, J., Harper, D., Kinderman, P., Longden, E., Pilgrim, D. and Read, J. (2018) *The Power Threat Meaning Framework: Towards the identification of patterns in emotional distress, unusual experiences and troubled or troubling behaviour, as an alternative to functional psychiatric diagnosis*. Leicester: British Psychological Society.

Kinderman, P. (2014) *A Prescription for Psychiatry: Why We Need a Whole New Approach to Mental Health and Wellbeing*. Basingstoke: Palgrave.

Mental Health Foundation (2022) 'Stigma and discrimination'. https://www.mentalhealth.org.uk/explore-mental-health/a-z-topics/stigma-and-discrimination. (accessed November 2022).

Middleton, H. (2015) *Psychiatry Reconsidered. From Medical Treatment to Supportive Understanding*. Basingstoke: Palgrave Macmillan.

Moncrieff, J. (2013) *The Bitterest Pills. The Troubling Story of Antipsychotic Drugs*. Basingstoke: Palgrave Macmillan.

Moncrieff, J. (2020) '"It Was the Brain Tumor That Done It!" Szasz and Wittgenstein on the Importance of Distinguishing Disease from Behavior and Implications for the Nature of Mental Disorder', *Philosophy, Psychiatry, & Psychology*, Vol. 27, No. 2, doi:10.1353/ppp.0.0023.

Moncrieff, J., Cooper, R. E., Stockmann, T., Amendola, S., Hengartner, M. P. and Horowitz, M. A. (2022) 'The serotonin theory of depression: a systematic umbrella review of the evidence', *Molecular Psychiatry*. doi:10.1038/s41380–41022–01661–0.

Pescosolido, B. A. (2011) 'Organising the Sociological Landscape for the next decades of health and health care research: The Network Episode Model III-R as Cartographic Subfield Guide'. In B. A. Pescosolido, J. K. Martin, J. D. McLeod and A. Rogers (Eds.) *Handbook of the Sociology of Health, Illness and Healing*. New York: Springer, pp. 39–66.

Porter, R. (1990) *A Social History of Madness*. New York: E. P. Dutton.

Read, J. and Dillon, J. (2013) *Models of Madness*. Second Edition. Hove: Routledge.

Ross, L.N. (2018) 'The doctrine of specific etiology', *Biology & Philosophy*, doi:10.1007/s10539–10018–9647-x

Scheff, T. J. (1966) *Being Mentally Ill. A Sociological Theory*. London: Weidenfeld and Nicholson.

Scull, A. (2022) *Desperate Remedies: Psychiatry and the Mysteries of Mental Illness*. London: Allen Lane.

Timimi, S. (2021) *Insane Medicine. How the Mental Health Industry Creates Damaging Treatment Traps and How you can Escape Them*. London: Independently published.

Van Os, J., Hanssen, M., Bijl, R. V. and Vollebergh, W. (2001) 'Prevalence of Psychotic Disorder and Community Level of Psychotic Symptoms', *Archives of General Psychiatry*, Vol. 58, pp. 663–668.

Whitaker, R. (2010) *Anatomy of an epidemic: Magic bullets, psychiatric drugs, and the astonishing rise of mental illness in America*. New York: Crown Publishers/ Random House.

World Health Organisation (2022) *International Classification of Diseases*. Eleventh Edition. Geneva: World Health Organisation.

1

SPOILED IDENTITY

One of the most distressing features of being someone who is troubled by psychotic experiences is how others respond. To be identified as someone with a mental illness is among the most disabling and life-changing events one might encounter. It may not seem that way to begin with. A 'diagnosis', a label, might initially provide a reassuring explanation of unwelcome and disturbing voices, strange beliefs, seemingly unshakeable misery or immobilising fears, but as time passes the limitations imposed by being assigned the identity of 'someone with a mental disorder' commonly become more damaging and restrictive than the experiences that led to the label in the first place. In one study (Rüsch et al. 2015), young people considered to be at high risk of developing 'Schizophrenia' were more likely to develop the condition if they perceived themselves as harmfully stigmatised. In another (Dubreucq et al. 2021), worsened clinical outcomes were associated with higher levels of experienced stigma.

There are many personal testimonies. Here is an example:

> For me, the scene has been repeated in many different settings: a supervisor who viewed my work and abilities as outstanding and my rate of productivity as very high before my illness, but who recommended disability retirement when I was depressed and less productive; a university that graduated me with high honours, admitted me into its graduate program with outstanding recommendations, and then sent me a form letter in response to my request for readmission (following my illness) saying, 'You do not meet our admission requirements'; and community mental health agencies that rejected my offers to be of assistance because I 'scared' mental health professionals.
>
> (Anonymous 1980, p. 546)

Relationships may be compromised, occupational opportunities can be damaged and there are myriad other ways in which lives are tainted and limited by the social consequences of being identified as someone suffering

DOI: 10.4324/9780429059094-2

with 'mental illness'. The issue is as old as humankind itself, and in one form or another discrimination against 'mad' people can be found wherever it has been sought (Cohen et al. 2016; Thornicroft et al. 2009). Indeed, social exclusion can be considered one of the defining features of 'being mad'. To emphasise this well-rehearsed point, here are some examples of published formal research and personal accounts that illustrate how deeply ingrained discrimination against people identified as suffering 'mental illness' is across all aspects of life.

Family, neighbors, and housing

Developing mental health difficulties, and particularly troubling psychotic experiences, has a profound effect upon family life. As a loved one begins to behave in an unfamiliar and even incomprehensible way, everyday routines become disrupted. This commonly becomes apparent in the neighborhood however hard a family might attempt to hide what is happening, and prejudicial reactions emerge. One survey (Struening et al. 2001) involving 461 caregivers in New York City explored experiences of these reactions as responses to statements beginning 'Most people …'; 391 (84%) agreed with the statement 'Most people look down on someone who once was a patient in a mental hospital.'. More than half agreed with 'Most people would not accept a person who once had a serious mental illness as a close friend.', and more than half agreed with 'Most people would rather not visit families that have a member who is mentally ill.', with 'Most people do not treat families with a member who is mentally ill in the same way they treat other families.' and with 'Most people feel that having a mental illness is worse than being addicted to drugs.'.

These neighborhood reactions also find expression in the readiness, or otherwise, with which people with a reputation of prior mental health difficulties might be accepted as local residents. During latter decades of the twentieth century significant numbers of people were moved from institutional care into smaller group homes, located alongside regular housing. These moves were commonly resisted by local residents. One investigation of this process was conducted in Montreal, Canada (Piat 2000). This was an attempt to understand community objections to such developments, and the most commonly encountered objection was that it was mistaken to argue in favor of deinstitutionalisation in the first place. One quote is particularly illustrative: 'They're not able to function. They don't function. They always have to be supervised. I'd say they're not able to live alone in an apartment, even if they've lived in this group home for years' (ibid, p. 133). The evidence, of course, is that most people who would otherwise be confined to an institution fare better in more naturalistic, community settings and many thrive (Chilvers et al. 2006). In England such resistance has also been associated with concerns for the market value of adjacent housing, something which had to result in a judicial ruling that 'public interest' outweighed such concerns (Thornicroft and Halpern 1993). Finally, a high proportion of adults with a 'diagnosis' of Schizophrenia have living arrangements that suggest something other than a household of their own making. Of 404 individuals identified across five European cities at the turn of the century, 278 (69%) were either living alone or with relatives, as opposed to living with a spouse or with others (Thornicroft et al. 2004).

Friendships, intimate relationships, and childcare

That a high proportion of individuals with a 'diagnosis' of Schizophrenia live alone or with relatives, might also reflect difficulties in forming and sustaining close relationships. Formal enquiry has established that people with so-called 'Serious Mental Illness' (SMI) have significantly smaller social networks than their peers. Koenders and colleagues (2017) compared social network size and relationship satisfaction of 211 Dutch SMI 'patients' with those of 949 control subjects. Social network size and composition were measured using the Social Network Questionnaire (Duurkoop 1991) which estimates the number of social contacts with friends, family members and acquaintances over a period of one month. Satisfaction with social relationships was recorded as answers to 'How satisfied are you with your social relationships?' rated on a seven-point scale from 'Very satisfied' to 'Very unsatisfied'. Among the SMI 'patients' there was an average of 4.75 contacts with family members, 2.78 with friends and 16.8 with acquaintances during a month, which contrasted with 10.45 family contacts, 8.63 contacts with friends and 45.56 contacts with acquaintances among the control subjects. Furthermore, satisfaction with social relationships was significantly higher among the control subjects. These differences could be attributed to the *effects* of SMI but the interaction is two-way, as illustrated by quotes collected in the course of more qualitative investigations, such as: 'Sometimes they don't understand. They don't understand, but they're still my friends. But sometimes it gets frustrating to talk, sometimes, because they don't understand' (Boydell et al. 2002, p. 128). Experiences such as these illustrate how expectations of social rejection may hinder the readiness with which friendships can be freely pursued.

In the arena of sexual relationships, marriage and parenthood a more complex picture emerges. There is evidence of risky sexual activity, enhanced rates of sexually transmitted disease, higher rates of promiscuity, lower rates of responsible contraception and sexual exploitation among those with mental health difficulties (Coverdale et al. 1997; Ramrakha et al. 2000). Possibly as a result, there is considerable ambivalence amongst mental health practitioners over the desirability of intimate relationships between psychiatric in-patients, despite human rights issues over attempting to prevent them (Ford et al. 2003). Once again, the reciprocity of these interactions and their associations with expectations of rejection is illustrated by a quote:

11

As a single person, it's very difficult to broach the subject of mental illness if you have just met someone you like. I've met people who have their own illness problems, and whilst they understand my difficulties better, now we find there's two sets of problems lurking, and a feeling that things could be very difficult if we both became ill. I find it hard to tolerate illness in a girl I've just met, so I know that people will find it hard to tolerate it in me.

(Thornicroft 2006, p. 34)

As far as childcare is concerned, there is evidence that women with SMI are at an enhanced risk of losing custody of their children (Howard 2005) but whether or not this is because of discrimination or because perceptions of the children's interests are being prioritised is unclear. However, there is some evidence of reluctance to provide enhanced support to mothers with mental health difficulties who might benefit from it (Craig & Bromet 2004), suggesting prejudice against them.

Discrimination in the workplace

Such prejudices extend into the workplace. There is consistent evidence that people who have, or who are, experiencing psychosis are less likely to be in competitive, paid work than the general population or even those with physical disability. Marwaha and Johnson (2004) identified twenty-seven studies that had reported rates of employment amongst those with a 'diagnosis' of Schizophrenia between 1958 and 2001. Most of these were from the UK, Europe and the USA but there had also been reports from Australia, India, Nigeria, Russia, Columbia and Taiwan. Among the later British, European, American and Australian studies employment rates ranged from 4% to 35%. Earlier reports, of data collected before 1990 tended to report higher rates as did reports from Russia and from less industrialised countries. Three British sites were able to provide data from two time points which revealed a fall in rates of employment amongst those with a 'diagnosis' of Schizophrenia between the 1980s and the 2000s. Aggregating all the British data suggested that rates of employment among 'patients' fell from around 40% in the 1960s to around 5% at the turn of the century. There are difficulties with these figures, not least of which are changes in formal policy towards people experiencing psychosis such as the provision of supported work for those coming to the end of long periods of institutionalisation, but they compare quite starkly with rates of 75%–80% among the general population over the same time. More recent data, from the 1966 Northern Finland Birth Cohort, give no reason to believe this has changed (Majuri et al. 2022).

Whether or not low rates of employment among those experiencing psychosis reflect prejudice, or possibly justifiable concerns over competence and reliability, is difficult to prove conclusively but the former seems the most likely explanation. In 2002, the Mental Health Foundation reported a survey of some 400 people with experiences of mental health difficulty. Findings included more than half of them believing they had been turned down for a job because of their record of having suffered mental health difficulties, and two-thirds feeling uneasy about disclosing such experiences in the course of a job application. A quarter felt that too much account was taken of their difficulties, and that they felt more patronised and more closely monitored than their colleagues; 15% believed that they had been passed over for promotion because of their difficulties, 10% believed that work colleagues had made sarcastic comments or avoided them and a third believed that bullying at work had added to their problems (Mental Health Foundation 2002).

Discriminatory health care

It is well established that individuals with a 'diagnosis' of Schizophrenia or other troubling experiences of psychosis have a reduced life expectancy. One review of the published literature estimated this to be some thirteen to fifteen years of potential life lost (Hjorthøj et al. 2017), with men more noticeably affected. Putative causes include higher rates of cardiovascular disease and diabetes (Laursen et al. 2012), tobacco smoking (Lasser et al. 2000), alcohol and illicit drug misuse (Toftdahl et al. 2016), sedentary lifestyle (Stubbs et al. 2016), poor dietary habits (Dipasquale et al. 2013), and the toxic effects of psychotropic medication (Young et al. 2016), but there are also reports of discriminatory behavior on the part of health care practitioners. One report from Quebec revealed poor access to general practitioners among individuals identified as suffering 'Severe Mental Illness', with a significant proportion relying upon psychiatrists or case workers without direct access to specialised medical advice and facilities (Fleury et al. 2010). From other sources there is evidence that when compared with the general population, such individuals have lower rates of surgical coronary re-vascularization (Druss et al. 2000), lower rates of guideline-consistent treatment for ischaemic heart disease (Kisely et al. 2009), less frequent admissions to hospital for diabetes (Sullivan et al. 2006), and poorer attention to basic assessments such as blood pressure measurement (Roberts et al. 2007).

A reason for this might be what has been described as 'diagnostic overshadowing', whereby patients' symptoms are interpreted differently when there is a background of mental health problems (Jones et al. 2008). With this is mind van Nieuwenhuizen and colleagues (2013) conducted a series of interviews with emergency department clinicians which confirmed often unconsciously mediated discriminatory practices:

> Once you have been labelled as having a psychiatric illness, it's very difficult to put that label to one side and to try essentially to deal with what you have in front of you.
>
> Junior doctor

If you presume the worst, presume that there is a real condition until you know that there isn't then you are much safer, but I know not everybody does that – people do make judgements – they shouldn't, but they do sometimes.

Senior nurse

Sometimes this can have fatal results:

She was discharged and then returned in less than 24 hours... and she actually didn't survive as a result of that... the decision was that her behaviour seemed compatible with the pre-existing mental health problem and therefore there was no need to investigate, it wouldn't have revealed anything, or wasn't expected to reveal anything untoward.

Senior doctor

In a complementary study Corrigan and colleagues (2014) considered the responses of 166 health care providers to a vignette describing a thirty-four-year-old male with 'Schizophrenia' and multiple other health problems including hypertension, obesity, disturbed sleep, and chronic low back pain attributed to arthritis. Current medications included Naproxen (500 mg twice a day for pain). He had reported finishing a Naproxen prescription for the month in twenty-five days and was wanting to have his prescription renewed early. Respondents also completed questionnaires assessing their comfort with mental health difficulties and attitudes to them (Olmsted and Durham 1976). They were asked to rate the 'patient' on the basis of personal qualities such as valuable–worthless, dirty–clean, and safe–dangerous, and whether or not he could be expected to 'adhere to medications', 'keep regular appointments' and 'renew his prescription on time'. Perhaps unsurprisingly there were strong associations between measures of discomfort with mental health difficulties, measures of stigmatising attitudes to people with them and judgements about the 'patient's' reliability and how best to provide treatment. Although it would be an extrapolation beyond available evidence to suggest that the undeniable excess mortality among people with experiences of psychosis is entirely due to discrimination in healthcare settings, there is evidence that such discrimination does occur, and that it can have adverse consequences.

Media portrayals

Widespread and reflexive judgement of people identified as suffering mental health difficulties; stereotyping, also extends into media portrayals. A study of newspaper items reporting on mental 'illness' that was conducted in New Zealand found that more than half depicted the mentally 'ill' person as dangerous; specifically, a physical danger to others, potentially criminal, unpredictable and/or a danger to themselves (Coverdale et al. 2002), and similar findings have emerged in the United States (Corrigan et al. 2005). In the UK, a survey of relevant headlines from nine daily newspapers revealed contrasting tones between those that referred to psychiatric disorders and those that referred to other aspects of medical practice. The former were significantly more critical than the latter. Furthermore, headlines referring to psychiatric disorders tended to be critical of 'patients', whereas critical headlines referring to other types of condition tended to be critical of practitioners (Lawrie 2000).

Reviews of television content are little different. In one content analysis of television characters, fictitious or otherwise, the portrayal of persons with mental disorders (largely portrayals of people with troubling experiences of psychosis) was highly correlated with the portrayal of violence. Overall, depictions of the mentally ill presented them as nearly ten times more likely to be violent than the general population of television characters. Furthermore, these rates were far higher than population and conviction rates would predict (Diefenbach 1997). Unsurprisingly, the media have a propensity to exaggerate risks associated with the occurrence of troubling psychotic experiences for dramatic purposes, and this feeds into more widely applicable concerns. Another investigation considered the relationship between watching television and reading the newspaper on the one hand, and the desire for social distance towards people with a diagnosis of 'Schizophrenia' on the other (Angermeyer et al. 2005). Using a fully structured personal interview, the investigators found that the desire for social distance from people with 'Schizophrenia' increases in line with the time spent watching television. The association between reading the newspaper and social distance was less pronounced and depended on the type of newspaper read. Given the adversely distorted portrayal of experiencing psychosis television and tabloid newspapers offer, this association between exposure to them and a desire to distance from people experiencing psychosis can, perhaps, be understood as a direct and harmful consequence of those portrayals.

Owen (2012) analysed the portrayal of 'Schizophrenia' in contemporary films. Forty-two characters from forty-one films were identified. Most displayed positive symptoms; delusions most commonly, followed by auditory and visual hallucinations. A majority displayed violent behavior, and nearly one-third of these were homicidal. A quarter committed suicide. Buday and colleagues (2022) have extended this into the world of video games, which are widely used by young people. They explored the best-selling video games released between 2002 and 2021, and came to the conclusion that around one in ten attempted to portray some symptoms of mental illness, largely in a negative and stereotyped way.

As is the case in relation to many other aspects of public discourse, newspapers, broadcast media and more recently social media deliberately attract attention (largely for reasons of advertising revenue) by appealing to pre-existing prejudices. This is generally achieved by confirming and dramatizing them, whereas the welfare of those experiencing psychosis might be better served by closer attention to the harms caused by unwarranted scaremongering.

Institutionalised discrimination

All of the above reflect the fact that people considered to be experiencing mental health difficulties, and in particular people known to be suffering troublesome psychotic experiences, are victims of discrimination across many domains of life, and suffer as a result. Indeed, for many the experiences of discrimination are as disabling, if not more so, than the direct effects of the 'mental illness' they might be experiencing. Apart from the emergent effects of discrimination upon relationships, housing, and employment, this also extends into formalised restrictions. Many who experience psychosis also experience limitations on their freedom to hold a driving licence. Sometimes this might be appropriate on the grounds of safety, but there appears to be inconsistent practice among psychiatrists when this issue is raised in the clinic (Wise and Watson 2001). Current UK legislation requires someone who has experienced troubling psychosis to have remained well and stable for at least three months, to be adhering to an agreed treatment plan and to be free from any medication effects that would impair driving. There is some evidence that the sedative effects of anti-psychotic medication wear off after the first few weeks (Brunnauer et al. 2021), but a judgement about such impairment is usually in the doctor's hands. Public opinion appears to be more restrictive.

Suffering a 'mental disorder' can be a reason for not being eligible for entry into the United States: 'Travelers to the United States who have been afflicted with a disease of public health significance, a mental disorder which is associated with a display of harmful behavior, or are a drug abuser or addict may be ineligible to receive a visa' (United States London Embassy 2022). Travel insurance may be difficult to obtain, or more costly, and for a variety of reasons which can include discrimination in the workplace, people seriously afflicted by mental 'illness' tend towards the lower end of the income spectrum; are three times more likely to be in debt and twice as likely to have difficulties managing their finances as the general population (Meltzer et al. 2000). In 1989 all of the fifty United States applied restrictions upon one or more of; jury service, voting, public office, parental and marriage rights. Ten years later the survey was repeated and there was no evidence of liberalisation, indeed legislation had become more restrictive (Hemmens et al. 2002). In Russia the status of 'legally incapacitated' which is commonly applied to those 'diagnosed' with serious mental illness means losing the right to manage property, choosing where to live, signing contracts, renting an apartment, being employed, voting in elections, marrying, or seeking judicial redress. In England, anyone who was suffering from a mental disorder, and on account of that was either resident in a hospital or a similar institution, or regularly attending for medical treatment was ineligible for jury service until 2013 (Mental Health Law Online 2022). This was a blanket, stereotypic restriction, in contrast to the eligibility of persons with physical disabilities, which is considered on a case-by-case basis by the judge concerned.

At the level of formal aspiration these injustices are recognised, and there are well meaning clauses in formal declarations such as the Universal Declaration of Human Rights (United Nations General Assembly 1948), the UN Principles for the Protection of Persons with Mental Illness (United Nations General Assembly 1991), the European Convention on Human Rights (European Court of Human Rights 1970, et seq.) and the English Human Rights Act (Equality and Human Rights Commission 1998). Unfortunately, these have yet to find full expression in everyday behavior and attitudes. Interviews with those attending community and day care facilities in North London revealed that about half had experienced verbal or physical abuse in public places, and the proportion was much higher among those who experienced psychosis (Dinos et al. 2004). A study of some 300 people in North Carolina found that people with a history of mental illness were two-and-a-half times more likely to be the victim of a violent crime than members of the general population (Hiday et al. 1999), and that has not changed over more recent years (Khalifeh et al. 2015). Despite a range of good intentions, people experiencing psychosis continue to suffer discrimination across a variety of settings in ways that can only be understood as 'institutional', and with significant consequences. One review (Hatzenbuehler 2016) found evidence that levels of institutional discrimination against people with 'mental illness' measurably enhance psychological reactions to it such as concealment and rejection sensitivity, impair the effectiveness of psychological interventions and contribute to adverse health outcomes.

Wounded identity

In *Stigma: Notes on the Management of Spoiled Identity*, Erving Goffman wrote:

> When the stranger is present before us, evidence can arise of his possessing an attribute that makes him different from others. ... and of a less desirable kind—in the extreme, a person who is quite thoroughly bad, or dangerous, or weak. He is thus reduced in our minds from a whole and usual person to a tainted, discounted one.
>
> (Goffman 1963, pp. 2–3)

17

Others' views and actions are contagious, and so it is hardly surprising that widespread and deeply entrenched discriminatory attitudes and approaches to people with mental health difficulties may influence how they see themselves. Social identity can be understood as the sense made of interactions with the social environment. 'Where do I fit in?' 'Whom can I trust and to what extent?' 'Will this or that approach to others succeed?' 'What, and how humiliating, would be the risk of rejection were I to ask that person out on a date?' Answers to these and related questions influence choices about who to mix with, and where to do it, about which jobs to apply for, about where to live and about how to invest time and energy. Experiencing the social environment as hostile, discriminatory and rejecting inevitably results in a sense of 'Who I am' that is limited, limiting and constrained. This is true for all who experience discrimination, whether it be on account of race, gender, sexual orientation, religious affiliation or for other reasons. There is awareness of these injustices in many contexts, and in many of them, interest in addressing them, but the limiting effects of discrimination against people with mental health difficulties remain obdurate and difficult to address with any noticeable success.

Overarching concepts such as self-esteem and locus of control have been used to explore this area quantitatively. Self-esteem is commonly quantified on the basis of responses to the Rosenberg Self Esteem Scale (Rosenberg 1989) which is a ten-item scale of items such as 'On the whole I am satisfied with myself', 'I feel that I have a number of good qualities' or 'All in all, I am inclined to think that I am a failure (scored negatively)'. Locus of control, also conceived of as self-agency or the subjective awareness of initiating, executing and controlling chosen actions, is commonly quantified on the basis of responses to Rotter's Internal versus External Control of Reinforcement Scale (Rotter 1966). Here respondents are asked to choose between contrasting statements such as 'Becoming a success is a matter of hard work, luck has little or nothing to do with it' and 'Getting a good job depends mainly on being in the right place at the right time', or 'No matter how hard you try some people just don't like you' and 'People who can't get others to like them don't understand how to get along with others'. Ciufolini and colleagues (2015) compared responses to these scales by 257 people troubled by psychotic experiences, with those of 341 closely matched control subjects. Self-esteem was lower and locus of control more 'external' (in other words, less personal control over their lives) amongst those with experiences of psychosis than amongst the control subjects.

MacDougall and colleagues (2016) explored the relationships between self-esteem and measures of Perceived Relational Evaluation, Social Dominance and Self-Stigma. Their Perceived Relational Evaluation Scale assessed participants' perceptions of the extent to which they were valued by others on the basis of responses to items exploring how much they felt family, friends, acquaintances and others valued them. Social Dominance was quantified using a scale in which respondents compared themselves to others in terms of six relevant adjective-anchored items such as; dominant ... timid, assertive ... submissive, strong ... weak. Self-Stigma was measured in terms of responses to 'self-concurrence' items of the Self-Stigma of Mental Illness Scale (Corrigan et al. 2006), which assess the degree to which negative stereotypes about people with serious mental illness are felt to apply to the respondent. Examples are responses to 'Because I am being treated at [name of the facility] for a mental illness' ... 'I am below average intelligence', 'I am dangerous' and so on.

One hundred and two people with troublesome experiences of psychosis provided their responses. Interestingly, self-esteem was not associated with these measures of self-stigma, but it was associated with the measures of relational evaluation and social dominance. These data suggest that it is not the experience of stigma *per se* that influences self-esteem, but whether or not, in that individual, it has led to experiences of social disadvantage and/or unsatisfactory experiences of relational evaluation. These might be more direct indices of social well-being. It would seem that the adverse effects of discrimination upon self-image (in this context, at least) are not so much a reflection of an awareness of discriminatory attitudes, but more a reflection of experiences of discriminatory actions. Understandably actions are likely experienced as more authentic reflections of others' evaluations than an awareness of their (possible) views, and therefore have greater impact.

Illness like any other ...?

This divergence between expressed, or more likely *partially suppressed* discriminatory attitudes towards those with mental health difficulties and their real-life experiences can be seen playing out in at least two contexts.

The first is what emerges when mental health professionals' attitudes to their clients are considered. Valery and Prouteau (2020) conducted a review of thirty-eight publications addressing this topic. Overall, they revealed significant negative beliefs and attitudes, and a desire for social distance in relation to all with mental health difficulties, and particularly in relation to those troubled by psychotic experiences. Several of the studies reported mental health practitioners consciously using such strategies as a defence against becoming too emotionally involved with their clients' suffering in order to avoid emotional exhaustion and burnout. This is understandable, but poignantly illustrated from the client's perspective in Neely Myers' detailed ethnography of an American day centre (Myers 2015), where peer support workers had been employed, precisely in order to address such problems. The aim was to overcome barriers to authentic, reciprocal relationships between 'staff' and 'clients'. The experience was that numerous institutional imperatives such as time constraints, cleanliness, paperwork,

19

organisational management and an evolving hierarchy undermined this and led to many disappointments. Setting provision for people experiencing psychosis (and other forms of mental health difficulty) within an institutional setting that is still, however broadly, seen as 'medical' inevitably constrains the extent to which its activities can separate from that tradition.

The second is what has emerged in relation to well-meaning attempts to address stigmatising attitudes to mental health difficulties in the wider population. Across the whole range of health problems, stigmatising attitudes and behavior are clearly more apparent in relation to mental health difficulties. Thus, one approach to that has been an attempt to re-frame mental health difficulties as 'illnesses like any other', such as that promoted by the Schizophrenia and Psychosis Action Alliance which proclaims that 'Schizophrenia is a treatable brain disease and should be treated like any other neurological illness' (Schizophrenia and Psychosis Action Alliance 2022). In the long run this may be counter-productive. Framing mental health difficulties as illnesses like any other legitimises the view that they can be construed in biomedical terms and treated accordingly. Indeed, recent years' enthusiasm for widening the range of what may or may not be identified as a mental health problem have not been associated with a parallel enthusiasm to widen the availability of talking therapies among healthcare providers, but it has been associated with continuing increases in the rates at which psychotropic medications are being prescribed for an increasingly wide range of indications (Shoham et al. 2021), consolidating the view that an increasingly wide range of unwanted mental states can be usefully construed as a biomedical disorder. Unfortunately, the research findings are that biomedical constructions of mental health difficulties, and in particular the troublesome experience of psychosis are associated with more, rather than less intensely stigmatising attitudes and behavior.

Angermeyer and colleagues (2011) identified thirty-three studies reporting attitudes towards people with mental illness and beliefs about those disorders. Biogenic, in other words inherited, abnormal brain chemistry or other biomedical explanations for the disorder were *not* associated with more tolerant attitudes and indeed were associated with less tolerant attitudes in those studies reporting attitudes towards people troubled by psychotic experiences. Larkings and Brown (2017) have reviewed similar, more recent literature and conclude with similar findings. Pescosolido and colleagues (2010) considered changes across time. Members of the general public rated their views of psychosis, depression or alcohol dependence on the basis of case vignettes in 1996 and in 2006. Respondents were asked whether they felt the vignette described someone who was experiencing 'a mental illness' and/ or 'the normal ups and downs of life', and whether they felt the condition was due to 'a genetic or inherited problem', a 'chemical imbalance in the brain', 'his or her own bad characteristics' and/or 'the way he or she was raised'. They were also asked how they would feel about the person working closely with them, living next door, spending an evening socialising, marrying into the family or being a friend. More endorsed a neurobiological explanation for the condition in 2006 than in 1996; in the case of 'Schizophrenia', a rise from 76% to 86% and in the case of 'Depression', a rise from 54% to 67%. The proportion attributing 'Depression' to 'the normal ups and downs of life' fell from 78% in 1996 to 67% in 2006. More 2006 respondents reported an unwillingness to have someone experiencing psychosis as a neighbor than in 1996, and despite a greater proportion endorsing the view that these conditions are the result of a neurobiological abnormality in the later survey, there was no evidence of a parallel *reduction* in any of the other measures of stigma or a desire for social distance. A separate study (Mehta et al. 2009) considered changes in attitude during the period 1993 to 2003 in the UK. This was across a period during which the Royal College of Psychiatrists had energetically promoted the 'illness like any other' framework (Crisp et al. 2005). Public attitudes towards people with mental illness in England and Scotland actually became *less* positive during 1994–2003, and especially so in 2000–2003. Finally, the Valery and Prouteau (2020) review of mental health practitioners' attitudes towards their clients referred to above, included two studies which explored aetiological beliefs about 'Schizophrenia'; whether it is best considered the result of biological or psycho-environmental causes. They found that biological beliefs were associated with more negative attitudes, such as exhibiting less empathy and more 'dehumanisation' (Lebowitz and Ahn, 2014; Pavon and Vaes, 2017).

Consequences of the sick role

This seems to be a robust if somewhat unexpected finding. It would appear humane, helpful and supportive to identify 'mental health difficulties' with other forms of 'illness'. Being unwell generally provokes concern, support and a charitable response from others. Why then is it that being 'mentally unwell' seems to provoke something less favorable? Someone experiencing troublesome psychosis might be pitied, might even be felt to be in need of care but all the evidence points to the fact that they are also likely to suffer discrimination which deepens their isolation and intensifies their disability.

One way of understanding this is to consider the distorting effect of the 'sick role'. The universality of discriminatory attitudes and behaviors towards people with 'mental health difficulties' suggests that they reflect a widely expressed social phenomenon, and a leading candidate has to be the 'sick role'. To consider a state of affairs an 'illness' is a very specific and influential step, identifying it as a particular form of deviance and defining associated power relations. Talcott Parsons' outline of the sick role (Parsons 1951) has stood the test of time and remains an effective summary of this social configuration. Simon Williams offers a more contemporary outline of the balance of rights and responsibilities it comprises:

21

From the point of view of the social system, too low a level of health and too high an incidence of illness is dysfunctional. Illness, in other words, given its interference with normal role capacity, becomes a form of social deviance that needs channelling, therefore, in an appropriate fashion through an institutionalized role or niche. The sick role, for Parsons, fulfils precisely these goals through a series of rights and obligations that its incumbents must recognize and respect. On the rights side of the equation, the patient (according to the severity of the illness) is exempt from normal role obligations, and is not deemed responsible for falling ill. On the obligations side of the equation, the patient must seek technically competent help and must want to get well. The doctor, for his or her part, must apply these technically competent skills in order to facilitate (a swift) recovery, guided as they are by the professional constellation of achievement, universalism, functional specificity, affective neutrality and collectivism ... The sick role, therefore, serves to discourage the secondary gains of illness and prevents a deviant subculture of sickness from forming. This reciprocal cluster of rights and obligations is intended to reintegrate the individual back into society through a return to normal role capacity (or an approximation thereof) as quickly as possible.

(Williams 2005, p. 124)

'Illness' is considered to be a form of deviance, but by providing an institutional response to it the social system negotiates a highly specific contract. The 'ill' person enjoys relief from responsibilities and access to care in exchange for a resignation of authority, submission to expertly defined treatment and dependency upon others. The ill person may resign command over most of their affairs but they still have power over others in the form of expectations of care and support. In exchange they give up their right to assumptions of full competence, and are at risk of assumptions of incapacity or incompetence. Despite criticisms, Williams argues, this combination of structural and relational features provides a good explanation of many interactions between individuals and healthcare practitioners. Substantive shortcomings only come to light when the arrangement is applied to circumstances that do not conform to a particularly formed pattern of illness.

Before the widespread introduction of sterile surgical techniques, effective antibiotics and immunisation during the second half of the nineteenth and the first half of the twentieth centuries, life-threatening illness commonly took the form of an acutely debilitating bacterial infection, such as pneumonia, puerperal sepsis or septicaemia from a gangrenous wound. Until very recently, from an historical perspective, common experience of serious illness was a fever that either 'broke' – in other words, resolved as the body's natural defences prevailed – or resulted in death. During the fever the victim would be incapacitated by pain and weakness, and personal hygiene,

22

nutrition and fluid intake would have to be supported by others. Under these circumstances it is adaptive to employ an institutionalised interaction between 'patient' and 'carers', in which the 'patient' temporarily surrenders autonomy in return for professional care and support which are realistically likely to improve their outcome, perhaps even save their life.

With the development of sterile surgical techniques and the availability of antibiotics, survival after serious injury, such as spinal transection causing paralysis, loss of a limb or a brain-damaging head injury, has become much more likely than had been the case. Mortality following surgical amputation of a limb stood at around 60% in the early nineteenth century. By 1910 it had fallen to some 10% (Alexander 1985). The need to accommodate the 'disabled but no longer ill' is a relatively new development that has only recently found full expression in the form of disability rights legislation, and progress towards realising this occupied much of the twentieth century. It includes redeeming the disabled from the status of 'patronised and dependent person' that is characteristic of a patient inhabiting the classic sick role, to that of 'autonomous and independent person' with full expectations of rights and responsibilities. Other developments in medical technology have altered the prognosis of many conditions from 'certainly very disabling and commonly life-threatening' to 'manageable provided certain regimes are followed'. Examples include diabetes, hypertension, asthma and epilepsy. Over a period of little more than 150 years the everyday experience of serious illness has widened from that of a time-limited episode resulting in either recovery or death, to include chronic physical disability; the presence of a persistent threat of life-endangering recurrence despite ongoing wellbeing, as in cancer in remission; steadily declining health beyond the reach of professional skills, such as the experience of progressive arthritis; and continuing wellbeing contingent upon a programme of professionalised intervention, such as controlled diabetes, asthma, hypertension or epilepsy. None of these is adequately accommodated by the classic sick role and all of them present challenges to the oversimplification that it represents. Nevertheless, the role has deep historical roots and it is a resilient social structure. It orders and legitimises influential institutions and power relations. When it is applied to situations that do not match its historical template, these may be unhelpful. Related power relations lose their legitimacy and the scene is set for tensions and dissatisfactions. Although these have begun to influence practice and have stimulated the introduction of supportive legislation in relation to physical conditions, the same has yet to happen in any measure within the mental health field. Thus, mental health service users experience institutions, practices and power relations that commonly reflect the ill-suited application of social arrangements derived from an illness ideology. In particular they experience paternalism, expectations of submission to professionalised interventions and all the other discriminating consequences of being identified as 'ill', and therefore socially located as deviant and incapacitated.

An 'illness' is generally considered categorically; one either has it or one doesn't. This is controversial in the context of mental health difficulties. It is widely accepted that 'psychotic' phenomena such as hallucinations or uncommon beliefs, otherwise considered pathognomonic of a psychotic *disorder* are experienced by many who are not or do not regard themselves as 'unwell' (e.g., van Os et al. 2001). Diagnostic criteria for 'clinical' depression, anxiety disorders, other affective disorders, substance misuse and personality difficulties all rest as much upon symptom intensity and impact as they do upon the presence of this, that or another 'diagnostic' feature. As a result, it is a legitimate and widely held view, that mental 'illnesses' are not categorical and distinct phenomena, as are for instance, a fractured humerus, a malignant tumor or a pneumococcal lung infection, but particularly intense instances of otherwise everyday psychic experiences. This view has become embedded in psychiatric discourse and is referred to as the *continuum* concept of mental health and mental illness. It assumes one dimension, from severe psychiatric 'symptoms' through subclinical (less disrupting), to nonexistent. Against this background a person with 'mental illness' might be seen as someone with familiar and everyday (though more intense) experiences, and therefore not categorically different. Viewed in this light they might not be so readily suited for the provisions of the 'sick role', not 'deviant', and therefore less susceptible to stigma and discrimination.

This possibility has been explored. Peter and colleagues (2021) were able to find thirty-three published studies in which the extent to which respondents 'stigmatised' or discriminated against an imagined 'patient' (mostly presented as a case vignette) could be related to the degree with which they held 'continuum' or 'categorical' views on the nature of mental 'illness'. Twenty-one provided quantitative data suitable for a meta-analysis. In eight studies respondents were asked to indicate how strongly they agreed with 'Basically we are all sometimes like [person described in a vignette]. It is just a question how pronounced this state is'. Six studies used a sixteen-item Continuum Beliefs Questionnaire, which emphasises the normalcy of psychotic experiences, and the remainder used one or another of several other established measures. Stigmatisation and/or other forms of discriminatory behavior and attitudes were assessed on the basis of responses to a social distance scale or to a scale measuring emotional reactions to people with mental 'illness'. The meta-analysis clearly showed an association between holding 'continuum' rather than 'categorical' views on the nature of mental 'illness' and less discriminatory and stigmatising attitudes and behavior.

In an earlier, related study, Corrigan and colleagues (2001) considered relationships between two cardinal features of the sick role; authoritarianism and benevolence, and behavioral discrimination, measured as preferred social distance. One hundred and fifty-one participants drawn from the general public completed measures of authoritarianism (the belief that persons with mental illness cannot care for themselves, and so a paternalistic health

24

system must do it for them) and benevolence (the belief that persons with mental illness are innocent and childlike). Preferred social distance was influenced by both of these, and in turn both were influenced by respondents' familiarity with mental 'illness'. There are clearly complex interactions between how mental 'illness' is perceived; an abnormality or an intense reaction, whether that mandates application of the 'sick role' and all its technical and social paraphernalia, and the extent to which doing so results in stigmatising and discrimination.

To summarise

How others respond to it is one of the key determinants of how a troubling experience of psychosis plays out. On occasion there may be non-judgemental supportive understanding, but in the vast majority of instances and life stories, being someone who experiences psychosis also means being someone whose life choices, relationship opportunities and sense of self-worth are all severely limited. There is copious evidence of this from studies of family life, employment, experiences of healthcare and media portrayals, and the perception of people who experience psychosis as somehow incompetent and possibly dangerous extends into legislation and challenges to their human rights.

Well-meaning attempts to address this based upon the charitable position that 'mental health difficulties' are 'illnesses like any other' appear to have foundered. The research findings are that following this approach appears to deepen and intensify discriminatory attitudes and behavior in the longer term. One way of understanding this apparent paradox is to consider the history and implications of the 'sick role'. The sick role confers certain rights upon the 'patient', but it also makes assumptions of incompetence and dependency, and in turn these legitimise paternalism and expectations of compliance with 'treatment'. The sick role has origins in much earlier times, when these might have been much more generally appropriate expectations than now. It is a deeply rooted social structure and it continues to exert considerable influence over healthcare practices and what is expected of them. The power and resilience of the sick role and its continuing consequences are particularly well illustrated by Henry Marsh's experience of 'crossing to the other side', as he contended with the shift in identity from prominent and renowned neurosurgeon to older person with cancer (Marsh 2022).

Whether or not troublesome experiences of psychosis are understood as 'illness', deserving of the sick role and its disempowering implications, is key to understanding their socially disabling consequences. Viewing mental health difficulties as discrete entities distinct from the turmoil of everyday life appears to be associated with a greater tendency to view them as 'illnesses' and justify the sick role and its consequences, and in turn that is associated with a higher probability of stigma and discrimination. In contrast, taking a dimensional perspective in which mental health difficulties are considered part of a continuum of subjective experiences that extends from the everyday to the less common appears to be associated with less damaging interactions. The consequences of experiencing a troubling episode of psychosis are powerfully determined by how others understand it. Indeed, others' understandings of what psychosis is and its implications may be a more important determinant of outcome than the experience itself. How others' understandings of what psychosis is and its implications might be best influenced is illustrated by an umbrella review of 216 review papers addressing various aspects of public and interpersonal stigma in relation to mental health difficulties (Thornicroft et al. 2022). The core finding was that social contact (direct or indirect) between people who do and those who do not have lived experience of mental health conditions is the most effective way to reduce stigmatisation. This emphasises the contextual nature of such 'knowledge'. *Vox pop* understandings of psychosis and its implications are generally derogatory and largely unjustified, but they have damaging consequences. These undoubtedly reflect discourses and the communities within which they are embedded. Such discourses and their consequences are susceptible to constructive change when they accommodate differing perspectives. Thus, how experiences of psychosis are understood and responded to are significantly influenced by who is involved and what views and perspectives they hold.

Understanding psychosis is not unique in this respect, though what it might be in any one setting can have a profound influence upon its consequences. The next chapter reflects upon ways in which 'understandings' arise in general; a framework from within which to consider how differing patterns of human interaction can result in differing understandings. This can be applied to how understandings of psychosis and its implications are generated. In turn this provides a rationale for exploring how psychotic experiences are construed by differing constituencies, and how these different constituencies might or might not result in harmful, even toxic, interactions with those who have acquired a reputation for them.

References

Alexander, J. W. (1985) 'The Contributions of Infection Control to a Century of Surgical Progress', *Annals of Surgery*, Vol. 201, No. 4, pp. 423–428.

Angermeyer, M. C., Dietrich, S., Pott, D. and Matschinger, H. (2005) 'Media consumption and desire for social distance towards people with schizophrenia', *European Psychiatry*, Vol. 20, No. 3, pp. 246–250.

Angermeyer, M. C., Holzinger, A., Carta, M. G. and Schomerus, G. (2011) 'Biogenetic explanations and public acceptance of mental illness: systematic review of population studies', *The British Journal of Psychiatry*, Vol. 199, pp. 367–372.

Anonymous (1980) 'First Person Account: After the Funny Farm', *Schizophrenia Bulletin*, Vol. 6, No. 3, pp. 544–546.

Boydell, K. M., Gladstone, B. M. and Stasiulis Crawford, E. (2002) 'The Dialectic of Friendship for People with Psychiatric Disabilities', *Psychiatric Rehabilitation Journal*, Vol. 26, No. 2, pp. 123–131.

Brunnauer, A., Herpich, F., Zwanzger, P. and Laux, G. (2021) 'Driving Performance Under Treatment of Most Frequently Prescribed Drugs for Mental Disorders: A Systematic Review of Patient Studies', *International Journal of Neuropsychopharmacology*, Vol. 24, No. 9, pp. 679–693.

Buday, J., Neumann, M., Heidingerová, J., Michalec, J., Podgorná, G., Mareš, T., Pol, M., Mahrík, J., Vranková, S., Kališová, L. and Anders, M. (2022) 'Depiction of mental illness and psychiatry in popular video games over the last 20 years', *Frontiers in Psychiatry*, https://doi.org/10.3389/fpsyt.2022.967992.

Chilvers, R., Macdonald, G. and Hayes, A. (2006) 'Supported housing for people with severe mental disorders', *Cochrane Database of Systematic Reviews*, Issue. 4, Art. No.: CD000453. doi:10.1002/14651858.CD000453.pub2..

Ciufolini, S., Morgan, C., Morgan, K., Fearon, P., Boydell, J., Hutchinson, G., Demjaha, A., Doody, G. A., Jones, P. B., Murray, R. and Dazzan, P. (2015) 'Self esteem and self agency in first episode psychosis: Ethnic variation and relationship with clinical presentation', *Psychiatry Research*, Vol. 227, pp. 213–218.

Cohen, A., Padmavati, R., Hibben, M., Oyewusi, S., John, S., Esan, O., Patel, V., Weiss, H., Murray, R., Hutchinson, G., Gureje, O., Thara, R. and Morgan, C. (2016) 'Concepts of madness in diverse settings: a qualitative study from the INTREPID project', *BMC Psychiatry*, Vol. 16, No. 388. doi:10.1186/s12888-016-1090-4..

Corrigan, P. W., Backs Edwards, A., Green, A., Lickey Diwan, S. and Penn, D. L. (2001) 'Prejudice, Social Distance, and Familiarity with Mental Illness', *Schizophrenia Bulletin*, Vol. 27, No. 2, pp. 219–225.

Corrigan, P. W., Watson, A. C., Gracia, G., Slopen, N., Rasinski, K. and Hall, L. L. (2005) 'Newspaper Stories as Measures of Structural Stigma', *Psychiatric Services*, Vol. 56, No. 5, pp. 551–556.

Corrigan, P. W., Watson, A. C. and Barr, L. (2006) 'The Self-Stigma of Mental Illness: Implications for Self-Esteem and Self-Efficacy', *Journal of Social and Clinical Psychology*, Vol. 25, No. 9, pp. 875–884.

Corrigan, P. W., Mittal, D., Reaves, C. M., Haynes, T. F., Han, X., Morris, S. and Sullivan, G. (2014) 'Mental health stigma and primary health care decisions', *Psychiatry Research*, Vol. 218, pp. 35–38.

Coverdale, J. H., Turbott, S. H. and Roberts, H. (1997) 'Family planning needs and STD risk behaviours of female psychiatric out-patients', *The British Journal of Psychiatry*, Vol. 171, No. 1, pp. 69–72.

Coverdale, J., Nairn, R. and Classen, D. (2002) 'Depictions of mental illness in print media: a prospective national sample', *Australian and New Zealand Journal of Psychiatry*, Vol. 36, pp. 697–700.

Craig, T. C. and Bromet, E. J. (2004) 'Parents with Psychosis', *Annals of Clinical Psychiatry*, Vol. 16, pp. 35–39.

Crisp, A., Gelder, M., Goddard, E. and Meltzer, H. (2005) 'Stigmatization of people with mental illnesses: a follow-up study within the Changing Minds campaign of the Royal College of Psychiatrists', *World Psychiatry*, Vol. 4, No. 2, pp. 106–113.

Diefenbach, D. L. (1997) 'The Portrayal of Mental Illness on Prime-Time Television', *Journal of Community Psychology*, Vol. 25, No. 3, pp. 289–302.

Dinos, S., Stevens, S., Serfaty, M., Weich, S. and King, M. (2004) 'Stigma: the feelings and experiences of 46 people with mental illness', *The British Journal of Psychiatry*, Vol. 184, pp. 176–181.

Dipasquale, S., Pariante, C. M., Dazzan, P., Aguglia, E., McGuire, P. and Mondelli, V. (2013) 'The dietary pattern of patients with schizophrenia: A systematic review', *Journal of Psychiatric Research*, Vol. 47, pp. 197–207.

Druss, B. G., Bradford, D. W., Rosenheck, R. A., Radford, M. J. and Krumholz, H. M. (2000) 'Mental Disorders and Use of Cardiovascular Procedures After Myocardial Infraction', *Journal of the American Medical Association*, Vol. 283, No. 4, pp. 506–511.

Dubreucq, J., Plasse, J. and Franck, N. (2021) 'Self-stigma in Serious Mental Illness: A Systematic Review of Frequency, Correlates, and Consequences', *Schizophrenia Bulletin*, Vol. 47, No. 5, pp. 1261–1287.

Duurkoop, W. R. A. (1991) 'Het sociale netwerk van chronisch psychiatrische patiënten'. In J. J. M. Dekker, S. J. A. M. van den Langenberg and L. A. J. M. van Eck (Eds) *Klinische psychiatrie*. Assen and Maastricht: Van Gorcum (n.p.).

Equality and Human Rights Commission (1998) https://www.equalityhumanrights.com/en/human-rights/human-rights-act (accessed September 2022).

European Court of Human Rights (1970, et seq.) https://www.echr.coe.int/Documents/Convention_ENG.pdf (accessed September 2022).

Fleury, M.-J., Grenier, G., Bamvita, J.-M. and Caron, J. (2010) 'Professional Service Utilisation among Patients with Severe Mental Disorders', *BMC Health Services Research*, Vol. 10, No. 141. https://doi.org/10.1186/1472-6963-10-141.

Ford, E., Rosenberg, M., Holsten, M. and Boudreaux, T. (2003) 'Managing Sexual Behavior on Adult Acute Care Inpatient Psychiatric Units', *Psychiatric Services*, Vol. 54, No. 3, pp. 346–350.

Goffman, E. (1963) *Sigma: Notes on the Management of Spoiled Identity.* New York: Simon & Schuster.

Hatzenbuehler, M. L. (2016) 'Structural Stigma: Research Evidence and Implications for Psychological Science', *American Psychologist*, Vol. 71, No. 8, pp 742–751.

Hemmens, C., Miller, M., BurtonJr., V. S. and Milner, S. (2002) 'The Consequences of Official Labels: An Examination of the Rights Lost by the Mentally Ill and Mentally Incompetent Ten Years Later', *Community Mental Health Journal*, Vol. 38, No. 2, pp. 129–140.

Hiday, V. A., Swartz, M. S., Swanson, J. W., Borum, R. and Wagner, H. R. (1999) 'Criminal victimization of persons with severe mental illness', *Psychiatric Services*, Vol. 50, pp. 62–68.

Hjorthøj, C., Stürup, A. E., McGrath, J. J. and Nordentoft, M. (2017) 'Years of potential life lost and life expectancy in schizophrenia: a systematic review and meta-analysis', *Lancet Psychiatry*, Vol. 4, pp. 295–301.

Howard, L. M. (2005) 'Fertility and pregnancy in women with psychotic disorders', *European Journal of Obstetrics & Gynecology and Reproductive Biology*, Vol. 119, pp. 3–10.

Jones, S., Howard, L. and Thornicroft, G. (2008) 'Diagnostic overshadowing': worse physical health care for people with mental illness', *Acta Psychiatrica Scandinavica*, Vol. 118, pp. 169–171.

Khalifeh, H., Johnson, S., Howard, L. M., Borschmann, R., Osborn, D., Dean, K., Hart, C., Hogg, J. and Moran, P. (2015) 'Violent and non-violent crime against adults with severe mental illness', *The British Journal of Psychiatry*, Vol. 206, pp. 275–282.

Kisely, S., Campbell, L. A. and Wang, Y. (2009) 'Treatment of ischaemic heart disease and stroke in individuals with psychosis under universal healthcare', *The British Journal of Psychiatry*, Vol. 195, pp. 545–550.

Koenders, J. F., de Mooij, L. D., Dekker, J. M. and Kikkert, M. (2017) 'Social inclusion and relationship satisfaction of patients with a severe mental illness', *International Journal of Social Psychiatry*, Vol. 63, No. 8, pp. 773–781.

Larkings, J. S., and Brown, P. M. (2017) 'Do biogenetic causal beliefs reduce mental illness stigma in people with mental illness and in mental health professionals? A systematic review', *International Journal of Mental Health Nursing*, Vol. 27, No. 3, pp 928–941.

Lasser, K., Wesley Boyd, J., Woolhandler, S., Himmelstein, D. U., McCormick, D. and Bor, D. H. (2000) 'Smoking and Mental Illness: A Population-Based Prevalence Study', *Journal of the American Medical Association*, Vol. 284, No. 20, pp. 2606–2610.

Laursen, T. M., Munk-Olsen, T. and Vestergaard, M. (2012) 'Life expectancy and cardiovascular mortality in persons with schizophrenia', *Schizophrenia*, Vol. 25, No. 2, pp. 83–88.

Lawrie, S. M. (2000) 'Newspaper coverage of psychiatric and physical illness', *Psychiatric Bulletin*, Vol. 24, pp. 104–106.

Lebowitz, M. S. and Ahn, W. (2014) 'Effects of biological explanations for mental disorders on clinicians' empathy', *Proceedings of the National Academy of Sciences*, Vol. 111, No. 50, pp. 17786–17790.

MacDougall, A. G., Vandermeer, M. R. J. and Norman, R. M. G. (2017) 'Determinants of self-esteem in early psychosis: The role of perceived social dominance', *Psychiatry Research*, Vol. 258, pp. 583–586.

Majuri, T., Alakokkare, A.-E., Haapea, M., Nordström, T., Miettunen, J., Jääskeläinen, E. and Ala-Mursula, L. (2022) 'Employment trajectories until midlife in schizophrenia and other psychoses: the Northern Finland Birth Cohort 1966', *Social Psychiatry and Psychiatric Epidemiology*. https://doi.org/10.1007/s00127-022-02327-6.

Marsh, H. (2022) *And Finally: Matters of Life and Death*. London: Vintage.

Marwaha, S. and Johnson, S. (2004) 'Schizophrenia and employment: A review', *Social Psychiatry and Psychiatric Epidemiology*, Vol. 39, pp. 337–349.

Mehta, N., Kassam, A., Leese, M., Butler, G. and Thornicroft, G. (2009) 'Public attitudes towards people with mental illness in England and Scotland, 1994–2003', *The British Journal of Psychiatry*, Vol. 194, pp. 278–284.

Meltzer, H., Bebbington, P., Brugha, T., Farrell, M., Jenkins, R. and Lewis, G. (2000) 'The reluctance to seek treatment for neurotic disorders', *Journal of Mental Health*, Vol. 9, No. 3, pp. 319–327.

Mental Health Foundation (2002) 'Out at work: A survey of the experiences of people with mental health problems within the workplace'. Online: The Mental Health Foundation.

Mental Health Law Online (2022) https://www.mentalhealthlaw.co.uk/Jury_service#cite_note-1 (accessed September 2022).

Myers, N. L. (2015) *Recovery's Edge: An Ethnography of Mental Health Care and Moral Agency*. Nashville: Vanderbilt University Press.

Olmsted, D. W., Durham, K. (1976) 'Stability of mental health attitudes: a semantic differential study', *Journal of Health and Social Behaviour*, Vol. 17, No. 1, pp. 35–44.

Owen, P. R. (2012) 'Portrayals of Schizophrenia by Entertainment Media: A Content Analysis of Contemporary Movies', *Psychiatric Services*, Vol. 63, No. 7, pp. 655–659.

Parsons T. (1951) *The Social System*. London: Routledge and Keegan Hall.

Pavon, G. and Vaes, J. (2017) 'Bio-genetic vs. psycho-environmental conceptions of schizophrenia and their role in perceiving patients in human terms', *Psychosis*, Vol. 9, No. 3, pp. 245–253.

Pescosolido, B. A., Martin, J. K., Long, J. S., Medina, T. R., Phelan, J. C. and Link, B. G. (2010) '"A Disease Like Any Other"? A Decade of Change in Public Reactions to Schizophrenia, Depression, and Alcohol Dependence', *American Journal of Psychiatry*, Vol. 167, No. 11, pp. 1321–1330.

Peter, L.-J., Schindler, S., Sander, C., Schmidt, S., Muehlan, H., McLaren, T., Tomczyk, S., Speerforck, S. and Schomerus, G. (2021) 'Continuum beliefs and mental illness stigma: a systematic review and meta-analysis of correlation and intervention studies', *Psychological Medicine*, Vol. 51, pp. 716–726.

Piat, M. (2000) 'The NIMBY Phenomenon: Community Residents' Concerns about Housing for Deinstitutionalized People', *Health & Social Work*, Vol. 25, No. 2, pp. 127–138.

Ramrakha, S., Caspi, A., Dickson, N., Moffitt, T. E. and Paul, C. (2000) 'Psychiatric disorders and risky sexual behaviour in young adulthood: cross sectional study in birth cohort', *British Medical Journal*, Vol. 321, pp. 263–266.

Roberts, L., Roalfe, A., Wilson, S. and Lester, H. (2007) 'Physical health care of patients with schizophrenia in primary care: a comparative study', *Family Practice*, Vol. 24, pp. 34–40.

Rosenberg, M. (1989) *Society and the Adolescent Self-Image*. Revised edition. Middletown, CT: Wesleyan University Press.

Rotter, J. B. (1966) 'Generalized expectancies for internal versus external control of reinforcement',*Psychological Monographs*, Vol. 80, pp. 1–28.

Rüsch, N., Heekeren, K., Theodoridou, A., Müller, M., Corrigan, P. W., Mayer, B., Metzler, S., Walitza, S. and Rössler, W. (2015) 'Stigma as a stressor and transition to schizophrenia after one year among young people at risk of psychosis', *Schizophrenia Research*, Vol. 166, pp. 43–48.

Schizophrenia and Psychosis Action Alliance (2022) https://sczaction.org/ (accessed September 2022).

Shoham, N., Cooper, C., Lewis, G., Bebbington, P. and McManus, S. (2021) 'Temporal trends in psychotic symptoms: Repeated cross-sectional surveys of the population in England 2000–14', *Schizophrenia Research*, Vo. 228, pp. 97–102.

Struening, E. L., Perlick, D. A., Link, B. G., Hellman, F., Herman, D. and Strey, J. A. (2001) 'The Extent to Which Caregivers Believe Most People Devalue Consumers and Their Families', *Psychiatric Services*, Vol. 52, No. 12, pp. 1633–1638.

Stubbs, B., Williams, J., Gaughran, F. and Craig, T. (2016) 'How sedentary are people with psychosis? A systematic review and meta-analysis', *Schizophrenia Research*, Vol. 171, pp. 103–109.

Sullivan, G., Han, X., Moore, S. and Kotrla, K. (2006) 'Disparities in Hospitalization for Diabetes Among Persons With and Without Co-occurring Mental Disorders', *Psychiatric Services*, Vol. 57, No. 8, pp. 1126–1131.

Thornicorft, G. and Halpern, A. (1993) 'Legal landmark for community care of former psychiatric patients', *British Medical Journal*, Vol. 307, pp. 248–250.

Thornicroft, G., Tansella, M., Becker, T., Knapp, M., Leese, M., Schene, A. and Vazquez-Barquero, J. L. (2004) 'The personal impact of schizophrenia in Europe', *Schizophrenia Research*, Vol. 69, pp. 125–132.

Thornicroft, G. (2006) *Shunned. Discrimination Against People with Mental Illness*. Oxford: Oxford University Press.

Thornicroft, G., Brohan, E., Rose, D., Sartorius, N. and Leese, M. (2009) 'Global pattern of experienced and anticipated discrimination against people with schizophrenia: a cross-sectional survey', *Lancet*, Vol. 373, pp. 408–415.

Thornicroft, G., Sunkel, C., Alikhon Aliev, A., Baker, S., Brohan, E., el Chammay, R., Davies, K., Demissie, M., Duncan, J., Fekadu, W., Gronholm, P. C., Guerrero, Z., Gurung, D., Habtamu, K., Hanlon, C., Heim, E., Henderson, C., Hijazi, Z., Hoffman, C., Hosny, N., Huang, F.-X., Kline, S., Kohrt, B. A., Lempp, H., Li, J., London, E., Ma, N., Mak, W. W. S., Makhmud, A., Maulik, P. K., Milenova, M., Morales Cano, G., Ouali, U., Parry, S., Rangaswamy, T., Rüsch, N., Sabri, T., Sartorius, N., Schulze, M., Stuart, H., Salisbury, T.T., San Juan, N. S., Votruba, N. and Winkler, P. (2022) 'The Lancet Commission on ending stigma and discrimination in mental health', *Lancet*, doi:10.1016/S0140-6736(22)01470-2..

Toftdahl, N.G., Nordentoft, M. and Hjorthøj, C. (2016) 'Prevalence of substance use disorders in psychiatric patients: a nationwide Danish population-based study', *Social Psychiatry and Psychiatric Epidemiology*, Vol. 51, pp. 129–140.

United Nations General Assembly (1948) https://www.un.org/en/about-us/universal-declaration-of-human-rights (accessed September 2022).

United Nations General Assembly (1991) https://digitallibrary.un.org/record/162032 (accessed September 2022).

United States London Embassy (2022) https://uk.usembassy.gov/visas/ineligibilities-and-waivers-2/medical-ineligibility/ (accessed September 2022).

Valery, K.-M. and Prouteau, A. (2020) 'Schizophrenia stigma in mental health professionals and associated factors: A systematic review', *Psychiatry Research*, Vol. 290. https://doi.org/10.1016/j.psychres.2020.113068.

van Nieuwenhuizen, A., Henderson, C., Kassam, A., Graham, T., Murray, J., Howard, L. M. and Thornicroft, G. (2013) 'Emergency department staff views and experiences on diagnostic overshadowing related to people with mental illness', *Epidemiology and Psychiatric Sciences*, Vol. 22, pp. 255–262.

van Os, J., Hanssen, M., Bijl, R. V. and Vollebergh, W. (2001) 'Prevalence of Psychotic Disorders and Community Level of Psychotic Symptoms', *Archives of General Psychiatry*, Vol. 58, pp. 663–668.

Williams, S. J. (2005) 'Parsons revisited: from the sick role to …?', *Health. An Interdisciplinary Journal for the Social Study of Illness and Medicine*, Vol. 9, pp. 123–144.

Wise, J. and Watson, J. P. (2001) 'Postal survey of psychiatrists" knowledge and attitudes towards driving and mental illness', *Psychiatric Bulletin*, Vol. 25, pp. 345–349.

Young, S. L., Taylor, M., and Lawrie, S. M. (2015) '"First do no harm." A systematic review of the prevalence and management of antipsychotic adverse effects', *Journal of Psychopharmacology*, Vol. 29, No. 4, pp. 353–362.

2

WHAT ARE WE DEALING
WITH, HERE?

Karl Popper, one of the twentieth century's most influential philosophers of science, is remembered among other things, for the pithy statement; 'Our knowledge can only be finite, while our ignorance must necessarily be infinite' (Popper 1960).

In June 1990 the *Los Angeles Times* reported on a conference that had taken place a couple of months earlier in Worcester MA, in an attempt to answer the question, 'What is Schizophrenia?' (Kohn 1990). Apparently the first speaker offered to list the established facts, and then projected an empty slide. Wry laughter rippled through the assembled experts. These included Manfred Bleuler, son of Eugene Bleuler who had coined the term in 1908, and some twenty other acknowledged experts; prominent psychiatrists, leading psychologists, renowned social scientists, anthropologists, philosophers and historians.

There was no consensus, other than to agree that the phenomenon 'Schizophrenia' resists a clear definition. The exchanges uncovered multiple, often conflicting uses of the term. For some of those present at the conference, it seemed to refer to certain kinds of people, for some, to certain kinds of behaviours, for others, to the consequences of certain biochemical events, and for some, to comprehensible psychological strategies. As one of the contributors subsequently pointed out, there were no contributions from a feminist perspective or from those with their own experiences of psychosis. Including these may have added further voices, but it is unlikely they would have led to a clearer consensus.

There was nothing new here, and nothing has emerged since then to bring these different perspectives together into a single frame. More than twenty years earlier Miriam Siegler and Humphry Osmond had outlined six 'models of madness' (Siegler and Osmond 1966). In 2013 John Read and Jacqui Dillon's *Models of Madness* (Read and Dillon 2013) enjoyed publication as a second edition and there have been many more contributions to this literature. They vary in emphasis but common threads are that 'Schizophrenia' or the troubling experience of psychosis can be seen from any one of many points of view, and that all of these are relevant. Siegler and Osmond (1966)

DOI: 10.4324/9780429059094-3

identified 'medical', 'moral', 'psychoanalytic', 'familial', 'conspiratorial' and 'social' models, each with their own assumptions of cause or aetiology, each with their own assumptions of approaches to 'treatment' and the respective responsibilities of 'patient' and 'therapist', and each with their own expectations of recovery. They emphasised the need for clarity around which model was guiding responses to someone experiencing psychosis. Each has its own strengths, weaknesses and most suitable applications, and each exerts covert as well as overt influences. Read and Dillon distinguish between an illness model, and social and psychological approaches to understanding 'madness'. The more recent *Power, Threat, Meaning Framework* (Johnstone and Boyle 2018) emphasises the same dichotomy.

All of these and many other related texts (however well researched and well argued) can suffer from being read as polemic contributions to a more 'political' debate about which professional grouping has the most to offer. Peter Kinderman's *A Prescription for Psychiatry: Why We Need a Whole New Approach to Mental Health and Wellbeing* (2014) is just that. It opens with

> Traditional thinking about mental health care is profoundly flawed, and radical remedies are required. Our present approach to helping people in acute emotional distress is severely hampered by old-fashioned and incorrect ideas about the nature and origins of mental health problems, and vulnerable people suffer as a result of inappropriate treatment. We must move away from the 'disease model', which assumes that emotional distress is merely a symptom of biological illness, and instead embrace a psychological and social approach to mental health and well-being that recognises our essential and shared humanity.
>
> (Kinderman 2014, p. 1)

Many would concur with this, but in the UK at least, rates at which psychiatric medicines are being prescribed and people are being subjected to coercive treatment show no signs of falling (Shoham et al. 2021; NHS Digital 2022). Those with mental health difficulties, and in particular those experiencing psychosis remain subject to disabling levels of stigma and discrimination, as outlined in the preceding chapter, and there is little evidence of the political and economic adjustments such as addressing socio-economic deprivation and inequality that critics of the status quo advocate. These unsatisfactory circumstances are undoubtedly rooted in how psychosis is understood, and it is clear that many views and explanations co-exist. Some might generate more toxic consequences, others less so, and how one person's experiences of psychosis might impact upon them will reflect whose views and whose influences they may have been subjected to. Firstly, a look at what those views might be and where they come from.

Knowledge concerning psychosis; a slippery fish

With findings that starkly contrast with Kinderman's (2014) and other critics' related positions, a differing series of reviews has summarised 'The Facts' concerning 'Schizophrenia'. Those authors conclude: 'We believe that there is sufficient evidence to call schizophrenia a disease related to brain abnormalities that are the final 'common pathway' caused by an assortment of specific genetic and/or environmental factors' (Tandon et al. 2008, p. 11). Unsurprisingly, according to institutional websites, those responsible for this conclusion all identify their primary research interests as the neurobiology and psychopharmacology of Schizophrenia and other related disorders. One reason why the 1990 conference in Worcester MA was unable to answer its eponymous title, 'What is Schizophrenia?', was that it included a range of specialists from differing professional and academic backgrounds. One of the participants commented:

> At the present time, a perusal of the literature on the meaning of schizophrenia is like a stroll through a street market in which various hawkers of what are proclaimed to be similar wares appeal to the consumer in their own idiosyncratic languages. The range of definitions is by no means exhausted by the following examples: a disorder of dopamine metabolism; an affective disturbance; a genetic disposition; a form of deteriorated functioning; a disturbance in familial interaction; a spoiling of identity; a learning of inappropriate responses; a regression caused by internal conflict; a relationship involving a pseudo-community and social exclusion; a disturbance in the ability to communicate, and a fortuitous labelling of people who are then socialized in the role of the mad patient.
>
> (Flack et al. 1991, p. 146)

A notable strength of the colloquium was that participants were able to contribute from these differing perspectives in an atmosphere of mutual respect and curiosity. As a result, their collective answer to 'What is Schizophrenia?' had to be 'We don't know'. There were many opinions but these reflected differing positions, research traditions, world views and, significantly, differing approaches to more fundamental questions such as, 'What is knowledge?', or 'Are certain forms of knowledge more privileged than others?' No one perspective, background or type of knowledge was given precedence, and as a result, they had to concur: 'It depends upon where you are coming from'. In summarising the event, the organisers commented:

> Specialists in the study of schizophrenia are not accustomed to identifying their preferences with respect to [the] philosophy of

science. In writing papers, most people seem to take it for granted that their viewpoints are shared by their colleagues. ... Picture the confusion, even frustration, that occurs in a discussion between two individuals, one of whom thinks in molar [widely embracing] concepts, is relativistic [knowledge is limited to its context] in interpretations of cross-cultural findings, and conducts minute-to-minute studies of patients' reports of their subjective states, on one hand; and another individual whose goal is a quest for a pathognomonic [identifying] feature and who is most comfortable with reductionistic [simplifying], objective, universally valid, and static concepts, on the other. There is no way of knowing, at this time, which orientations are most conducive to progress ...

(Flack et al. 1991, p. 261)

Answers to questions such as 'What is Schizophrenia (or Psychosis)?', 'What do we know about Schizophrenia (or Psychosis?)', or 'What is the best way to respond when someone experiences psychosis?' depend more upon who is asking or answering them, why they are asking, and where and how the knowledge in question was generated, than it does upon the accuracy or validity of what is put forward.

Uncertainty in the field

This absence of consensus matters. Troublesome psychotic experiences are not uncommon, frequently distress those having them and their associates, and attract the attention of statutory and other arrangements designed to respond to them. Furthermore, how they are understood in popular culture has a defining effect upon how those with such experiences relate to others. How psychotic experiences are understood matters to a lot of people and frequently determines what can happen in what are, usually, emotionally charged circumstances. If that understanding – knowledge concerning psychotic experiences – is a slippery fish which can wriggle this way or that depending upon how it is held, or how it is generated and who is providing it, then difficulties can arise.

Those experiencing psychosis vary in how they understand the experience, and this understanding will be influenced by their social and cultural context. Some might be comfortable with the view that it is the result of 'abnormal brain chemistry', and with submitting to a regime of medical treatment. Some might consider their psychotic experiences to be rogue intrusive thoughts best addressed by psychological 'retraining' such as cognitive behaviour therapy. Some might experience them as a way of making sense of things. Some may find them religiously or spiritually meaningful, and some may experience them as a comforting companion. Many are overwhelmed and distressed by the otherwise inexplicable experience of intrusive and critical voices, disturbing images, tortuous and threatening beliefs, or uncomfortable bodily sensations.

Close associates commonly experience concerns for safety, frustration, anger, guilt, and challenges to their attempts to empathise. How these are expressed will reflect their own understandings of what it means and implies to be experiencing psychosis. Less close associates might offer support and advice, but as often as not, commonly respond by keeping their distance. As the previous chapter has outlined, mental health difficulties commonly result in social distancing. When sought, professional interventions can range from a minimal; 'wait and see' through supportive understanding, routine anti-psychotic medication and/or a formally structured psychological therapy, to coercive hospital admission and heavy sedation. Which of these is followed depends upon a complex interaction between anxieties raised among profes-sionals ('clinical' risk), anxieties raised among the 'patient's' associates and the wider public, the availability and inclinations of support staff, and the general tenor or clinical ideology of the organisation providing care when that happens. Given the confusing array of ways in which an experience of psychosis can be understood, it is barely surprising that responses to it do not always fulfil everyone's expectations, and conflicts arise, conflicts which more often than not worsen the situation. The person experiencing psychosis might become estranged from friends and family because they do not share their associates' concerns about what is happening. Professionals might become frustrated and dismissive because what they have available or are choosing to offer does not chime with either the 'patient's' or their associates' expectations. There might be expressions of public concern over safety which can generate more public debate, and even calls for changes in practice (Piat 2000, p. 133).

As with all instances of conflict, these situations become unhelpfully inflamed when and if participants dig in their heels: 'Leave me alone, there is nothing wrong with me.' 'That person could be dangerous and should be put away.' 'This is nothing a few weeks in hospital on an anti-psychotic can't sort out.' 'This is the clinical pathway we follow under such circumstances', and so on. Furthermore, the heightened interpersonal tensions that commonly accompany troublesome experiences of psychosis drive a need for 'some-thing' to be done. In the presence of so much uncertainty and common dis-agreement over what that should be in any one instance, it is barely surprising that mental health services have such a poor reputation.

'Knowledge'... or differing 'opinions'?

Given this plethora of differing, and often conflicting opinions about psy-chotic experiences, there is a pressing need to dig a little deeper. As the organisers of 'What is Schizophrenia?' pointed out, specialists in the study of psychosis tend to investigate, publish and communicate within their own subfield; neurobiology, psycho-pharmacology, cognitive science, social psychology, sociology and so on. This is not peculiar to the study of psychosis. It is a feature of systematic research across all fields of enquiry, and it reflects the fact that the growth of 'knowledge' is collective, slow and incremental. An investigation builds upon its predecessors. One experiment, survey or review will establish some facts and reveal new uncertainties. These are then, in their turn, addressed by a further investigation. Truly new knowledge only emerges by carefully looking again at what has already been agreed, and how those interpretations might be criticised. Different interpretations (hypotheses) are tested; by experimentally manipulating certain molecules, cellular mechanisms, subatomic particles or material objects, by re-defining a survey and/or applying it to a particular population, by re-excavating a known historic site, or by reviewing documents and other utterances in a slightly different way. In other words, generating new knowledge; resolving uncertainties, rests upon painstakingly going over old ground in search of the gaps, and devising fresh ways of collecting information that might fill them. Every doctoral student discovers this, and, equally, discovers that their success is going to depend upon becoming deeply immersed in the details of what is already agreed within their chosen, narrow, self-contained field of study.

Inevitably this process generates and maintains communities of narrow specialism focused upon this, that, or another area of knowledge which are relatively isolated from one another. Individual participants might be aware of, and may even respect others' fields of interest, but the business of conducting genuine, cutting-edge research is inescapably carried out by relatively small, tightly focused communities of interest which exclude most people who are not, and cannot be, party to the necessary level of detail. This may be of little consequence in fields such as atomic physics, archaeology or primary archival research where cutting-edge research has only indirect effects upon mundane lives. The uninitiated might be intrigued to know more about the nature of matter, the mysteries of the universe, how Ancient Egyptians lived or exactly what Anne Boleyn wrote in her letters, but none of these is likely to have a direct effect upon everyday life. That is not the case in relation to knowledge concerning the experience of psychosis or, indeed a range of other topics. Medicine, psychology, climate science, economics, engineering and many other enterprises all have direct effects upon the lives of those who are not necessarily fluent with their fine details. For most people, what they 'know' about this, that or another aspect of these and similar enterprises is a simplified digest of what the most knowledgeable are currently considering. As such it tends to overlook underpinning uncertainties, and the nuances of debate among the cognoscenti who are attempting to resolve them.

Scholarship and scientific institutes exist to house and enable such debates. Experiments, surveys, or a review of existing information are ways of adjudicating between opinions. Although it is conventional to believe that there are experts out there that 'know' about this, that or the other area of expertise, in truth, the better informed the expert, the more keenly they will be aware of prevailing controversies and uncertainties. From this perspective 'knowledge' is not and never can be fixed, established and immutable. It is better seen as a moving boundary between how things are understood at present, given the results of experiments, surveys and other sources of information *to date*, and uncertainties mulled over in the course of careful, detailed questioning by those minded and equipped to do so. In this sense true 'knowledge' about *anything* is a destination yet to be reached. All that is available in the most well-informed circles, is the cut and thrust of prevailing debate; the process of sharing, challenging and testing differing opinions.

Viewing knowledge as a destination yet to be reached does not help very much if it is to be used as a guide to action. Shaping and directing any action presupposes a choice from available options, and that in turn presupposes shutting down debate about their relative merits. Whether or not this, that or another line of action is the best one to follow is a judgement that has to accept some uncertainty, because there never can be full closure of debate. Obviously, most of most people's lives is conducted on the basis of safe assumptions. Newton's laws of motion (1687), for instance, are sufficient to guide a cricketer or a footballer, driving a car and most engineering projects, but they have been found wanting as a way of understanding and predicting the nature of sub-atomic particles, or explaining some of astronomy's observations. They apply in a wide range of terrestrial circumstance but beyond that, debate and uncertainty continue (see, for instance Hawking, 2018). Knowledge guiding action in less rarefied contexts is inevitably even more uncertain and provisional, and most courses of action have to be chosen without recourse to the sort of detailed debate that characterises theoretical physics. Coronary heart disease has to be identified or ruled out, before a fatal heart attack occurs. Bank interest rates have to be adjusted in response to economic ebbs and flows if the smooth exchange of goods and services is to continue; action is needed if atmospheric pollution is to be contained, and so on.

Most usually, when someone experiences psychosis, a lot of uncomfortable and uncontainable emotion is generated within and around them. Jim Buchanan (2020) provides one of many accounts of his own confusion, disturbing behaviour, and the effects these had on those close to him. All of these and more generate pressures to act. Knowledge informing what that might be is unavoidably provisional and imperfect. It is not 'knowledge' as 'knowledge' is broadly understood; an abstract, disembodied phenomenon, universally available and universally applicable. It is inescapably one or more of many embodied opinions. Opinions guiding how to understand any one experience of psychosis and how to respond to it, are necessarily determined by the context in which it is occurring, who is involved and how they relate to one another. Do some, as experts, hold power that is either formally or unconsciously acknowledged by others, or attempt to exert expert power that others do not recognise? Is this particular experience of psychosis a new development or a familiar one? What are the prior relational configurations between participants? What other relational and material commitments do they each have? What are the wider social and economic circumstances? What cultural backgrounds do participants share, and which do they find difficult to share? Which genders, ages, and social classes are at play? It is barely surprising the 1990 'What is Schizophrenia?' conference was unable to come to a united conclusion, or that anyone else has since. Currently, there is no alternative to concluding that understanding what an episode of psychosis is and deciding what to do about it, depends upon many things, but primarily, upon who is involved in making those judgements.

There is little new here. Arguing that 'knowledge' is inescapably fluid and provisional reflects Popper's more detailed treatise (Popper 2002), and recognising linkages between 'knowledge', power and how human affairs are conducted across time and contexts, is a core feature of Michel Foucault's many analyses (see, for instance, Mambrol 2017). Giving attention to 'who is involved' in relation to understanding and responding to any one episode of psychosis sharpens focus upon the parts they are playing, their background and allegiances, the opinions these have generated, and the power and 'authority' of such roles and opinions.

This can be envisaged as an 'economy of opinions'; who holds which opinions, how have they arisen, and how do participants interact; how do they 'trade' opinions with one another. Bernice Pescosolido's Network Episode Model (Pescosolido 2011) offers a way of thinking about interactions among those around a person experiencing psychosis. These are likely to include their immediate social circle, mental health 'experts', and the wider social context in which an episode of psychosis might be playing out. The Network Episode Model offers a way of considering how these various participants might interact, and together generate whatever that response might be. What has come to be known as Symbolic Interactionism (Blumer 1969) offers a more generalised framework that outlines how all meanings, understandings and opinions are shaped and generated through human interactions, including those implicated in an episode of psychosis. The next two sections offer more detailed outlines of these frameworks, and there then follows a discussion of how bringing them together offers a way of considering how this, that or another understanding of psychosis and its implications might arise in this, that or another set of socially determined circumstances.

Pescosolido's Network Episode Model

This model (Pescosolido 2011) elevates the experience of 'illness' and its 'treatment' from the conventional, mechanistic construct of a biological disturbance more or less responsive to expert intervention, to the outcome of complex interactions between social and somatic influences. In particular, it pays attention to ways in which the experience of 'illness' is subject to the opinions and reactions of the ailing person's immediate social circle; that these in turn are subject to the institutional setting – the availability, accessibility and perceived value of healthcare and other support; and that these in their turn are subject to the wider geographic, political and historic context in which they are embedded. It can be thought of as a more detailed and contextually defined way of considering how the sick role (Parsons 1951) is playing out in a defined set of circumstances. It also acknowledges that these interactions can extend *into* the individual in the form of altered physiological activity and even changes in gene expression; what has come to be known as epigenetics. Thus, the model outlines a seamless set of interactions which impinge upon the living individual from without, and from within. Though seamless, insofar as boundaries between them are difficult to define, external influences can be helpfully conceptualised as: the 'patient's' immediate personal network; people with whom they have direct personal contact, institutions and organisations; formal social structures that influence the opinions, choices and activities of that network in relation to healthcare, and the wider social context; historical, political and geographic legacies and influences that shape those structures. The model envisages an individual whose experience of 'illness' is primarily determined by the actions and opinions of their immediate personal network, that these actions and opinions are strongly influenced by how institutional healthcare arrangements and other formal social structures are experienced and perceived, and that such institutional settings are themselves reflections of history, politics, geography and other determinants of the 'time' and the 'place' in which events are occurring. Internal influences upon the experience of 'illness' might include physiological or anatomical disturbances, such as coronary artery disease, the growth of a cancer, the consequences of an injury or an infection, or the effects of medication. In relation to troublesome experiences of psychosis, family, friends and perhaps work colleagues will each have their own views on what they imply, and of the 'patient'. They will have differing relationships with the 'patient' and with one another, and they will have a variety of views, experiences and opinions concerning available mental health professionals. Available and participating mental health professionals will have their own views, experiences and opinions. Most probably they will be employees bound, to a greater or lesser extent, by their employing organisations' obligations, expectations and resources. These in turn will be shaped by the prevailing ideological, historical and political landscape within which such organisations are embedded; responsibilities for 'risk management', adherence or otherwise to an 'illness' model of mental health difficulties, commercial pressures, and public and political expectations. From within, the 'patient' might be influenced by the effects of prescribed psycho-pharmaceuticals, recreational drug use, alcohol, the effects of 'stress', or the consequences of disturbed access to an appropriate diet and other home comforts. The Network Episode Model focuses upon how these many influences impinge upon an individual, and determine how an episode of 'illness' is experienced and conducted. The actors and their roles might differ, but given its scope and flexibility, it is as applicable to an experience of psychosis as it might be to, say, a coronavirus infection.

Symbolic interaction

Running through the Network Episode Model (Pescosolido 2011), and through real-world experiences of 'illness' and their 'treatment' it is designed to mimic, is emphasis upon the human interactions that populate and shape them. Symbolic Interactionism is a generic approach to the way in which meanings and understandings are generated through human interactions (Blumer 1969). As such it offers a framework from within which to explore, for instance, how different ways of understanding an experience of psychosis might develop.

The approach has a long and respected history among social scientists with an interest in mental health difficulties. It is detectable in the work of Charles Cooley (1864–1929), George Herbert Mead (1863–1931), Erving Goffman (1922–1982) and Thomas J. Scheff (b. 1929) (Scheff 2005; Fink 2016), although the term itself came later. Scheff's profound and enduring exposition of how 'mental illness' can be understood as a consequence of human responses to 'deviance', *Being Mentally Ill,* was first published in 1966, as a second edition in 1984 and as a third edition in 1999 (Scheff 1999). Although Scheff does not directly use the term 'symbolic interaction', his thesis explicitly outlines how self-perceptions, role adoption and the fate of someone suffering 'mental illness' are critically determined by their interactions with others, and the words 'symbolic' and 'interaction' both occur repeatedly, throughout the book.

The term 'symbolic interactionism' was coined by Herbert Blumer (1969) who has summarised the framework in the form of three underpinning principles.

Firstly, that humans act toward things on the basis of the meanings they ascribe to those things. This emphasises the central part derived meaning plays in determining how an individual behaves towards other people, physical objects, actions, concepts or whatever other phenomena they might encounter. How the world is *understood* rather than how it *is*, is what determines how someone responds to it.

Secondly, such understandings, or meanings, are derived from, and arise out of, human interactions. People interact with each other by interpreting one another's utterances and actions, rather than simply responding to them. What something – a pile of rubbish, a military parade, the experience of hearing voices or whatever else is being considered – appears to mean, represent or symbolise to others is discerned from what they say about it and

41

how they respond to it. How it is understood and what it means to oneself takes this into account, may or may not influence existing meanings, and will influence further rounds of interacting behaviours and debate. How and in what ways one individual's understanding of a particular phenomenon influences another's will be subject to the nature of their relationship: can I trust them? Are they an acknowledged expert in this field? What do others have to say about this? And so on.

Thirdly, meanings accumulate and are continuously modified through this process. Successive encounters with a particular phenomenon and other's reactions to it provide the grist of an interpretive process by which the subjective meanings, or implications of a particular situation are developed and form the basis of action. Sudden pain will likely result in rapidly withdrawing the offending thumb and inspecting it. Recognising that the pain was due to clumsy use of a hammer, to clumsy use of a knife or to a wasp that is just flying away will result in different interpretations of the pain, and different resulting actions. A small child as yet unable to distinguish between these differing interpretations and their implications may, instead, remain in a state of less differentiated distress. How others respond to this will play a strong part in determining how they interpret and respond to similar experiences in the future.

Viewed through this particular lens, 'knowledge', meaning or understanding, concerning anything, are not independent, external things, out there to be acquired in full or totally ignored. Instead, they are the outcome of interactions with others. 'Knowledge', meaning or understanding apply to the sense someone makes of whatever it is they have in their sights at the time. That might be something common, straightforward and uncontroversial such as a can opener. It might be a film, a play or a piece of music, it might be a person, it might be a worrying symptom such as chest pain, it might be a political manifesto or an academic argument, or it might be the experience of voices, an unconventional point of view or someone else undergoing those experiences. Symbolic Interactionism draws attention to the fact that whatever sense is made of these (or of anything else) is not just a sterile, personal opinion. It is the outcome of interacting with others ... over how can openers work and can be used; sharing the experience of an evening's entertainment, discussing it, reading reviews and perhaps comparing it with similar performances; gossiping about someone or sharing an experience of their company with others; discussing the pain with the family, browsing the internet or seeking a medical opinion; political or academic discussion, perhaps with people who are known and liked, perhaps with people who are less convivial; or attempting to make sense of troublesome psychotic experiences by trying to share them with others' experiences, by approaching professionals, by searching the internet, or through reading others' accounts. The emphasis is, that the sense we make of anything, is the outcome of interactions with others.

Psychotic experiences such as voice-hearing and/or unconventional beliefs might be experienced as benign or even pleasant. They might just as easily be experienced as something dreadful, that others could be so concerned about that they might result in coercion and sedation. Under the latter circumstances they are much more likely to be threatening, troublesome and, perhaps, something to be kept hidden. Where a 'patient's' close associates might be in relation this range of opinions, and how and in what way they might influence the 'patient's' understanding will reflect their own understandings of psychosis. These are likely drawn from previous experiences, reading, whatever popular discourse they engage with, and the nature of their relationships with the 'patient' and others involved, including health and social care professionals. Symbolic interactionism firmly locates 'how something is understood' and the consequences that follow, in their social context. It is not necessarily the psychotic experience itself that is troublesome, but how it is understood that does or does not make it so.

By way of illustration, consider how the choice to adopt a vegan diet might be experienced. It reflects a decision to avoid foods in any way derived from animals. Against the background of conventional western dietary habits this might be considered deviant but choices such as this are generally considered 'personal' and respected. Why someone might make this choice will be the result of many influences and how they are received; animals are seen as co-inhabitants of the planet and deserve respect, most commercial animal husbandry is cruel and exploitative, animal farming is a major contributor to environmental degradation, eating meat and other animal products is nutritionally harmful, and perhaps there might be religious or other spiritual contributions to the choice. How any of these, or other considerations, contribute to a personal understanding of animal-product-eating as a bad thing will depend upon human interactions around it; with whom it has been discussed, what has been read about it, with whom one usually eats, previous experiences of meat eating, financial considerations, and more. How these influences are brought together by and within one individual will or will not result in the conclusion that 'animal-product-eating is not for me'. There is nothing intrinsically poisonous or biologically harmful about animal-product-eating; it would not have become established were that the case, but for the vegan, for any of many possible reasons, their reading of them and how they have read others' views, the symbolic meaning they attach to animal-product-eating is that it is not a good idea. Not everyone agrees, but when it is expressed, it is generally respected and, increasingly, it is accommodated by restaurants and other food outlets. What about responses to someone experiencing psychosis?

Psychosis, symbolic interactions and an economy of healthcare 'knowledge'

Were it the case that animal-product-eating was more widely considered a core feature of everyday life, as it is among certain pastoral cultures such as the Maasai, then someone choosing to give it up would be considered significantly deviant. What then would be made of evidence concerning the effects of animal farming upon the environment, of commercial animal farming, of the ecological relationships between humans and other creatures, or of the nutritional benefits or otherwise of animal-product-eating? What interactions and conversations would the putative vegan have with other people? What myths about dangerous or depraving vegans might develop? What 'treatments' might be devised to turn people away from being a vegan?

Of course, none of this happens, because although strict veganism is still confined to a minority who might, by some, be regarded as unusual, it does not and never has had the historical legacy the experience of psychosis carries. From biblical accounts of demonic possession through to present day 'diagnoses', voice hearing and unusual beliefs have been widely viewed as evidence of something unacceptable. Result; on the one hand, 'If you want to give up animal-product-eating, fine, but don't expect me to join you.', and on the other, 'Goodness, are you hearing voices? We need to do something about that.' Clearly the human interactions each of these are going to generate will be entirely different. They will result in quite different symbolic interpretations, or understandings of the 'deviance' and, quite likely, entirely different outcomes.

The nature and content of human interactions involving individuals experiencing psychosis reflect this legacy. The Network Episode Model usefully simplifies the complex interactions that come to bear upon someone who is standing out, whether as a result of illness or overt disability or, indeed for any other reason. This 'deviance' will be most noticeably experienced by those they are most closely associated with; usually friends, family, or work colleagues. Each of these constituencies will have their own prior opinions about what it means to be hearing voices, holding unconventional beliefs or whatever else it is that has raised concern. Uncomplicated experiences of voice-hearing or unconventional beliefs are not uncommon (e.g. van Os et al. 2001), and if they are understood as a feature of internal debate, option appraisal or rehearsal of a past or future encounter, then they can be accommodated as a feature of everyday life and a manifestation of 'normal'. They only become troublesome and subject to the label of 'psychotic experiences' if and when interactions with others generate that view.

The opinions of friends, family, work colleagues and others immediately associated with the person will be the result of their own, individual interactions with what voice hearing or unconventional beliefs symbolise. Do they mean that so and so is having a hard time? Do they mean that so and so has been smoking too much weed? Do they mean that so and so is developing Schizophrenia? Which of those, or other interpretations they adopt will reflect what they have heard, what they recall from similar prior experiences and what they see, hear and read about others' reactions. Prominent among these are likely to be their reading of positions taken by appointed experts in this field. They may have read or heard something about chemical imbalances, they may be aware of someone else like this who was committed to hospital, or be prompted by concerns for safety fuelled by media representations of the 'mad'. All of these and other influences upon what voice hearing and unusual beliefs symbolise for our 'patient's' immediate associates will influence their interactions with them, and in turn influence what these experiences mean to our 'patient', and how they might respond to them. These interactions will also be influenced by the nature and quality of the relationships within which they are embedded, and by the identities and backgrounds of those who form them. Thus, from a symbolic interactionist perspective, otherwise untroubling experiences of voices or challenging beliefs can come to be understood and experienced as unwanted and possibly damning evidence of a severe mental illness, not because that is an inevitable outcome written into the natural history of a disease called 'Schizophrenia', but because that is the discursive context within which they have been considered by those directly involved in the episode.

Naturally, healthcare professionals are prominent and influential contributors to that discursive context, but theirs is a very specific perspective. Their understanding of psychotic experiences is part of an arduously obtained professional qualification. They have access to what society has chosen to make available in order to provide for the 'mad', and their qualifications and experience mark them out as experts with more and better experience of the subject than others. Mental healthcare professionals embody the next tier of Pescosolido's model (Pescosolido 2011), or economy of opinions, as it might be applied to the experience of psychosis. Theirs is not usually knowledge derived from experiencing psychosis or from living alongside someone who is. Their knowledge and understanding of it reflect a distillation of science and other forms of research that will have found their ways into training schemes, programmes of professional development, and intra-professional conversation and discourse. Their practices are almost always embedded in a large healthcare organisation, with its own momentum and needs for self-preservation. Mental healthcare professionals hold and exert considerable power as experts in the field, but the expertise they hold is narrowly defined by training curricula which, for reasons of formal approval, tend to prioritise certain forms and sources of 'knowledge'; certain bodies of opinion. Furthermore, what they are paid for and supported in doing is often quite narrowly prescribed by expectations of adherence to the 'scientific' evidence base. From a symbolic interactionist perspective mental healthcare professionals exert considerable influence over how voice-hearing, challenging thoughts or other 'symptoms' of psychosis are understood, but this influence is from a very specific perspective; one determined by ways in which they and the organisations they inhabit are themselves embedded in their wider socio-political context.

The over-arching layer of Pescosolido's model (Pescosolido 2011), the upper tier of our economy of opinions, is what she defines as the 'community core subsystem' but for present purposes can be better envisaged, as Michel

Foucault might, as underpinning, wider and not necessarily consciously articulated discourses that define the general tenor, values, and the resulting distribution of power found in a given socio-political context. In relation to experiences of psychosis this refers to historically longstanding and widely applied habits of distaste and discomfort in relation to certain kinds of people who are 'different' or who are behaving in an unfamiliar way. It applies to intolerances of the economically unproductive, unless they are suitably certified as 'disabled'. It applies to the view that formal authority should be applied to contain these challenges to social order, and it applies to the licencing, employment and organising of a specialised workforce to carry this out. These discourses find expression in various forms of public policy and the institutions they generate and support. Until relatively recently those experiencing psychosis were sequestered in the asylum or suppressed in other ways (Scull 2022). More recently they have been defined by 'diagnosis' and, effectively, socially excluded as essentially flawed (see Chapter 1). A whole industry has grown up around them, comprising a hugely profitable trade in psycho-pharmaceuticals, and a plethora of professionals and their infrastructure. In most jurisdictions there is mental health legislation which authorises the use of force to detain someone who is deemed to be a challenge to personal or public safety on account of mental health difficulties. From a symbolic interactionist perspective these formal and institutionalised reactions to someone experiencing psychosis have a powerful effect upon how they are viewed by others, how they experience others' interactions with them and as a result, how they view themselves. Of course, many are uncomfortable and distressed, but there are numerous accounts of the extent to which this is felt to be the result, not the cause, of the social alienation they experience as a result of everyday interactions with others (see Chapter 1.). Concerns about the risk of violence posed by people experiencing psychosis provide an illustration.

It is estimated that around 6% of all homicides in the UK are attributed to someone with a 'diagnosis' of Schizophrenia (Baird et al. 2010). This is an excess, given the fact that people with a 'diagnosis' of Schizophrenia account for less than 1% of the population, and it readily feeds concern that people with 'Schizophrenia' are dangerous. However, some 49% of all UK homicides are also considered attributable to a quarrel, a revenge attack or a loss of temper (Office for National Statistics 2020). To what extent is the excess rate of homicides found among people with a 'diagnosis' of Schizophrenia due in some way to the condition itself, or to the fact that the experience of being unreasonably shunned by others nurtures anger, a sense of rejection and/or a short fuse? We don't know, because we tend not to look at the question this way round. The assumption is that people with 'Schizophrenia' are dangerous, but it could just as readily be that such people are subject to human interactions coloured by discrimination and social exclusion, which of themselves generate anger and frustration that can lead to violence.

Toxic interactions

There is no widely agreed definition of troubling psychotic experiences. There are numerous opinions, and which is held by whom depends very much upon where they are coming from and what they want to know. Knowledge concerning *anything* is a slippery fish which wriggles this way and that depending upon who is holding it. Cutting edge research is best understood as a set of ongoing debates, albeit slow and painstaking, and punctuated by repeated references to experimental data or other sources of confirmation and refutation. Such debates are conducted by numerous groups of interacting cognoscenti who commonly approach the field of interest from different starting points, and whether or not a particular position prevails over others depends upon the perceived authority of its adherents. Where such debates are largely contained within the narrow confines of academia, that authority is relatively unchallenged and 'expert opinion' holds sway. In relation to understandings of psychosis, such debate is much more wide-ranging and widely dispersed. As a result, a much wider range of views and interpretations contribute to the human interactions that form any one person's understanding of the experience, whether they be observer or participant. This is not a random process. Views and interpretations contributing to interactions around someone experiencing psychosis will reflect the identities and propensities of those amongst whom the interactions are taking place, and these in turn reflect the institutional, educational and socio-political environment in which the events are playing out. Not all of these are convivial and constructive. There is scope for toxic interactions, whereby otherwise harmless and possibly fleeting subjective experiences can become demonised as a result of others' interpretations of them, whereby the identity of 'disabled person' becomes entrenched and self-fulfilling, whereby an unjustified reputation for violence can develop, whereby commitments are made to long-term, possibly harmful medication, or whereby other debilitating consequences might follow.

Recent years have seen the accumulation of considerable quantities of epidemiological data that link the risk of experiencing psychosis, or at least of obtaining a 'diagnosis' of Schizophrenia, to a range of social circumstances. These include migration, ethnic status, and urban living. They also include associations with adverse childhood experiences, certain other features of family life, acute trauma and accumulated distress. All of these can interact, but it remains unclear how their individual or collective impacts result in or contribute to the phenomenon identified as 'the troublesome experience of psychosis'. How do migration, urban living, adverse childhood experiences and other vicissitudes 'cause' psychosis, or any other form of mental health difficulty?

The conventional approach to that question is to turn to a notion of stress that results in or triggers a biologically mediated reaction (Johnstone and Boyle 2018). A more parsimonious approach might be to consider the troublesome experience of psychosis not as an identifiable 'thing', made more likely by certain circumstances, but a derived understanding of certain subjective experiences and propensities, and as a result, a derived (and degraded) understanding of who and what one is (as Scheff does). This avoids the need to impute intervening biological mechanisms other than the generalised biological embodiment of all human behaviour. It also allows closer linkage between the details of contributing human interactions and their possible contribution to unwelcome consequences. Experiences of psychosis can be thought of as (usually) unhelpful ways of understanding subjective experiences and the implications these have for experiencing identity. Symbolic interactionism argues that the unravelling of how unhelpful ways of understanding subjective experiences might have come about would benefit from focusing upon the human interactions that have led to them. Critically this has to include clarifying who those interactions are amongst, the views they articulate (overtly or otherwise), their perceived authority, how readily such interactions can occur, in what ways they develop, and levels of trust between participants.

Within such a framework there is wide scope to consider the possibility of associations between social circumstances, and the risk of developing the entrenched patterns of concern, confusion and distress that often characterise troubling psychotic experiences. Migration, urban life and difficult life circumstances all represent or result in particular patterns of human interaction. Adverse childhood experiences and other features of family life leave their stamp on how readily or otherwise someone might relate to others, or what their choice of associates might be. People with mental health difficulties, in particular those experiencing psychosis, are profoundly discriminated against, with defining effects upon the human interactions they can expect, and much of what is emerging from psychotherapy research in this area suggests that the most effective interventions are those which unravel the consequences of toxic interactions such as these.

Given the accumulation of epidemiological and other data identifying associations between certain social conditions and the risk of troubling psychotic experiences, it seems appropriate to review them. Given the collapse in credibility of the biomedical framework which has served as a principle around which to organise thinking about psychosis for so long, it seems timely to consider an alternative. Considering how the epidemiological data might reflect particular patterns of human interaction, and how such interactions might have unintended toxic effects offers that alternative. Inevitably this is speculative, but it is presented as an approach which might reward future empirical investigators.

References

Baird, A., Webb, R. T., Hunt, I. M., Appleby, L. and Shaw, J. (2020) 'Homicide by men diagnosed with schizophrenia: national case–control study', *The British Journal of Psychiatry Open*, Vol. 6, No. e143, pp. 1–8.

Blumer, H. (1969) *Symbolic Interactionism. Perspective and Method*. Berkeley: University of California Press.

Buchanan, J. (2020) 'What Is It Like to Have Psychosis?'. https://www.psychreg.org/experience-psychosis/ (accessed October 2022].

Fink, E. L. (2016) 'Symbolic Interactionism'. In C. R. Berger and M. E. Roloff (Eds.) *The International Encyclopedia of Interpersonal Communication. First Edition*. New York: Wiley-Blackwell, pp. 1–13.

Flack, W. F. Jr., Miller, D. R. and Wiener, M. (1991) *What Is Schizophrenia?* New York: Springer-Verlag.

Hawking, S. (2018) *Brief Answers to the Big Questions*. London: John Murray.

Johnstone, L. and Boyle, M. with Cromby, J., Dillon, J., Harper, D., Kinderman, P., Longden, E., Pilgrim, D. and Read, J. (2018) *The Power Threat Meaning Framework: Towards the identification of patterns in emotional distress, unusual experiences and troubled or troubling behaviour, as an alternative to functional psychiatric diagnosis*. Leicester: British Psychological Society.

Kinderman, P. (2014) *A Prescription for Psychiatry: Why We Need a Whole New Approach to Mental Health and Wellbeing*. Basingstoke: Palgrave.

Kohn, A. (1990) 'Getting a Grip on Schizophrenia'. *Los Angeles Times*. June 25th 1990.

Mambrol, N. (2017) 'Key Theories of Michel Foucault'. https://literariness.org/2017/03/28/key-theories-of-michel-foucault/ (accessed October 2022).

Newton, I. (1687) *Philosophiæ Naturalis Principia Mathematica*. London: Edmund Halley.

NHS Digital (2022) 'Mental Health Act Statistics, Annual Figures – 2020–2021'. https://digital.nhs.uk/data-and-information/publications/statistical/mental-health-act-statistics-annual-figures/2020-21-annual-figures (accessed October 2022).

Office for National Statistics (2020) 'Homicide in England and Wales: year ending March 2020'. https://www.ons.gov.uk/peoplepopulationandcommunity/crimeandjustice/articles/homicideinenglandandwales/yearendingmarch2020 (accessed October 2022).

Parsons, T. (1951) *The Social System*. London: Routledge and Keegan Hall.

Pescosolido, B. A. (2011) 'Organising the Sociological Landscape for the next decades of health and health care research: The Network Episode Model III-R as Cartographic Subfield Guide'. In B. A. Pescosolido, J. K. Martin, J. D. McLeod and A. Rogers (Eds.) *Handbook of the Sociology of Health, Illness and Healing*. New York: Springer, pp. 39–66.

Piat, M. (2000) 'The NIMBY Phenomenon: Community Residents' Concern about Housing for Deinstitutionalized People', *Health & Social Work*, Vol. 25, No. 2, pp. 127–138.

Popper, K. R. (1960) 'Lecture to British Academy, 20th January 1960', *Proceedings of the British Academy*, Vol. 46, p. 69.

Popper, K. R. (2002) *Conjectures and Refutations. The Growth of Scientific Knowledge*. London: Routledge and Kegan Paul.

Read, J. and Dillon, J. (2013) *Models of Madness*. Second Edition. Hove: Routledge.

Scheff, T. J. (1999) *Being Mentally Ill*. Third edition. New York: Routledge.

Scheff, T. J. (2005) 'Looking-Glass Self: Goffman as Symbolic Interactionist', *Symbolic Interaction*, Vol. 28, No. 2, pp. 147–166.

Scull, A. (2022) *Desperate Remedies. Psychiatry and the Mysteries of Mental Illness*. London: Allen Lane.

Shoham, N., Cooper, C., Lewis, G., Bebbington, P. and McManus, S. (2021) 'Temporal trends in psychotic symptoms: Repeated cross-sectional surveys of the population in England 2000–14', *Schizophrenia Research*, Vol. 228, pp. 97–102.

Siegler, M. and Osmond, H. (1966) 'Models of Madness', *British Journal of Psychiatry*, Vol. 112, pp. 1193–1203.

Tandon, R., Keshavan, M. S. and Nasrallah, H. A. (2008) 'Schizophrenia, "Just the Facts": What we know in 2008 Part 1: Overview', *Schizophrenia Research*, Vol. 100, pp. 4–19.

Van Os, J., Hanssen, M., Bijl, R. V. and Vollebergh, W. (2001) 'Prevalence of Psychotic Disorder and Community Level of Psychotic Symptoms', *Archives of General Psychiatry*, Vol. 58, pp. 663–668.

3

CHILDHOOD ADVERSITY AND TROUBLING PSYCHOTIC EXPERIENCES

Although it now seems impossible to think otherwise, it is only relatively recently that a link between adverse or abusive childhood experiences and adult psychological wellbeing has become widely acknowledged. It is claimed that Sigmund Freud considered his clients' accounts of sexual abuse to be fantasies (Rush 1980). Even as recently as 1972 the frequency of incest was being reported as occurring in only one in a million families (Henderson 1972). The first systematic survey investigating the frequency of childhood sexual abuse unearthed the fact that 27% women and 16% men could recall some form of what would now be regarded as sexual abuse during childhood (Finkelhor et al. 1990). Historical denials of this served to obscure the activities of several notorious abusers who were able to hide in plain sight. This has changed and associations between the experience of adversity and/or abuse in childhood and a wide range of adult difficulties, including the propensity to experience psychosis are now widely acknowledged. In large part this reflects general acceptance of a mountain of empirical data which are worth reviewing. A landmark is Varese and colleagues' 2012 meta-analysis of data from studies that had investigated associations between the experience of childhood adversities and the occurrence of psychotic experiences later in life (Varese et al. 2012a). This was not the first such report and it is unlikely to be the last, but it lays down a clear marker. It brings together findings from case control studies in which comparisons are made between those with troubling experiences of psychosis and 'control subjects', cross-sectional studies in which those with experiences of psychosis have been investigated in further detail, and prospective studies in which those with troublesome experiences of psychosis have been followed over time. Some details of these follow.

Case control studies.

Agid and colleagues (1999) compared the incidence and form of early parental loss amongst Israeli patients classified as suffering 'Major Depression',

DOI: 10.4324/9780429059094-4

'Bipolar Disorder' or 'Schizophrenia' with the incidence and form of early parental loss among matched controls. Patients were drawn from an inpatient population and controls were selected on the basis of gender, age, immigration status and ethnicity. Of the seventy-six patients classified as suffering with 'Schizophrenia', seventeen had suffered the loss of one or both parents by death or by permanent separation by the age of sixteen; fourteen of them by the age of eight. Only six of their matched controls had suffered a similar loss.

Bartels-Velthuis and colleagues (2012) followed up participants in a population-based survey of 3,870 seven- to eight-year-olds in Groningen, The Netherlands, that was conducted during the 2002/2003 school year. They explored the experience of voice-hearing. In 2007/2008, 170 of the original voice hearers and 165 of the original non-voice hearers were reviewed and assessments made of their experiences of trauma such as sexual abuse, internet blackmailing or witnessing a serious accident, injury or threat, and their experiences of stress such as parental separation or death, serious illness or victimisation. These assessments were conducted by trained interviewers. Some 80% of those who had continued to hear voices between the two surveys, or who had begun to hear voices between them, reported at least one such traumatic experience. In contrast, only 40% of those who had not heard voices throughout, or who had stopped hearing voices between the surveys, reported such experiences, and overall, these were reported as less intense.

Cohen and colleagues (2010) were interested in suicidal thinking and behaviour amongst older New York State residents: 198 people aged fifty-five or older holding a 'diagnosis' of Schizophrenia for at least ten years before the investigation were compared with 113 from a community sample who were matched to them in pairs by age, gender, race and income. Adverse earlier life experiences were quantified as scores on a Lifetime Trauma and Victimisation scale (Cohen et al. 1997). This reflects reports of one or more of twelve potential adverse experiences, such as being the victim of assault, sexual abuse or rape, or witnessing a violent death. Not only was there an association between suicidality and scores on this scale, but those with a 'diagnosis' of Schizophrenia scored higher than their controls.

Convoy and colleagues (1995) considered the frequency of sexual abuse before the age of fifteen among psychiatric patients in Prague by interview and anonymous questionnaire. These included 100 people troubled by psychotic experiences who were compared with 100 'controls'; people with no experience of mental health services recruited from healthcare facilities and other workplaces. Of the 'psychotics' sixteen reported such experiences as opposed to eleven 'controls'.

Dell'Erba and colleagues (2003) compared thirty-five male and nineteen female Italian inpatients with a DSM-IV (1994) classification of Schizophrenia, with twenty-eight men and thirty-two women enrolled from hospital staff. At interview and from medical records thirty of the patients but only ten of the controls were identified as having suffered adverse childhood experiences such as early parental loss, institutionalisation or abuse.

Fennig and colleagues (2005) compared forty Israeli adolescents with a 'diagnosis' of Schizophrenia, with twenty recruited from nearby schools who were matched by age and gender. They reported the number of life events (from a fifty-one-item scale), and the occurrence of sexual abuse. The average number of negative life events among the 'Schizophrenic' patients was 8.82 as opposed to 5.05 amongst the controls. Experience of sexual abuse was elicited using a Hebrew version of screening questions developed in the US during the late 1980s (Finkelhor et al. 1990). The 'Schizophrenic' adolescents reported a higher frequency of such experiences than their controls though, interestingly, absolute numbers were not reported.

Fisher et al. (2010) used British data collected in the course of the Aetiology and Ethnicity in Schizophrenia and Other Psychoses (ÆSOP) study. The Childhood Experience of Care Abuse Questionnaire (CECA.Q, Bifulco et al 2005) was used to register experiences of sexual abuse, parental neglect, antipathy or physical abuse before the age of seventeen. Of the 390 'cases' and 391 'controls' recruited into the overall study, 182 'cases' and 246 'controls' completed the CECA.Q. Maternal abuse, antipathy and neglect were more common among the 'cases' than among the controls; 14% vs 5.4%, 13% vs 7.3% and 11% vs 7.3% respectively.

Friedman and Harrison (1984) investigated the sexual history of 'Schizophrenic' women by comparing twenty inpatients so classified with fifteen 'controls' matched by race, age and religious affiliation. Information was obtained using a semi-structured interview based upon a self-report questionnaire (Frank et al. 1978). Twelve of the 'Schizophrenic' patients reported having been sexually abused as a child, as opposed to two of the 'controls'.

Furukawa et al. (1998) compared the rate of childhood parental loss, by death or permanent separation, between 225 Japanese people classified as 'Schizophrenic' at the time of their first hospital attendance, and 122 healthy controls taken from a separate epidemiological study. In this instance there was no significant difference between the two groups.

Giblin et al. (2004) compared fourteen subjects with a classification of 'Late onset psychosis' and thirteen subjects with a classification of 'Late onset depression', who were all receiving psychiatric care in London, with eighteen healthy volunteers recruited from a variety of community sources. All were over the age of sixty. Adverse experiences in childhood and adult life were explored using a questionnaire based upon the Social Readjustment Scale (Holmes and Rahe 1967). It was designed to detect seven threatening experiences or fragile relationships such as abuse or illegitimacy, nine forms of loss such as parental death or miscarriage, four health-related adversities such as injury or disability and seven other forms of hardship such as frequent moves in childhood or financial problems. Overall, both patient groups reported more experiences of adversity than the healthy volunteers. When only childhood adversities were considered, 'Late onset psychosis' subjects reported more such experiences than both the 'Late onset depression' subjects and the heathy volunteers.

Heins and colleagues (2011) considered 272 patients with a 'diagnosis' of Nonaffective Psychotic Disorder who were being seen as outpatients or inpatients across the southern part of the Netherlands and Belgium. 227 comparison subjects were recruited through random mailings and local newspaper advertisements. The occurrence of adverse childhood experiences was assessed using a shortened Dutch version of the Childhood Trauma Questionnaire (Bernstein et al. 1997). Subjects indicated the extent to which they experienced a range of emotional, physical, and general childhood abuses and emotional or physical neglect resulting in a score for abuse, a score for neglect and an overall trauma score. On all three scales, not only was there an association between the degree of abuse, neglect or overall trauma and the probability of experiencing psychosis, there was also evidence that the more intense these were, the stronger the association.

Husted et al. (2010) were interested in the interaction between the presence of a family history suggesting genetic influences on the experience of psychosis, and a history of childhood adversity. Seventy-nine adult Canadian subjects fulfilling formal classificatory criteria for 'Schizophrenia' were compared with eighty-six unaffected adults from the same family background. Childhood adversity was defined as a threat to physical, emotional or sexual integrity, a victim of serious injury or illness, or a witness to violence. Information was obtained by in-depth interview, from medical, social services and legal records, and from collateral information from relatives. These data were coded by trained investigators who determined whether there was evidence of physical abuse, neglect, sexual abuse, verbal abuse, a victim of life-threatening accident, major disaster such as flood or fire, physical assault outside the family or witnessing such events, all before the age of nineteen. Sixty-five of the 'Schizophrenic' subjects and forty-five of the unaffected subjects were deemed to be at 'genetic risk'. Sixteen of the 'Schizophrenic' subjects, but only seven of the unaffected, had suffered adverse childhood experiences identified in this way. 'Genetic risk' had no effect upon the relationship between adverse childhood experiences and the probability of experiencing psychosis.

McCabe and colleagues (2012) considered 675 Australian subjects; 408 were classified as suffering 'Schizophrenia' by ICD-10 (1994) criteria and 267 were considered healthy controls. Adverse childhood experiences were assessed using a modification of the Childhood Adversity Questionnaire (Rosenman and Rodgers 2004). This measures six aspects of parental emotional availability: parental affection, and mental health difficulties or substance abuse; detects a background of household tension and conflict or parental separation; makes nine measures of abuse, neglect or overly authoritarian rearing, and three of parental indifference. 'Schizophrenia' subjects were more likely to have experienced fifteen of these twenty forms of childhood adversity before the age of eighteen than the healthy controls. Experiences that were not associated with a higher probability of troublesome psychotic experiences were parental divorce, parental loss, poverty or financial hardship and loss of a sibling.

Morgan and colleagues (2007) did find that parental loss by death or separation before the age of sixteen was more common among those experiencing psychosis for the first time. Of the 390 'cases' recruited into the ÆSOP programme, 190 had experienced one or other of these, whereas either of these had occurred among only ninety-four of the 391 'controls'. When these data were considered by race, the same heightened risk pertained for both Black British Caribbeans and White British, but the rate of parental loss was much higher amongst Black British Caribbeans irrespective of whether they were 'cases' or not; 48% 'White' 'cases' and 21% 'White' 'controls' had experienced early parental loss as opposed to 59% 'Black' 'cases' and 33% 'Black' 'controls'.

Rubino and colleagues (2009) compared 173 Italian adult inpatients with DSM-IV (1994) classifications of 'Schizophrenia' with 310 volunteers from the general population. Four types of childhood abuse and various forms of parental adversity such as discord, separation, death or mental health difficulties were considered. All adversities apart from sexual abuse and parental death were associated with a 'diagnosis' of Schizophrenia, and greater the number of adversities, the greater the probability of diagnosis.

Varese and colleagues (2012b) were interested in the relationships between childhood trauma, dissociation and the experience of hallucinations. Forty-five patients with experiences of psychosis were recruited from in-patient and out-patient mental health services in North Wales, and compared with twenty healthy controls recruited as volunteers from among university staff and students. The experience of childhood adversity was assessed using the Child Abuse and Trauma Scale (Sanders and Becker-Lausen 1995). This asks subjects to rate the frequency ('Never', 'Rarely', 'Sometimes', 'Often' or 'Always') with which each of thirty-eight potential adversities such as 'As a child did you feel unwanted or emotionally neglected?', 'Were there traumatic or upsetting sexual experiences when you were a child or teenager that you couldn't speak to adults about?' or 'Did you witness the physical mistreatment of another family member?' are recalled. It provides an overall abuse and trauma score and four subscale scores reflecting experiences of sexual abuse, punishment or physical abuse, neglect or an adverse home environment and emotional abuse. A version of the Launay–Slade Hallucination Scale (Bentall and Slade, 1985) was used to quantify the experience of both auditory and visual hallucinations. Subjects were asked to rate how certainly each of twelve items such as 'No matter how hard I try to concentrate, unrelated thoughts always creep into my mind', 'Sometimes my thoughts seem as real as actual events in my life' or 'I often hear a voice speaking my thoughts aloud' apply to them. Patients scored higher on the Child Abuse and Trauma Scale than controls, and, irrespective of clinical status, higher scores on the Hallucination Scale were associated with higher levels of abuse and trauma.

Weber and colleagues (2008) recruited thirty-two subjects with an ICD-10 (1994) classification of 'Schizophrenia' from a psychiatric clinic in Southern Germany, and compared them with thirty-one control subjects matched by age and gender. The Early Trauma Inventory (Bremner et al. 2000) was used to assess adverse childhood experiences. This is a fifty-six-item semi-structured interview which assesses the experience of physical, emotional, and sexual abuse, and traumatic experiences such as parental loss and natural disaster. For each item the frequency of abuse or trauma, the age of the subject at its onset and termination, the identity of the perpetrator, and its past and current impact are all explored. As well as the overall number of adverse events, this information allows a Childhood Trauma Severity Index to be derived for different periods of development. When compared with the control subjects, patients classified as suffering 'Schizophrenia' had modestly higher Childhood Trauma Severity Indices for the period before six years of age, the period between the age of six and puberty, and the period between puberty and age at the time of interview.

Cross-sectional studies

Bebbington and colleagues (2011) considered data from the third British Adult Psychiatric Morbidity Survey which was conducted in 2006 and 2007. This was designed to be representative of the adult population in terms of age, gender and region. Sampling was based upon postcode addresses. This resulted in 13,171 eligible addresses which yielded 7,353 willing subjects who were interviewed by trained social investigators. Those interviews were considered suggestive of troubling psychotic experiences on the basis of responses to the Psychosis Screening Questionnaire (Bebbington and Nayani 1995), that the participant was currently taking antipsychotic medication, or that they had been admitted to a hospital or ward specialising in mental health problems at any time. 313 met these criteria of whom 190 agreed to a further interview, and twenty-three of these formally fulfilled ICD-10 (1994) criteria for 'Non-organic psychosis' during the year prior to the second interview. Experience of childhood sexual abuse had been explored during the first interview as answers to three questions: 'Has anyone talked to you in a sexual way that made you feel uncomfortable?', 'Has anyone touched you, or got you to touch them, in a sexual way without your consent?' and 'Has anyone had sexual intercourse with you without your consent?' The ages at which abuse had happened were recorded and considered as; during childhood (before the age of sixteen), or during adulthood. Answers to the 'before sixteen' questions among the twenty-three definite 'cases' of troublesome psychosis and among the twenty who endorsed two or more items of the psychosis screen were compared with those of the full survey population who were not considered to have psychotic experiences. 29% of the 'cases' but only 10.2% of the 'controls' endorsed the first question, 25.8% of the former but only 8.2% of the second, and 16.1% and 1.8%, the third, respectively.

Kelleher and colleagues (2008, and Harley et al. 2010) explored interactions between adverse childhood experiences, the use of cannabis and the likelihood of troublesome psychotic experiences: 211 adolescents aged between twelve and fifteen years and their parents were investigated using a semi-structured interview which enquired into adverse childhood experiences, cannabis use and psychiatric symptoms in adolescence; the Schedule for Affective Disorders and Schizophrenia for School-Age Children (Kaufman et al. 1996). Children were asked the following in relation to physical abuse: 'When your parents got mad at you, did they hit you?' 'Have you ever been hit so that you had bruises or marks on your body, or were hurt in some way?' 'What happened?' In relation to sexual abuse, they were asked: 'Did anyone ever touch you in your private parts when they shouldn't have?' 'What happened?' 'Has someone ever touched you in a way that made you feel bad?' Parents were asked the same questions appropriately modified. A disclosure of physical or sexual abuse by a parent was taken as evidence of a history of child abuse, regardless of whether it was also disclosed by the child. There were no cases where the parent disputed the occurrence of abuse that had been disclosed by the child. Exposure to domestic violence was assessed in the following way: 'Some kids' parents have a lot of nasty fights. They call each other bad names, throw things, and threaten to do bad things to each other. Did your parents ever get in really bad fights?' 'Tell me about the worst fight you remember your parents having.' 'What happened?'. Again, parents were asked the same questions, appropriately modified. A disclosure of physical violence between parents/step-parents by a parent was taken as evidence of a history of domestic violence. There were no cases where the parent disputed the occurrence of domestic violence that had been disclosed by the child. Bullying was explored on the basis of parents' and children's answers to 'Have you (Has your child) ever been bullied?' and 'Have you (Has your child) ever been accused of being a bully?' Again, a positive response from either the parent or child was taken as evidence of a history of being a bully or being a victim of bullying, and there were no instances of young people reporting these experiences that were denied by their parents. Both adolescent and parent were asked whether the adolescent had ever used cannabis. If the answer was yes, then frequency of use in the past six months and frequency ever used were recorded. Fourteen adolescents gave unequivocal evidence of psychotic experiences. Of these eight reported neither cannabis use or trauma, one reported only cannabis use, two reported only trauma, and three reported both. Intriguingly five of the fourteen children identified as experiencing psychotic symptoms were considered to have been accused of bullying.

Houston and colleagues (2008) were also interested the possibility of an interaction between cannabis use and childhood sexual trauma, and the likelihood of experiencing psychotic symptoms. Data were taken from Part II of the National Comorbidity Survey (Kessler 1994) reflecting responses from 5,877 individuals. A history of childhood sexual trauma was deemed to be present on the basis of answers to two questions; 'Were you raped (someone had sexual intercourse with you when you did not want to by threatening you or using some degree of force)?' and 'Were you sexually molested (someone touched or felt your genitals when you did not want them to)?' The experience of psychotic symptoms was identified on the basis of responses to an adapted version of the Structured Clinical Interview for the DSM-III-R (1987). Cannabis use before the age of sixteen was identified on the basis of answers to 'Have you ever used either marijuana or hashish, even once?' and 'How old were you the first time (you used marijuana or hashish)?' Forty-two subjects were deemed to have experienced troubling psychotic symptoms, twenty-six of whom had neither experienced childhood sexual trauma or used cannabis before the age of sixteen, eight had experienced childhood sexual trauma but had not used cannabis before the age of sixteen, four had used cannabis before the age of sixteen but had not experienced child-hood sexual trauma and four had experienced both. In other words, psychotic experiences were identified in 12% of the thirty-two subjects who reported both childhood sexual trauma and the use of cannabis early in life.

Kim and Kim (2005) were interested in the prevalence and consequences of incest in the Korean population: 1,053 adolescents were recruited from mainstream middle and senior schools, and 619 so-called 'delinquent' adolescents were recruited from juvenile corrective institutions. The occurrence of incest was identified by the victim articulating a clear and conscious memory of at least one incident of unwanted sexual penetration of a bodily orifice by an older blood relative occurring either by threat or by force. Defined in this way incest had been experienced by twenty-eight of the mainstream school students (2.7%) and thirty-four (5.5%) of the 'delinquent' adolescents. Psychological difficulties were assessed using a Korean translation of Derogatis and Melisaratos' Brief Symptom Inventory (Derogatis and Melisaratos 1983). On this basis thirty subjects had experienced psychotic symptoms, twenty-one of whom had also experienced incest.

Murphy and colleagues (1988) conducted a relatively early study of the relationship between childhood sexual abuse and psychological difficulties later in life. This involved 391 female South Carolina residents who agreed to a detailed assessment. When screening questions suggested that sexual abuse had occurred, more detailed information was obtained concerning the first, the most recent and the most distressing experiences of rape, attempted rape, molestation, attempted molestation or other forms of unwanted sexual approach. Psychological distress was assessed on the basis of responses to the Derogatis Symptom Check List 90 (revised) (Derogatis 1977). Thirty-eight subjects reported childhood (before the age of twelve) sexual abuse, forty-eight, adolescent (between the ages of twelve and eighteen) sexual abuse, eighty-one sexual abuse as an adult, and thirty-four both before and after the age of eighteen. The multiple, adult and adolescent sexual abuse groups reported higher levels of paranoid ideation that the non-victims group, and the multiple and adult abuse groups reported higher levels of 'psychoticism' than the non-victims.

Nishida and colleagues (2008) were interested in the prevalence and associations of psychotic-like experiences (PLEs) amongst Japanese school children. Full data sets were obtained from 4,984 twelve- to fifteen-year-olds recruited through their schools. PLEs were deemed to be present on the basis of a positive answer to at least one of the following: 'Some people believe in mind reading or being psychic. Have other people ever read your mind?', 'Have you ever had messages sent to you through the television or the radio?', 'Have you ever thought that people were following you or spying on you?' or 'Have you ever heard voices other people cannot hear?'. Of these, 746 reported at least one definite PLE. A number of potentially associated experiences were also explored, including the experiences of violence in the home and being bullied. Both of these were more frequent amongst subjects reporting PLEs.

Shevlin and colleagues have published three reports on data taken from the National Comorbidity Survey and its replication, and from the British Psychiatric Morbidity Survey. In the first of these (Shevlin et al. 2007), data from 5,877 respondents were considered. Childhood abuse was identified on the basis of responses to five questions: 'Were you seriously neglected as a child?', 'Were you physically abused as a child?', 'Were you seriously physically attacked or assaulted?', 'Were you raped (someone had sexual intercourse with you when you did not want to by threatening you or using some degree of force)?' and 'Were you sexually molested (someone touched or felt your genitals when you did not want them to)?'. The experience of psychotic symptoms was detected on the basis of responses to the Composite International Diagnostic Interview (Robins et al. 1988). In this data set only childhood physical abuse was associated with an increased risk of troubling psychotic symptoms, but the effects of other forms of childhood trauma were apparent in that as the number of traumas increased, so did the risk of experiencing troubling psychosis. In the second report (Shevlin et al 2008) this was extended and associations strengthened by inclusion of data from the British Psychiatric Morbidity Survey. Both data sets revealed a strong dose-response relationship between the number of different forms of traumatic experience and the probability of experiencing psychosis. The third (Shevlin et al. 2011) considered data from the National Comorbidity Survey Replication (Kessler and Merikangas 2004). This was conducted across a number of sites in the US between 2001 and 2003. After initial screening 5,692 subjects were investigated further, including exploration of the possibility they might have suffered childhood trauma. Of these a random sample of 2,353 were questioned about the experience of psychotic symptoms. This was registered on the basis of responses to two questions prefaced by the following: 'These questions are about unusual things, like seeing visions or hearing voices. We believe that these things may be quite common, but we don't know for sure because previous research has not done a good job asking about them. So please take your time and think carefully before answering', and then the following questions were asked: 'The first thing is seeing a vision: that is, seeing something that other people who were there could not see. Did you ever see a vision that other people could not see?' and 'The second thing is hearing voices that other people could not hear. I don't mean having good hearing, but rather hearing things that other people said did not exist, like strange voices coming from inside your head talking to you or about you, or voices coming out of the air when there was no one around. Did you ever hear voices in this way?'. The experience of childhood trauma was registered on the basis of answers to 'As a child, were you ever badly beaten up by your parents or the people who raised you?', 'Concerning rape; We define this as someone either having sexual intercourse with you or penetrating your body with a finger or object when you did not want them to, either by threatening you or using force, or when you were so young that you didn't know what was happening'. 'Did this ever happen to you?' and 'Other than rape, were you ever sexually assaulted where someone touched you inappropriately, or when you did not want them to?'. The occurrence of childhood trauma in the larger sample was related to the experience of psychotic symptoms in the smaller sample, and the probability of experiencing the latter was significantly increased where there was a history of childhood trauma.

Van Nierop and colleagues (2012) have provided data from the second Netherlands Mental Health Survey and Incidence Study (De Graaf et al. 2010). Altogether 6,646 subjects were involved, of whom 1,084 self-reported at least one psychotic experience and 384 were felt to have experienced 'true' psychosis on the basis of a clinical interview. There was a significantly higher rate of having experienced sexual abuse, physical abuse, emotional abuse, psychological abuse and/or regular peer victimisation amongst those self-reporting psychotic experiences and amongst those considered to have experienced 'true' psychosis than amongst those reporting neither.

Kaiser Permanente have initiated large scale surveys investigating relationships between adverse childhood experiences (ACEs) and a range of health and social outcomes. Amongst these have been the experience of hallucinations; data reported by Whitfield and colleagues (2005). These data include information about a comprehensive range of ACEs pertaining to respondents' first eighteen years of life:

> Emotional abuse. 'How often did a parent, step-parent, or adult living in your home swear at you, insult you, or put you down?' or

'How often did a parent, step-parent, or adult living in your home act in a way that made you afraid that you might be physically hurt?'

Physical abuse. 'How often did a parent, step-parent, or adult living in your home push, grab, slap, or throw something at you?' or 'How often did a parent, step-parent, or adult living in your home hit you so hard that you had marks or were injured?'

Sexual abuse. 'During the first eighteen years of life, did an adult, relative, family friend, or stranger ever touch or fondle your body in a sexual way, have you touch their body in a sexual way, attempt to have any type of sexual intercourse with you (oral, anal, or vaginal) or actually have any type of sexual intercourse with you (oral, anal, or vaginal)?'

Battered mother. 'How often did your father (or step-father) or mother's boyfriend do any of these things to your mother (or step-mother); push, grab, slap, or throw something at her, kick, bite, hit her with a fist, or hit her with something hard, repeatedly hit her over at least a few minutes, or threaten her with a knife or gun, or use a knife or gun to hurt her?'

Household substance abuse. Two questions clarified whether or not, during childhood, the respondent lived with a problem drinker, an alcoholic or someone who used street drugs.

Mental illness in the household. 'Was anyone in your household mentally ill or depressed?' or 'Did anyone in your household attempt to commit suicide?'

Parental separation or divorce. 'Were your parents ever separated or divorced?'

Incarcerated household member. Exposure to a household member who was incarcerated.

Answers to these questions provided an ACE count of 0–8.

The experience of hallucinations was registered on the basis of answers to 'Have you ever had or do you have hallucinations (seen, smelled, or heard things that weren't really there)?' Across a total sample of 17,337 respondents only 36% (6,241) reported no ACEs. 26% reported one, 15.9% two and 1%; 173 individuals seven or more. 2% whole sample had experienced hallucinations. This rose to more than 8% as the number of reported ACEs rose from zero to seven or more.

Prospective studies

Arsenault and colleagues (2011) have reported on data obtained from the Environmental Risk Longitudinal Twin Study (E-Risk), which is tracking the development of a nationally representative birth cohort of 2,232 British children. The sample was collected in 1999 and 2000, when 1,116 families with same-sex five-year-old twins participated in home-visit assessments. In 2007, when the children were twelve years old, the experience of psychotic symptoms was explored through questions about delusional experiences: 'Have you ever believed that you were sent special messages through TV or radio?', 'Have you ever felt like you were under the control of some special power?', 'Have other people ever read your thoughts?', 'Have you ever thought you were being followed or spied on?', 'Have you ever known what another person was thinking, even though that person was not speaking, like read their mind?', and hallucinations: 'Have you heard voices that other people cannot hear?' and 'Have you ever seen something or someone that other people could not see?'

Information that could reveal evidence of maltreatment by an adult was obtained from mothers who were asked: 'When [name] was a toddler, do you remember any time when [he or she] was disciplined severely enough that [he or she] may have been hurt?' and 'Did you worry that you or someone else [such as a babysitter, a relative or a neighbour] may have harmed or hurt [name] during those years?'. Where appropriate these probes were followed up with more detailed enquiry. Bullying by peers was also explored with mothers. It was defined as another child or children saying mean and hurtful things, making fun, or calling someone mean and hurtful names; completely ignoring or excluding someone from their group of friends, or leaving them out of things on purpose; hitting, kicking or shoving someone, or locking them in a room; telling lies or spreading rumours, or other hurtful actions such as these, all, both frequently and in ways that are difficult for the victim to stop. Additionally, the experience of seriously harmful or frightening accidents was explored, examples being involvement in a house fire, a car crash or being bitten by a dog. A complete set of data was obtained from 2,127 subjects, of whom 125 had had at least one psychotic experience. Of these twenty (16%) had experienced maltreatment by an adult, fifty-three (42%) bullying and forty-nine (39%) a serious accident. Comparison figures for the 2,002 subjects who had no experience of psychosis were 101 (5%), 435 (22%) and 598 (30%).

Cutajar and colleagues (2010) followed up children who had been the subject of legal enquiries following formal allegations of sexual abuse. Information from records covering the period between 1964 and 1995 concerning cases in which sexual penetration before the age of sixteen had been suspected was obtained from the Australian State of Victoria's Police Surgeon's Office and Institute of Forensic Medicine. This identified 2,759 victims of childhood sexual abuse. A comparison group of 2,677 individuals, matched for age and gender was obtained from electoral records. The occurrence of one or more episodes classified as either 'Schizophrenia' or other forms of psychotic disorder on the basis of ICD criteria was obtained from the state psychiatric case register. Seventy-eight (2.8%) of the childhood sexual abuse subjects but only thirty-seven (1.4%) of the comparison group were identified as having experienced psychosis.

De Loore and colleagues (2007) conducted a follow-up study involving children in the Netherlands using data from the Youth Care Divisions of the Public Health Services' data. Information was obtained from data collected when they were aged thirteen to fourteen years and from data collected two years later. The presence of psychotic experiences, on both occasions, was identified on the basis of answers to: 'Some people believe in mind reading or being psychic. Have other people ever read your mind?', 'Have you ever had messages sent just to you through television or radio?', 'Have you ever thought that people are following you or spying on you?', and 'Have you ever heard voices other people cannot hear?'. Bullying was assessed on the basis of answers to the question: 'How many times have you been the victim of bullying in the past year?' and considered to have occurred if the answer was 'once a week', or more. Sexual trauma was assessed on the basis of answers to 'Have you ever had an unpleasant sexual experience?' and considered to be present if the answer was 'yes'. The possibility of other negative life events was explored in relation to children's family circle and school on the basis of answers to: 'Did you experience important and unpleasant events in the past year?' and 'How much did this event influence your daily life?'. These answers were rated 0=no event; 1=little to moderate influence; 2 = a lot of influence. Ratings from the two domains (family and school) were combined. Data was obtained on both occasions from 1,129 subjects. 207 reported psychotic experiences at the age of thirteen to fourteen, and 202 two years later. Fifty reported being bullied at the age of thirteen to fourteen, and of these 15 (30%) reported psychotic experiences two years later. Twenty-four reported sexual trauma at the age of thirteen to fourteen, and of these thirteen (54%) reported troubling psychotic experiences two years later.

Another Dutch study used data from The Netherlands Mental Health Survey and Incidence Study in which subjects were interviewed on three occasions: 1996, 1997 and 1999 (Janssen et al 2004). Data were derived from 4,045 subjects, from whom 4,007 provided a full data set. The experience of psychosis was rated on the basis of a telephone re-interview conducted by a clinician with subjects who screened positive for 'psychosis' at an initial interview based upon a Dutch version of the Composite International Diagnostic Interview. The re-interview was based upon the Brief Psychiatric Rating Scale (Lukoff et al. 1986). It explored the degree and implications of 'unusual thought content' and 'hallucinations' that might have been present. Abuse before the age of sixteen was established on the basis of answers to: 'Do you think that there was any kind of emotional neglect, such as people at home didn't listen to you, that your problems were ignored, or that you had the feeling of not being able to find any attention or support from the people in your house?', 'Do you think there was any kind of psychological abuse, such as being sworn at, lesser treatment compared to brothers or sisters, unjustified punishment or blackmail?', 'Do you think there was any kind of physical abuse, such as being beaten, kicked, punched or other forms of physical abuse?' and 'Were you ever approached sexually against your will, in other words, were you ever touched sexually by anyone against your will or forced to touch anybody sexually; were you ever pressured into sexual contact against your will?'. In 1999 (at a mean age of 41.4) 412 subjects reported childhood abuse of one form or another. Of these eleven (2.4%) were considered to be troubled by psychotic experiences, which contrasts with twenty-seven of the 3,595 (0.7%) who did not report childhood abuse.

A prospective Finnish study explored associations between parental loss and single parent status, and the subsequent development of mental health difficulties (Mäkikyrö et al. 1998). 11,017 individuals of 12,058 who were born in Northern Finland in 1966 were identified at the age of sixteen and still living in the country. From these, those appearing in the Finnish Hospital Discharge Register were identified and their DSM-III-R (1987) classification extracted. In total 149 had acquired a 'diagnosis' of Schizophrenia, Schizophrenia Spectrum Disorder or Other Psychosis. Of these 111 had grown up, at least until the age of fourteen, with two parents. Statistics confirmed that these data do not reflect an association between growing up in a single parent household and the later experience of psychosis.

Schreier and colleagues (2009) explored data from the Avon Longitudinal Study of Parents and Children. This is information concerning children born in South West England between 1991 and 1992. This study was based upon 6,115 children who were questioned about the experience of psychosis when assessed between the ages of twelve and thirteen. A semi-structured interview explored the experience of visual and auditory hallucinations and various forms of 'delusion'. The experience of peer victimisation (bullying) was explored with the aid of a structured interview; The Bullying and Friendship Interview Schedule (Wolke et al. 2000), which was administered when the child was eight and again when they were ten. It explores the occurrence of overt victimization; having property taken, being threatened or blackmailed, being hit or beaten up, being tricked, and being called nasty names, and relational victimization; children refusing to play with them, children trying to get them do something they did not want to do, children telling lies or nasty things about them, and children spoiling games to upset them. 2,823 children reported some form of victimization, and of them 479 (17%) were considered to have psychotic experiences. This contrasts with 336 (10.2%) of the 3,292 who did not report victimization.

Spauwen and colleagues (2006) explored data collected in Germany in the course of The Early Developmental Stages of Psychopathology study (Lieb et al, 2000); 2,524 subjects between the ages of fourteen and twenty-four recruited as a randomly selected, representative sample were interviewed on two occasions some forty-two months apart. The experience of psychosis at the second interview was assessed by trained interviewers using the using a computer-assisted version of the Munich Composite International Diagnostic Interview (Wittchen et al. 1998). Self-reported exposure to a range of

CHILDHOOD ADVERSITY AND ADULT PSYCHOSIS

potentially traumatic experiences; war, physical threat, rape, sexual abuse, natural catastrophe, serious accident, imprisonment or kidnap, or another form of terrible event prior to the first assessment was determined by reference to visual cues. 491 reported such an experience and 106 of these (21.6%) also reported psychotic experiences. Of the 2,033 who did not report experiencing trauma, only 335 (16.5%) also reported psychotic experiences.

Wigman and colleagues (2011) used data from the Dutch Tracking Adolescents' Individual Lives Survey which were collected at three times in the lives of 1,816 adolescents; when they were around eleven years old, when they were around fourteen years old, and when they were around sixteen years old. Their focus was upon the presence and trajectory of 'subclinical' psychotic experiences which were explored by questionnaire asking about the occurrence of 'thought problems': taking one's mind off things, thinking about self-harm, hearing things that others do not, twitching/nervous behaviour, repeating certain behaviours, seeing things that others do not, displaying behaviour that others find strange, having ideas that others find strange, and sleeping problems. The occurrence of adverse experiences before the age of eleven was registered on the basis of parental report covering house moves, hospitalization, sickness or death, parental divorce, or parental absence for other reasons for at least three months, and self-rated recollections of other adversities such as victimization or bullying, violence, gossip or sexual harassment. Subjects were classified into four groups on the basis of how the intensity of their 'thought problems' progressed with time. 1,804 subjects made up the 'low' group who reported few or no 'thought problems', 204 made up a 'decreasing' group in whom the intensity of 'thought problems' fell as they moved from age eleven to age sixteen, 169 an 'increasing' group amongst whom it rose during that time, and forty-one a 'persistent' group in whom a relatively high level of 'thought problems' was present at age eleven and continued. Of the 'low' group 616 (34%) were rated high on the childhood adversity scale, amongst the 'decreasing' group this figure was 108 (53%), amongst the 'increasing' group 82 (48%), and amongst the 'persistent' group 30 (81%).

Meta-analysis

Varese and colleagues (2012a) were able to draw this considerable set of data together. Altogether the case control studies had compared experiences of childhood adversity in 2,048 individuals with troublesome experiences of psychosis with those of 1,856 unaffected individuals. The cross-sectional studies had explored the likely association of later psychotic experiences and adverse childhood events across an overall study population of 35,546, and the prospective, follow-up studies addressed the same question in an overall study population of 41,803. Meta-analysis involves a number of assumptions, in particular, that the measured and reported variables are roughly comparable across the included studies. The relative familiarity of troubling psychotic experiences and the use of established ways of detecting their presence, albeit frequently in the form of diagnostic criteria provides confidence that their presence or otherwise was detected in broadly similar ways across the studies. The same is largely true for evidence of adverse childhood experiences. The studies varied in terms of the emphasis given to different forms of adversity; sexual abuse, parental neglect, family breakdown and so on, but in all of the studies, evidence of a range of adversities was sought. Furthermore, it is both intuitive and evidenced that, in general, when childhood abuse does happen, it tends to manifest in a variety of forms at the same time and in the same context. Therefore, it is justifiable to assume that the occurrence of any form of abuse, particularly as detected by one or another of the various approaches used in these studies is broadly equivalent to the occurrence of another. This was supported by separate analyses (see below), and so it is justifiable to draw all these data together into a single statistic; an odds ratio reflecting the extent to which any form of significantly adverse childhood experience increases the likelihood of troubling, subsequent psychotic experiences. That odds ratio was 2.78 with a 95% confidence interval of 2.34 to 3.31. What that means is that with more than 95% certainty, the occurrence of adverse childhood experiences nearly triples the likelihood of being troubled by psychotic experiences later in life.

Where the data allowed, the meta-analysis also considered any distinctions there might be between the consequences of differing forms of adverse experience. Apart from parental death, other forms of adversity had roughly equivalent effects upon the likelihood of subsequent psychosis. Sexual abuse, physical abuse, emotional abuse, bullying and neglect all came up with statistically highly significant odds ratios of between 2.4 and 3.4. In other words, where any one of them had been detected the risk of being troubled by psychotic experiences later in life was between two-and-a-half and three-and-a-half times what it was among those who had not been abused.

To summarise

Combining studies which, together reflected findings from some 80,000 subjects, Varese and colleagues' meta-analysis has concluded that the experience of one or more adverse experience in childhood nearly triples the risk of being troubled by psychotic experiences later in life. It is an interesting reflection on 'we only see what we want to see' that it has taken until the beginning of the twenty-first century to widely appreciate the need to protect children from abuse, of a range of forms. The effect of not doing so extends well beyond an increase in the likelihood of experiencing psychosis, to include higher rates of other forms of 'mental illness', academic and occupational progress, relationship stability and self-esteem. Clearly the quantitative data that has established these associations are largely retrospective self-reports of variously defined adverse childhood experiences and they do not, of themselves, offer further understanding of how these associations may have come about. Possibly the most robust approach to this is to consider the effects of abuse upon the development of secure and effective social and emotional attachments between the child and their care-givers (Bowlby 1988). Secure and effective childhood attachments are considered to shape and sustain beliefs about the wider social world. The nature and quality of early attachments have enduring effects upon how we relate to others, empathise with and understand them. Disruptions, in the form of adverse childhood experiences, can therefore be understood as having an enduring effect upon how subsequent human interactions are chosen, experienced and conducted. Advancing an understanding of the association between the risk of troublesome psychotic experiences and a history of abuse in childhood will look towards unpicking what those effects and their consequences might be.

References

Agid, O., Shapira, B., Zislin, J., Ritsner, M., Hanin, B., Murad, H., Troudart, T., Bloch, M., Heresco-Levy, U. and Lerer, B. (1999) 'Environment and vulnerability to major psychiatric illness: a case control study of early parental loss in major depression, bipolar disorder and schizophrenia', *Molecular Psychiatry*, Vol. 4, pp. 163–172.

Arseneault, L., Cannon, M., Fisher, H. L., Polanczyk, G., Moffitt, T. E. and Caspi, A. (2011) 'Childhood Trauma and Children's Emerging Psychotic Symptoms: A Genetically Sensitive Longitudinal Cohort Study', *American Journal of Psychiatry*, Vol. 168, pp. 65–72.

Bartels-Velthuis, A. A., van de Willige, G., Jenner, J. A., Wiersma, D. and van Os, J. (2012) 'Auditory hallucinations in childhood: associations with adversity and delusional ideation', *Psychological Medicine*, Vol. 42, pp. 583–593.

Bebbington, P., Jonas, S., Kuipers, E., King, M., Cooper, C., Brugha, T., Meltzer, H., McManus, S. and Jenkins, R. (2011) 'Childhood sexual abuse and psychosis: data from a cross-sectional national psychiatric survey in England', *The British Journal of Psychiatry*, Vol. 199, pp. 29–37.

Bebbington, P. and Nayani, T. (1995) 'The Psychosis Screening Questionnaire', *International Journal of Methods in Psychiatric Research*, Vol. 5, pp. 11–19.

Bentall, R. P. and Slade, P. D. (1985) 'Reliability of a scale measuring disposition towards hallucination: a brief report', *Personality and Individual Differences*, Vol. 6, No. 4, pp. 527–529.

Bernstein, D. P., Ahluvalia, T., Pogge, D. and Handelsman, L. (1997) 'Validity of the Childhood Trauma Questionnaire in an Adolescent Psychiatric Population', *Journal of the American Academy of Child and Adolescent Psychiatry*, Vol. 36, No. 3, pp. 340–348.

Bifulco, A., Bernazzani, O., Moran, P. M. and Jacobs, C. (2005) 'The childhood experience of care and abuse questionnaire (CECA.Q): Validation in a community series', *British Journal of Clinical Psychology*, Vol. 44, pp. 563–581.

Bowlby, J. (1988) *A Secure Base: Parent-Child Attachment and Healthy Human Development*. London: Basic Books.

Bremner, J. D., Vermetten, E. and Mazure, C. M. (2000) 'Development and Preliminary Psychometric Properties of an Instrument for the Measurement of Childhood Trauma: The Early Trauma Inventory', *Depression and Anxiety*, Vol. 12, pp. 1–12.

Cohen, C. I., Abdallah, C. G. and Diwan, S. (2010) 'Suicide attempts and associated factors in older adults with schizophrenia', *Schizophrenia Research*, Vol. 119, pp. 253–257.

Cohen, C. I., Ramirez, M., Teresi, J., Gallagher, M. and Sokolovsky, J. (1997) 'Predictors of Becoming Redomiciled Among Older Homeless Women', *The Gerontologist*, Vol. 37, No. 1, pp. 67–74.

Convoy, H., Weiss, P. and Zvĕrina, J. (1995) 'Sexual abuse experiences of psychiatric patients', *Medicine and Law*, Vol. 14, No. 3–4, pp. 283–292.

Cutajar, M. C., Mullen, P. E., Ogloff, J. R. P., Thomas, S. D., Wells, D. L. and Spataro, J. (2010) 'Schizophrenia and Other Psychotic Disorders in a Cohort of Sexually Abused Children', *Archives of General Psychiatry*, Vol. 67, No. 11, pp. 1114–1119.

De Graaf, R., Ten Have, M. and van Dorsselaer, S. (2010) 'The Netherlands Mental Health Survey and Incidence Study-2 (NEMESIS-2): design and methods', *International Journal of Methods in Psychiatric Research*, Vol. 19, No. 3, pp. 125–141.

De Loore, E., Drukker, M., Gunther, N., Feron, F., Deboutte, D., Sabbe, B., Mengelers, R., van Os, J. and Myin-Germeys, I. (2007) 'Childhood negative experiences and subclinical psychosis in adolescence: a longitudinal general population study', *Early Intervention in Psychiatry*, Vol. 1, pp. 201–207.

Dell'Erba, G., Venturi, P. and Tallarico, V. (2003) 'Childhood stressful experiences in familial and sporadic schizophrenic patients' [in Italian], *Italian Journal of Psychopathology*, Vol. 9, pp. 32–39.

Derogatis, L. R. (1977) *SCL-90: Administration, scoring, and procedure manual for the R (revised) version.* Baltimore: John Hopkins University School of Medicine.

Derogatis, L. R. and Melisaratos, N. (1983) 'The Brief Symptom Inventory: an introductory report', *Psychological Medicine*, Vol. 13, pp. 595–605.

Fennig, S., Horesh, N., Aloni, D., Apter, A., Weizman, A. and Fennig, S. (2005) 'Life events and suicidality in adolescents with schizophrenia', *European Child and Adolescent Psychiatry*, Vol. 14, pp. 454–460.

Finkelhor, D., Hotaling, G., Lewis, I. A. and Smith, C. (1990) 'Sexual Abuse in a National Survey of Adult Men and Women: Prevalence, Characteristics, and Risk Factors', *Child Abuse and Neglect*, Vol. 14, pp. 19–28.

Fisher, H. L., Jones, P. B., Fearon, P., Craig, T. K., Dazzan, P., Morgan, K., Hutchinson, G., Doody, G. A., McGuffin, P., Leff, J., Murray, R. M. and Morgan, C. (2010) 'The varying impact of type, timing and frequency of exposure to childhood adversity on its association with adult psychotic disorder', *Psychological Medicine*, Vol. 40, pp. 1967–1978.

Frank, E., Anderson, C. and Rubinstein, D. (1978) 'Frequency of sexual dysfunction in "normal' couples"', *The New England Journal of Medicine*, Vol. 299, pp. 111–115.

Friedman, S. and Harrison, G. (1984) 'Sexual Histories, Attitudes, and Behavior of Schizophrenic and "Normal" Women', *Archives of Sexual Behavior*, Vol. 13, No. 6, pp. 555–567.

Furukawa, T., Mizukawa, R., Hirai, T., Fujihara, S., Kitamura, T. and Takahasi, K. (1998) 'Childhood parental loss and schizophrenia: evidence against pathogenic but for some pathoplastic effects', *Psychiatry Research*, Vol. 81, pp. 353–362.

Giblin, S., Clare, L., Livingston, G. and Howard, R. (2004) 'Psychosocial correlates of late-onset psychosis: life experiences, cognitive schemas, and attitudes to ageing', *International Journal of Geriatric Psychiatry*, Vol. 19, pp. 611–623.

Harley, M., Kelleher, I., Clarke, M., Lynch, F., Arseneault, L., Connor, D., Fitzpatrick, C. and Cannon, M. (2010) 'Cannabis use and childhood trauma interact additively to increase the risk of psychotic symptoms in adolescence', *Psychological Medicine*, Vol. 40, pp. 1627–1634.

Heins, M., Simons, C., Lataster, T., Pfeifer, S., Vermissen, D., Lardinois, M., Marcelis, M., Delespaul, P., Krabbendam, L., van Os, J. and Myin-Germeys, I. (2011) 'Childhood Trauma and Psychosis: A Case-Control and Case-Sibling Comparison Across Different Levels of Genetic Liability, Psychopathology, and Type of Trauma', *American Journal of Psychiatry*, Vol. 168, pp. 1286–1294.

Henderson, D. J. (1972) 'Incest: A Synthesis of Data', *The Canadian Journal of Psychiatry*, Vol. 17, pp. 299–313.

Holmes, T. H. and Rahe, R. H. (1967) 'The Social Readjustment Rating Scale', *Journal of Psychosomatic Research*, Vol. 11, No. 11, pp. 213–218.

Houston, J. E., Murphy, J., Adamson, G., Stringer, M. and Shevlin, M. (2008) 'Childhood Sexual Abuse, Early Cannabis Use, and Psychosis: Testing an Interaction Model Based on the National Comorbidity Survey', *Schizophrenia Bulletin*, Vol. 34, No. 3, pp. 580–585.

Husted, J. A., Ahmed, R., Chow, E. W. C., Brzustowicz, L. M. and Bassett, A. S. (2010) 'Childhood trauma and genetic factors in familial schizophrenia associated with the NOS1AP gene', *Schizophrenia Research*, Vol. 121, pp. 187–192.

Janssen, I., Krabbendam, L., Bak, M., Hanssen, M., Vollebergh, W., de Graaf, R. and van Os, J. (2004) 'Childhood abuse as a risk factor for psychotic experiences', *Acta Psychiatrica Scandinavica*, Vol. 109, pp. 38–45.

Kaufman, J., Birmaher, B., Brent, D., Rao, U. and Ryan, N. (1996) *The Schedule for Affective Disorders and Schizophrenia for School Aged Children: Present and Lifetime Version*. Pittsburgh: University of Pittsburgh, Western Psychiatric Institute and Clinic.

Kelleher, I., Harley, M., Lynch, F., Arseneault, L., Fitzpatrick, C. and Cannon, M. (2008) 'Associations between childhood trauma, bullying and psychotic symptoms among a school-based adolescent sample', *The British Journal of Psychiatry*, Vol. 193, pp. 378–382.

Kessler, R. C. (1994) 'The National Comorbidity Survey of the United States', *International Review of Psychiatry*, Vol. 6, pp. 365–376.

Kessler, R. C. and Merikangas, K. R. (2004) 'The National Comorbidity Survey Replication (NCS-R): background and aims', *International Journal of Methods in Psychiatric Research*, Vol. 13, No. 2, pp. 60–68.

Kim, H.-S. and Kim, H.-S. (2005) 'Incestuous Experience Among Korean Adolescents: Prevalence, Family Problems, Perceived Family Dynamics, and Psychological Characteristics', *Public Health Nursing*, Vol. 22, No. 6, pp. 472–482.

Lieb, R., Isensee, B., Sydow, K. V. and Wittchen, H.-U. (2000) 'The early developmental stages of psychopathology study (EDSP): a methodological update', *European Addiction Research*, Vol. 6, pp. 170–182.

Lukoff, D., Nuechterlien, K. and Ventura, J. (1986) 'The Brief Psychiatric Rating Scale. Manual for the Expanded Version', *Schizophrenia Bulletin*, Vol. 13, pp. 261–276.

Mäkikyrö, T., Sauvola, A., Moring, J., Veijola, J., Nieminen, P., Järvelin, M.-R. and Isohanni, M. (1998) 'Hospital-Treated Psychiatric Disorders in Adults with a Single-Parent and Two-Parent Family Background: A 28-Year Follow-up of the 1966 Northern Finland Birth Cohort', *Family Process*, Vol. 37, pp. 335–344.

McCabe, K. L., Maloney, E. A., Stain, H. J., Loughland, C. M. and Carr, V. J. (2012) 'Relationship between childhood adversity and clinical and cognitive features in schizophrenia', *Journal of Psychiatric Research*, Vol. 46, pp. 600–607.

Morgan, C., Kirkbride, J., Leff, J., Craig, T., Hutchinson, G., McKenzie, K., Morgan, K., Dazzan, P., Doody, G. A., Jones, P., Murray, R. and Fearon, P. (2007) 'Parental separation, loss and psychosis in different ethnic groups: a case-control study', *Psychological Medicine*, Vol. 37, pp. 495–503.

Murphy, S. M., Kilpatrick, D. G., Amick-McMullan, A., Veronen, L. J., Paduhovich, J., Best, C. L., Villeponteaux, L. A. and Saunders, B. E. (1988) 'Current Psychological Functioning of Child Sexual Assault Survivors', *Journal of Interpersonal Violence*, Vol. 3, No. 1, pp. 55–79.

Nishida, A., Tanii, H., Nishimura, Y., Kajiki, N., Inoue, K., Okada, M., Sasaki, T. and Okazaki, Y. (2008) 'Associations between psychotic-like experiences and mental health status and other psychopathologies among Japanese early teens', *Schizophrenia Research*, Vol. 99, pp. 125–133.

Robins, L. N., Wing, J. and Wittchen, H. U. (1988) 'The Composite International Diagnostic Interview: An Epidemiologic Instrument Suitable for Use in Conjunction With Different Diagnostic Systems and in Different Cultures', *Archives of General Psychiatry*, Vol. 45, No. 12, pp. 1069–1077.

Rosenman, S. and Rodgers, B. (2004) 'Childhood Adversity in an Australian Population', *Social Psychiatry and Psychiatric Epidemiology*, Vol. 39, pp. 695–702.

Rubino, I. A., Nanni, R. C., Pozzi, D. M. and Siracusano, A. (2009) 'Early Adverse Experiences in Schizophrenia and Unipolar Depression', *The Journal of Nervous and Mental Disease*, Vol. 197, No. 1, pp. 65–68.

Rush F. (1980) *The Best Kept Secret: The Sexual Abuse of Children*, Englewood Cliffs: Prentice Hall.

Sanders, B. and Becker-Lausen, E. (1995) 'The Measurement of Psychological Maltreatment: Early Data on the Child Abuse and Trauma Scale', *Child Abuse and Neglect*, Vol. 19, No. 3, pp 315–323.

Schreier, A., Wolke, D., Thomas, K., Horwood, J., Hollis, C., Gunnell, D., Lewis, G., Thompson, A., Zammit, S., Duffy, L., Salvi, G. and Harrison, G. (2009) 'Prospective Study of Peer Victimization in Childhood and Psychotic Symptoms in a Nonclinical Population at Age 12 Years', *Archives of General Psychiatry*, Vol. 66, No. 5, pp. 527–536.

Shevlin, M., Dorahy, M. J. and Adamson, G. (2007) 'Trauma and Psychosis: An Analysis of the National Comorbidity Survey', *American Journal of Psychiatry*, Vol. 164, pp. 166–169.

Shevlin, M., Houston, J. E., Dorahy, M. J. and Adamson, G. (2008) 'Cumulative Traumas and Psychosis: an Analysis of the National Comorbidity Survey and the British Psychiatric Morbidity Survey', *Schizophrenia Bulletin*, Vol. 34, No. 1, pp. 193–199.

Shevlin, M., Murphy, J., Read, J., Mallett, J., Adamson, G. and Houston, J. E. (2011) 'Childhood adversity and hallucinations: a community-based study using the National Comorbidity Survey Replication', *Social Psychiatry and Psychiatric Epidemiology*, Vol. 46, pp. 1203–1210.

Spauwen, J., Krabbendam, L., Lieb, R., Wittchen, H.-U. and van Os, J. (2006) 'Impact of psychological trauma on the development Impact of psychological trauma on the development of psychotic symptoms: relationship with psychosis proneness', *British Journal of Psychiatry*, Vol. 188, pp. 527–533.

Van Nierop, M., van Os, J., Gunther, N., Myin-Germeys, I., de Graaf, R., ten Have, M., van Dorsselaer, S., Bak, M. and van Winkel, R. (2012) 'Phenotypically Continuous With Clinical Psychosis, Discontinuous in Need for Care: Evidence for an Extended Psychosis Phenotype', *Schizophrenia Bulletin*, Vol. 38, No. 2, pp. 231–238.

Varese, F., Smeets, F., Drukker, M., Lieverse, R., Lataster, T., Viechtbauer, W., Read, J., van Os, J. and Bentall, R. P. (2012a) 'Childhood Adversities Increase the Risk of Psychosis: A Meta-analysis of Patient-Control, Prospective- and Cross-sectional Cohort Studies', *Schizophrenia Bulletin*, Vol. 38, No. 4, pp. 661–671.

Varese, F., Barkus, E. and Bentall, R. P. (2012b) 'Dissociation mediates the relationship between childhood trauma and hallucination-proneness', *Psychological Medicine*, Vol. 42, pp. 1025–1036.

Weber, K., Rockstroh, B., Borgelt, J., Awiszus, B., Popov, T., Hoffmann, K., Schonauer, K., Watzl, H. and Pröpster, K. (2008) 'Stress load during childhood affects psychopathology in psychiatric patients', *BMC Psychiatry*, Vol. 8, No. 63. https://doi.org/10.1186/1471-244X-8-63.

Whitfield, C. L., Dube, S. R., Felitti, V. J. and Anda, R. F. (2005) 'Adverse Childhood Experiences and Hallucinations', *Child Abuse and Neglect*, Vol. 29, pp. 797–810.

Wigman, J. T. W., van Winkel, R., Raaijmakers, Q. A. W., Ormel, J., Verhulst, F. C., Reijneveld, S. A., van Os, J. and Vollebergh, W. A. M. (2011) 'Evidence for a persistent, environment-dependent and deteriorating subtype of subclinical psychotic experiences: a 6-year longitudinal general population study', *Psychological Medicine*, Vol. 41, pp. 2317–2329.

Wittchen, H.-U., Lachner, G., Wunderlich, U. and Pfister, H. (1998) 'Test-retest reliability of the computerized DSM-IV version of the Munich-Composite International Diagnostic Interview (M-CIDI) ', *Social Psychiatry and Psychiatric Epidemiology*, Vol. 33, pp. 568–578.

Wolke, D., Woods, S., Bloomfield, L. and Karstadt, L. (2000) 'The Association between Direct and Relational Bullying and Behaviour Problems among Primary School Children', *Journal of Child Psychology and Psychiatry*, Vol. 41, No. 8, pp. 989–1002.

4

FAMILY LIFE

It is virtually unchallenged folklore that 'madness' runs in families, and the early decades of the twentieth century saw some horrendous consequences of this. In Europe and in America, during the 1920s and 1930s proponents of eugenics encouraged the sterilisation, sequestration, and under the Nazi regime, even the murder of people with mental health difficulties (e.g. Llewellyn et al. 2020). The rationale was that this would 'breed out' genes responsible for 'madness' and other so-called deficiencies, and thereby improve the human gene pool (ibid). Although policies derived from it are no longer quite as alarming, the view that 'madness' is inheritable continues to hold considerable sway. Some cultures continue to regard a family history of 'madness' as a taint which should inhibit marriage for fear of it recurring in offspring (Sharma et al. 2013). Simplified understandings of how inheritability 'works' have made a considerable contribution to the notion that mental health difficulties reflect biological abnormalities such as aberrations of brain chemistry which are best addressed medically. Careful scrutiny of the evidence supporting all of this raises some important questions.

More than 100 years' research has repeatedly shown that the risk of troubling psychotic experiences (usually as having acquired a 'diagnosis' of Schizophrenia) is substantially increased where there are one or more first degree relatives who have had similar experiences. However, there is a conundrum. Despite a century of robust and repeated findings which support the informal view, that 'madness runs in families', clear evidence of a credible genetic basis for it remains elusive.

'Nature' or 'Nurture'?

Earlier approaches to the 'inheritability' of psychosis centred around attempts to dissect apart 'Nature' and 'Nurture'. Convincing evidence that this might be worthwhile came from simple family studies. Kendler and Diehl (1993) found seven such studies which they felt to be of good quality (an identified control group, personal interviews and blind diagnosis) that were published between 1985 and 1993. Summing the results of all seven

    DOI: 10.4324/9780429059094-5

studies amounted to 116 cases of 'Schizophrenia' in 2,418 lifetimes at risk among the first-degree relatives (parents, siblings or children) of individuals with a 'diagnosis' of Schizophrenia. Among control subjects (first degree relatives of individuals without a 'diagnosis' of Schizophrenia) there were fifteen instances of such a 'diagnosis' in 3,035 lifetimes at risk. In other words, on the basis of these figures, someone who has a first degree relative with a 'diagnosis' of Schizophrenia is nearly ten times more likely to acquire such a diagnosis themselves than someone who hasn't.

Against this background twin studies exploited the opportunity identical twins offer to compare rates of concordance (similar outcomes) between them and between dizygotic, non-identical twins. Identical twins are assumed to have the same genetic composition, and that of non-identical twins differs. As it is also assumed that pairs of identical twins and pairs of non-identical twins share the same family environment, differences in the rate of concordance between them can be attributed to a genetic influence. Gottesman and colleagues (1987) reviewed and combined studies providing such data. Of 261 identical twin sets where one had a broadly defined 'diagnosis' of Schizophrenia, 119 or 45.6% of their co-twins acquired such a diagnosis at some stage, whereas comparable figures among 329 non-identical twin sets were forty-five, or 13.7%. On the basis of the assumption that the only relevant difference between identical and non-identical twin sets is that the former share the same genetic endowment, this appears to more than triple the risk of experiencing troublesome psychosis.

A more direct approach to the 'Nature' or 'Nurture' debate has been the use of adoption studies. These address the possibility that growing up in a family where one or more family members might be afflicted by the experience of psychosis could in itself increase the risk of that happening to others in the family. It is argued that offspring of those with troubling experiences of psychosis will carry any genetic contribution to the risk of that happening to them, but if they are adopted into a family without such a background, they will not grow up in a family influenced by any potentially relevant environmental contributions. If the offspring of those with troublesome experiences of psychosis who have been adopted out of that family into one where there is no such background do have an enhanced risk of troubling psychotic experiences, then this must be due to their genetic endowment. On the face of it this appears to be a powerful way of dissecting apart environmental and genetic contributions, and a series of studies conducted from the 1960s to the 1990s exploited this. They appeared to confirm that the risk of troubling psychotic experiences psychosis was, in part, genetically mediated.

Main contributors to this were studies of the (well-documented) Danish population conducted in partnership with several American collaborators. Summarised in 1992 (Kety and Ingraham 1992), their findings were as follows. 14,427 Danish individuals were identified who had been legally adopted by non-biologically related families between 1924 and 1948. This yielded

73

forty-six adoptees with a 'diagnosis' of Schizophrenia whose biological relatives could be traced, and evidence of 'Schizophrenia' was found in eight (17%) of their families of origin. This contrasted with evidence of 'Schizophrenia' in only one of the families of origin of a group of control adoptees without comparable evidence of troublesome psychosis. Given the large original sample size, these findings were statistically significant, and have probably done more than any others to drive the conviction that the risk of troublesome psychotic experiences is in part genetically mediated. However, as mentioned above, this has resulted in a conundrum. More recent, and more technically sophisticated approaches to genetic research such as genome wide association studies have so far failed to identify convincing candidate genes that might be responsible for this.

Surveying candidate genes.

It is now possible to determine the molecular details of DNA samples, compare them between individuals and obtain estimates of their similarities and differences. It has also become possible to acquire and manipulate such data from large numbers of cases. Furthermore, it is becoming possible to 'drill down' and determine what the molecular and therefore biologically relevant effects of different genes, alleles or strings of DNA might be, once they have been identified. In theory, therefore, genetic mapping and surveys of similarities and differences between different groups offer a route to identifying variations in molecular biology associated with the occurrence of a particular condition that might provide a pathway to identifying targets for drug treatments. For instance, the inheritance of Cystic Fibrosis is clearly due to the configuration of a single piece of genetic material which, if passed on by both parents, results in abnormality of an identified enzyme implicated in mucus production (National Heart, Blood and Lung Institute 2022). As a result, mucus is stickier than it would otherwise be, and this leads to the lung, pancreatic, intestinal and other problems characteristic of the disease. Medical treatments based on this understanding are under investigation. Nothing even approaching this clarity of understanding has emerged from attempts to explain the 'inheritance' of a propensity to suffer troubling psychotic experiences.

The Schizophrenia Working Group of the Psychiatric Genomics Consortium have used such a framework to seek associations between a 'diagnosis' of Schizophrenia and genetic configurations, in the hope of finding configurations particular to the risk of experiencing psychosis that could become the focus of medical treatments. Their available dataset is a large one but their findings have been disappointing. In a comparison between 36,989 'cases' and 113,075 'controls' (Schizophrenia Working Group of the Psychiatric Genomics Consortium 2014) there were 108 genetic configurations that were more likely to be found in 'cases' than they were in 'controls'. In most of these the differences between rates among 'cases' and rates among 'controls' were small and likely only statistically significant because of the huge sample size. Additionally, only ten of these variations were in genetic material that is known to directly influence a protein structure and thereby a potentially identifiable biological effect. Others appear to be involved in influencing the activity of genetic material that is not, in itself, in any way likely to influence the risk of experiencing psychosis. The strongest association between genetic configuration and a 'diagnosis' of Schizophrenia emerging from this work has been variations in the configuration of DNA associated with the expression of immune system activity. Speculatively this could be implicated in synaptic pruning (Sekar et al. 2016), a process whereby neuronal circuits are refined in response to experience in the course of psychological maturation. In terms of the human life cycle, synaptic pruning tends to occur most actively during later adolescence and early adulthood, when psychotic experiences commonly first occur. However, these associations are tentative and not beyond dispute.

Lam and colleagues (2019) have compared linkages between genetic configurations and the risk of experiencing psychosis between European and Asian populations, and although most of the weaker associations between genetic configuration and the risk of troublesome psychotic experiences were similar in both groups, that was not the case for strings of DNA associated with immune system activity. That association was absent in samples from the Asian population, although its presence among Europeans was replicated. Mariaselvam and colleagues (2021) focused more specifically upon DNA coding for C4 complement. This underpins the manufacture of molecules critical for normal brain development and synaptic pruning. Comparisons were made between 271 European, Israeli and Australian subjects after a first presentation with troublesome experiences of psychosis, and 221 age and gender-matched 'controls'. In this study there was no association between configurations of DNA coding for C4 complement and the risk of experiencing psychosis. In other words, even at this detailed level and with large samples, genetic configurations reliably associated with the risk of troubling psychotic experiences are proving hard to identify.

Epigenetics

This could be that traditional ways of conceptualising distinctions between 'Nature' and 'Nurture' are unduly simplistic. It is now clear that the pathway from parental DNA to the offspring's biology is far more complex than Crick and Watson envisaged in 1953, and one of the insights into this has been the recognition of 'epigenetics'. Although DNA might hold a full set of codes for this, that or another protein which, when produced by a cell, could in turn determine what that cell might or might not do in the body, many influences can alter whether or not a particular code is activated. At a molecular level there are several identified mechanisms whereby gene expression can be influenced in this way, including methylation, acetylation, and histone reconfiguration. In principle these processes can be responsive to the influence of environmental factors, and so at this level of analysis there is no clear distinction between 'Nature' and 'Nurture'. Environmental influences (Nurture) can alter the activity of genetic DNA (Nature), and reciprocally, by ultimately contributing to an organism's activities, which include interactions with its environment, genetic DNA impacts upon 'Nurture'. Once again, the natural world has proved to be far more complex and interactive than simple twentieth century models have supposed.

In relation to the occurrence of psychotic experiences and their propensity to 'run in families' epigenetics offers some hints. The study of how the activation of particular genes might be influenced by a cell's environment is rooted in attempting to understand how a complex organism made up of many different types of cell, each carrying out different functions and behaving in a wide range of ways, can grow from a single cell which was formed at conception and which holds a complete template of that individual's definitive DNA. During gestation and on into independent life, whether or not a particular string of DNA is active and driving this, that or another cellular activity will depend upon that cell's location, its molecular environment and therefore its role in the complex interaction of cellular functions that makes up a living organism. The genetic material brought together at the time of conception cannot simply express itself repeatedly and in the same way over and over again. How it expresses itself has to be flexible and responsive to the circumstances of the particular cell.

The operation of this flexibility can be detected by determining whether or not, at any particular time and within any particular cell, particular strings of DNA have been inactivated by mechanisms such as methylation, acetylation or histone reconfiguration. This has allowed epigenetic research to extend beyond influences upon gene expression attributable to the micro-molecular environment of individual cells into investigations of how the whole organism's environment might influence gene expression. For instance, several features of human lifestyle, including diet, obesity, physical activity, tobacco smoking, alcohol consumption, environmental pollutants, psychological stress and working night shifts have all been shown to be associated with differing patterns of gene expression (Alegría-Torres et al. 2011). Other forms of psychological trauma or challenge are credible contenders. There is experimental evidence of this in animal models, and of the possibility that epigenetic modifications of gene expression can be passed from generation to generation. In one example, male rats subjected to maternal separation in early childhood fathered offspring which, though reared 'normally' themselves, nevertheless showed signs of disturbed behaviour characteristic of having suffered maternal deprivation. These behavioural phenomena were associated with molecular evidence of epigenetic influences upon the activity of DNA coding for aspects of stress-related cortisol release (Franklin et al. 2010). Yehuda and colleagues (2016) were able to study Holocaust survivors and their offspring who had been conceived after 1945. They found that patterns of epigenetic methylation found in the survivors, and presumed to be attributable to their wartime sufferings, were also present their offspring in a similar genetic 'place', and where they might have an effect upon responses to 'stress'. At a conceptual level, the study of epigenetics forces a radical review of the relationship between 'Nature' and 'Nurture'. How the corner-stone of their DNA, their 'natural' endowment, expresses itself in an individual is susceptible to environmental influences, and the effect of these influences might not be limited to that individual but may be transmissible across generations.

Understandings of how the risk of experiencing psychosis may or may not be 'inherited' have to embrace a much more complex set of possibilities than earlier frameworks were able to. Large databases and sophisticated molecular analyses have not uncovered one or even a small number of genes (genetic variations) undeniably associated with the occurrence of psychosis; a 'Psychosis Gene'. There are weak associations with many, but none have emerged as reliable candidates for the title. Furthermore, and perhaps most significantly, the processes of gene expression and intergenerational transmission appear to be much more susceptible to external influences. Popular perceptions tend to differentiate nature and nurture. A biological phenomenon such as height, weight, or sensitivity to 'stress', is widely considered to be due to interactions between an inherited and fixed genetic endowment, and a variety of external influences. The emerging picture is that these are much less distinct. 'Nurture' can directly influence 'Nature', and alter the way in which it is expressed. One generation's experiences can have a biological effect upon their offspring, and so what was 'Nurture' in one setting, becomes 'Nature' in another. The distinction between 'Nature' and 'Nurture' is, perhaps, best seen as arbitrary and context-specific. There *is* robust epidemiological evidence that 'madness' runs in families, but it is no longer helpful to retreat into simply assuming that this, even partly, reflects a genetic contribution that can only be addressed by selective breeding or gene therapy.

Revisiting twin and adoption studies

Growing up in a family that may have been disrupted by one or more family members' experiences of psychosis, or where there was a longer family history of such experiences can be, in and of itself, disturbing and quite possibly stigmatising. That is why investigators sought ways of dissecting environmental or even relational influences from potential genetic influences in the form of twin and adoption studies. Although their findings appeared to point to evidence of a genetic contribution, careful scrutiny suggests there might be more to 'madness runs in families' than simply the handing on of troublesome DNA.

Twin studies found higher rates of concordance among mono-zygotic (identical) twins than among di-zygotic (non-identical) twins, and traditionally this was considered to reflect the operation of genetic influences because that was thought to be the only relevant difference between them. Conventionally, pairs of mono-zygotic (MZ) twins and pairs of di-zygotic (DZ) twins each share the same family and developmental experiences and the only distinction between them is that the former are genetically identical, whereas the latter are not. This is the so-called equivalent environment assumption (EEA) and there are good reasons to believe that it is flawed. It is readily observable that identical twin pairs are treated more alike and are socialized to be more alike than di-zygotic twin pairs. Half of all di-zygotic twin pairs are boy-girl sibships, whereas, clearly, all mono-zygotic twin pairs are same sex sibships. Earlier twin researchers Scarr and Carter-Saltzman concluded that 'the evidence of greater environmental similarity for MZ than DZ twins is overwhelming' (Scarr and Carter-Saltzman 1979, p. 528). Another investigator also found that 'identical twins are indeed treated more alike – they are dressed alike more often, are more often together at school, play together more, and so-forth' (Loehlin 1978, p. 72). Others have pointed to identical twins' greater psychological closeness, identity confusion, and 'ego-fusion' when compared with DZ pairs (Dalgard and Kringlen 1976).

With these reservations about the validity of the EEA in relation to twin studies exploring the genetics of psychosis in mind, Fosse and colleagues (Fosse et al. 2015) reviewed literature reporting on the experiences of relevant forms of abuse among twin pairs. They were able to identify eleven studies where the authors had assessed twin pair similarity during childhood or adolescence for experiences of sexual abuse, physical abuse, emotional neglect, emotional abuse, bullying, and other types of family difficulty. Overall, these eleven studies included twenty-four pairs of correlations for these exposure types; one of each pair estimated the extent to which MZ twin pairs experienced difficulties to the same degree, and one of each pair, the extent to which DZ twin pairs' experiences correlated. Overall data were obtained from 9,119 twin pairs. There was clear evidence of closer correlations between MZ twins' experiences of such difficulties than between DZ twins' experiences. In other words, when abuse did occur it was more likely to be suffered by both if they were identical twins than if they were non-identical twins. Higher rates of concordance for the subsequent experience of troublesome psychosis could just as easily be explained by higher rates of concordant victim-hood or other forms of childhood adversity among MZ twins as they might be by any genetic similarities they could share.

Adoption studies' rationale is that the only endowment an adoptee transfers from their biological background into their adopted family is their DNA. It is only if this holds that differential rates of subsequent troublesome

78

psychotic experiences between those originally from a family with a history of psychosis and those without that background can be credibly attributed to a genetic influence. There is considerable evidence that this does not hold. The real-world process of adoption introduces a number of influences upon the adoptee which include exposure to emotional and possibly physical hardships that may have debilitating effects.

Many of the data concerning adoption studies have come from Denmark (e.g. Kety and Ingraham 1992) where, for much of period in question, formal and informal practices that discriminated against people with mental health difficulties could have influenced the adoption process. For instance, it is not possible to rule out with any certainty, that prospective adopting parents, formally informed of their potential adoptee's background, would not have discriminated against children from a background that included troubling experiences of psychosis. Thus, the process of adoption may have been influenced by instances of the most loving and emotionally stable potential adoptive parents, informed of 'deviance' in the adoptee's family background, not 'choosing' children 'tainted' by a family history of mental disorders. Furthermore, when children from a background of 'biological' vulnerability to psychosis *were* adopted, there seems to have been little investigation into the possibility that that was by families that differed in subtle but possibly relevant ways from those adopting children who did not have such a background.

A second set of unanswered questions about these adoption studies revolve around the adoptees' experiences of the process. Ideally this should be minimal, including in such a study only those who were separated from their biological mother at the time of birth and adopted into their definitive family immediately afterwards. Even this would not control for any non-genetic antenatal influences but it would be methodologically sounder than the background to many of the reported studies. Adoption is commonly a messy process, and a significant proportion of the adoptees were separated from their birth mothers, weeks or even months after their birth, and many spent significant periods in institutional care before joining their adoptive families. Although control cases might have suffered similar experiences there has been no attempt to control for these possibilities in the presented analyses, and where there was a delay between birth and separation, those from a 'Schizophrenic' background might well have spent that time in a 'Schizophrenic' environment.

Family life

A separate series of studies conducted in Finland (Tienari et al. 1987, 1994, 2000, 2004) has investigated the possibility that the adopted home environment might influence the risk of subsequently experiencing troubling psychosis, and they have found that it did. They also found that this effect is more noticeable amongst adoptees who came from a 'Schizophrenic' background. These studies have been widely quoted as evidence of a gene/environment interaction but the same criticisms pertain. Here too, there were inevitable delays in adoption and the adoption process was selective. As a result, index (psychosis-experiencing family of origin) adoptees' pre-adoption developmental environments were not certainly the same as the control (non-psychosis-experiencing family of origin) adoptees', and so differences between them in the rate of troubling psychotic experiences later in life cannot, necessarily, be reliably attributed to a genetic influence. What this research has done, however, is focus attention upon aspects of family life which do emerge as being associated with a later risk of troubling psychotic experiences.

The programme of research was explicitly presented as an investigation into the experiences and outcomes of adoption. This meant that adopting families could be legitimately approached from that perspective rather than from one which foregrounded mental health difficulties, with all their attendant stigmatising difficulties. Detailed case registers and information from adoption agencies made it possible to screen the entire Finnish population for suitable subjects, and the investigators were able to identify 170 women who had received a 'diagnosis' of Schizophrenia or Paranoid Psychosis in the course of a hospital admission, and who had given up at least one child for adoption. This identified 186 adopted individuals who had a biological background that included the experience of psychosis (index cases). They had been adopted into 185 distinct families. Records of a national adoption agency were scrutinised in order to identify the next listed adoptee and their adoptive family that matched each index case on the basis of age and gender, adoptive parents' ages and gender, adoptee's age at adoption, socioeconomic status and family structure (both parents or single mother). This resulted in 201 mothers who had not appeared in the psychiatric case register and who had, in total, given up 203 children for adoption into 203 distinct families. Thus, the research could be based upon 388 families, 185 adopting children from a family background that included a maternal experience of troublesome psychosis, and 203 which adopted children without such a background. A full family assessment was possible in 303 (78%) of these.

These assessments were exhaustive. They occupied some fourteen to sixteen hours spread over two days, in the course of which psychiatrists of a family therapy background conducted tape recorded joint interviews with the whole family, with the parental couple, and semi-structured interviews with individual family members. Standardised assessments included a measure of communication deviance, a personality inventory and a brief measure of IQ. Central to the assessment was a summary of family function developed in the course of this research, the Oulun Perhe Arviointi Skaala (OPAS) or Oulu Family Rating Scale.

The OPAS was developed from considerations of pre-existing family evaluations such as the Beavers' Family Evaluation Scales (Lewis et al. 1976), and theorising about the forms of family dysfunction that might result in later vulnerability to troublesome psychotic experiences. Eventually thirty-three sub-scales of family function were developed. Examples include 'rigid family structure', 'lack of empathy', 'lack of humour', 'disruptive communication', 'parental conflict', 'suspicious of extrafamilial context', 'unclear family roles' and 'inadequate daily problem solving'. These thirty-three sub-scales have been grouped as five dimensions: *Family structure,* which reflects issues of power, leadership, authority, control, interpersonal role differentiation, and parental coalition; *Communication,* which refers to the quality, flexibility and appropriateness of observed verbal and other communications amongst family members; *Affect,* which refers to the intensity, or inappropriate lack of intensity in the family's emotional climate; *The nuclear family's boundaries and attitude towards the outer world,* which reflects the capacity of family members to engage with extended family members and persons in the community; and *Binding and expelling.* Binding refers to practices whereby a family member influences another family member's inner world so that his or her thoughts, needs, feelings, goals and fantasies are changed to conform to the other's interpretations of them. Expelling refers to practices as a result of which there is little or no supportive influence on another family member's inner world and development, and a family member may be cut off from participation in family relationships.

Each of the thirty-three sub-scales is rated 1–4 or 5, with 1 referring to the most 'healthy' pattern of practices. For instance 'rigid family structure' would be rated 1 if the family was considered to be well-organised, leadership shared in accord with the task and individual ability and there was evidence of a well-functioning parental coalition, 3 if there was evidence of a somewhat rigid structure and with some inappropriate dominance/submission, and 5 if the family structure was observed to be extremely rigid, leadership invariant regardless of circumstances and there were patterns of fixed dominance/submission. 'Suspicious of extrafamilial context' would be rated 1 if there was evidence of a realistic, trustful attitude towards the outer world involving significant interaction with a social network of both extended family and non-family members, 3 if there was evidence of some suspiciousness and reduced contact with others, and 4 if the family displayed high levels of suspicion and was isolated from social contacts, including both extended family and non-familial contacts. Altogether this process has been able to rate families in a semi-quantitative way across a wide range of qualities, with reasonable levels of inter-rater reliability. The result has been to find that people growing up in families deemed to be relatively 'unhealthy' in these ways have an increased risk of troubling psychotic experiences later in life. Conventionally this research has been reported as evidence of a gene/environment interaction because the effects of family environment upon the risk of subsequently experiencing psychosis were stronger among adoptees from a background that included a family history of 'Schizophrenia'. As already noted, this interpretation is vulnerable to the same criticisms of earlier adoptive studies in that adoptions were likely to have been selective and it is impossible to adequately control for the pre-adoption family environment or experiences of care. Nevertheless, this exhaustive research does point very clearly to an interaction between observable features of family life and the risk of subsequently troublesome experiences of psychosis. If the influence of potential genetic susceptibility is removed from the analysis, the risk of experiencing psychosis is still strongly influenced by 'unhealthy' OPAS scores (Tienari et al. 2004).

A 'Schizophrenogenic' family?

This is controversial territory, not least because such conclusions can direct responsibility for a person's experiences of psychosis towards their parents, carers or other aspects of their developmental background. Prompted by psychoanalytic theories concerning the importance of developmental difficulties in leading to later psychological differences, early twentieth century-clinicians explored the families of 'Schizophrenic' patients in search of what might be causing their difficulties. One 1930s' study (Kasanin et al. 1934) reported maternal rejection in two patients and maternal overprotection in 33 out of 45 'Schizophrenic' patients. The idea that a mixture of maternal overprotection and maternal rejection could cause 'Schizophrenia' gained traction, and in 1948 Frieda Fromm-Reichmann named these so-called rejecting and overprotective mothers 'schizophrenogenic'. She wrote '[t]he schizophrenic is painfully distrustful and resentful of other people, due to the severe early warp and rejection he encountered in important people of his infancy and childhood, as a rule, mainly in a schizophrenogenic mother' (Fromm-Reichmann 1948, p. 265). Mothers with their own psychological problems, it was thought, gave birth to healthy children and then literally drove them mad. In these homes, according to Fromm-Reichmann, the mother and her delusional ideas dominated, making her unaware of the needs of other family members. 'Schizophrenic' behaviours were a way for the child to make sense of this toxic home environment.

Taken at face value this is a damning indictment and its wide unacceptability was one of the drivers encouraging a more exclusively genetic explanation for the familial transmission of 'madness', and a reluctance to further pursue relational family research. Frank (1965) considered the many studies that had been published in this field over the preceding three decades. He found a wealth of methodological shortcomings including the weaknesses of basing conclusions on self-report questionnaires, the intrusions of other forms of familial vicissitude such as parental loss, poor comparisons with appropriate control groups and imprecise definitions of 'schizophrenogenic'. He concluded that 'no factors were found in the parent-child interaction of schizophrenics, neurotics, or those with behaviour disorders which could be identified as unique to them or which could distinguish one group from the other, or any of the groups from the families of controls' (Frank 1965, p. 191).

Ten years later Jacob (1975) reviewed reports of methodologically more exacting family studies. He focused upon studies in which findings had been derived from direct observation of orchestrated interactions between family members and which could be rated on the basis of several methodological requirements; comparisons had been made between socio-demographically comparable families in which there either was or was not at least one member (father, mother or child) with a 'diagnosis' of Schizophrenia, those rating (largely) tape-recorded interactions were blind to participants' diagnostic status, there was evidence of good inter-rater reliability, children's gender was taken into account, and observations and recordings had been made under standardised conditions. Thirty such studies were identified. Few fulfilled all these methodological requirements to an acceptable standard but nevertheless they were the data available at the time. Judgements about the nature of family interactions were made on the basis of four dimensions; conflict, dominance, affect (or emotionality), and clarity of communications. Across the included studies, findings were inconsistent. In relation to *Conflict,* of sixteen comparisons between 'Schizophrenic' families and controls, nine yielded no reliable differences between groups, three indicated more interrupting behaviour in 'Schizophrenic' families than amongst controls, three suggested more conflict and disagreement in the 'Schizophrenic' families, and one indicated more disagreement in 'normal' families. In relation to *Dominance,* seventeen comparisons were identified. Seven yielded no clear group differences, one indicated that fathers of 'Schizophrenics' were more dominant than their 'normal' counterparts, four pointed in the other direction and five produced a mixed bag of findings. There were thirty-one group comparisons of the amount or quality of *Affective* expression. Fourteen were unable to distinguish between 'Schizophrenic' and 'normal' families, three only reported a difference when a 'non-schizophrenic' sibling was present, two suggested that 'normal' families were more emotionally expressive than 'Schizophrenic' families, three suggested that 'normal' families expressed more positive affect than did 'Schizophrenic' families and the nine remaining comparisons, again, produced a mixed bag. In contrast, comparisons of *Communication Clarity* were more revealing. Nine studies assessed 'Schizophrenic' and 'normal' families in terms of communication clarity over a total of twenty-four comparisons. Only five reported no reliable group differences. 'Normal' families were found to communicate more clearly and effectively than 'Schizophrenic' families across a wide range of measures. However, this was a wide range of measures and Jacob concluded that:

the available data assessing communication clarity and accuracy generally suggest that schizophrenic families communicate with less clarity and accuracy than do normal families. The major exception to this conclusion, however, is that the more objective and less inferential measures of disruptions in communication reveal few reliable differences between groups.

(Jacob 1975, p. 55)

Although the body of work summarised by Jacob in 1975 undoubtedly laid foundations for the OPAS and its findings, it also revealed the conceptual and methodological challenges facing investigators interested in trying to establish the effect and nature of so-called 'schizophrenogenic' families (or even mothers). It encouraged those who, quite understandably, wanted to put the very idea of 'blaming' families, or even specific parents, for the later occurrence of troubling psychotic experiences among their offspring to one side, and inhibited further research. In 2012 Ann Harrington wrote:

Fear of giving any energy to discredited models of family blaming means that, today, cultural and psychosocial questions relating to schizophrenia are rarely discussed. I consider it axiomatic that all human beings, even those with biological vulnerabilities that put them at risk of schizophrenia, are embedded in a cultural and interpersonal world that gets under their skin and affects them.

(Harrington 2012, p. 1293)

Gene-environment interactions

Mainstream epidemiology continues to follow the line developed by the Finnish programme referred to above; a search for developmental experiences that might interact with an assumed genetic predisposition to the risk of troubling psychotic experiences. This circumvents the otherwise uncomfortable prospect of appearing to seek 'causes' for the subsequent experience of psychosis amongst developmental experiences, and thereby, however indirectly, implicating family and friends.

Van Os and colleagues (2004) revisited Danish case records and sought associations between urbanicity as a proxy developmental influence and a family history of 'Schizophrenia' as a proxy for genetic risk. They found that the effect of increasingly urban developmental settings upon the risk of subsequently being troubled by psychosis was stronger among those with a family history of 'Schizophrenia' than among those without it. Fisher and colleagues (2014) explored the interaction between a family history of troublesome psychosis, again, a proxy for genetic risk, and the recollection of maternal physical abuse upon the risk of subsequently experiencing psychosis. Their data were taken from the Aetiology of Schizophrenia and Other Psychoses (Æsop) case-controlled study. Within this sample, a history of psychosis in at least one parent was around seven times more common

84

among participants with their own troublesome experiences of psychosis, than among community controls. Those with a parental history of psychosis had an enhanced likelihood of suffering severe physical abuse at the hands of their mother before the age of twelve, and this experience of maternal abuse was associated with the enhanced risk of subsequently experiencing psychosis. Nevertheless, this effect upon risk was not influenced by the presence or absence of a family history of psychosis. Thus a parental history of troubling psychotic experiences enhanced the likelihood of suffering abuse in childhood, and abuse in childhood was associated with subsequent experiences of psychosis. However, abuse in childhood was not confined to those with a family history of psychosis and it appeared to exert its own established effect whether or not there was such a family history. Although these data agreed with established associations of family history and childhood abuse with the experience of psychosis, they failed to identify a gene-environment interaction, suggesting that the two influences were operating independently. Adding to the mix, Pedersen & Mortensen (2006) considered whether or not the effects of an urban upbringing upon the risk of subsequently experiencing psychosis reflected an influence rooted in the individual or in the family. Again, using Danish data, they identified 2,720 individuals who had developed 'Schizophrenia' between 1970 and 2001. They explored whether or not the nearest older sibling's place of birth had an independent effect upon the risk of 'Schizophrenia' and found that it did. This has been interpreted to suggest that the effect of urban upbringing upon the risk of troubling psychotic experiences may, in part, be mediated through influences acting upon the family as a whole rather than acting specifically upon the subsequently afflicted individual. Shevlin and colleagues (Shevlin et al. 2016) also used Danish data to explore the independence of familial factors (advanced paternal age, family dissolution, parental psychosis) environmental factors (urbanicity, deprivation), psychological factors (experience of having been in care as a child), and gender upon the risk of subsequently experiencing troubling psychosis. Seven binary (yes/no) variables were abstracted from the records of 54,458 Danish residents born in 1984. Multivariate binary logistic regression was used to establish the independent and related effects of each of these upon the risk of subsequently experiencing troubling psychosis. Paternal age and gender failed to reach significance but the remaining five potential determinants did, with family history and having been in care exercising the strongest effect. Once again, these data point to complex interactions between a family history of psychosis, which may represent genetic risk or might reflect some other form of familial transmission, and more clearly evident environmental influences. Finally, Grech and colleagues (2017) explored the effects upon the risk of experiencing psychosis of interactions between supposed genetic influences (in the form of a sibling who had experienced psychosis), and the urbanicity of life before the age of fifteen. Overall, the risk of reporting psychotic experiences (on the basis of the

Community Assessment of Psychic Experiences, Konings et al. 2006) among subjects who had a sibling with a 'diagnosis' of Schizophrenia was higher than amongst those without. Strikingly, however, this was a much weaker effect amongst those who had grown up in a rural environment than amongst those who had grown up in an urban environment.

In the absence of convincing and credible candidates for the role of 'Schizophrenia Psychosis Gene', these studies are limited by their dependence upon proxy measures, most usually the presence or otherwise of one or more first-degree relatives who have suffered troubling psychotic experiences themselves. These cannot be independent of other more indirect consequences of such a family history, for instance the stigma and discrimination that commonly accompany them, effects upon the stability and warmth of family life, and more. Until or unless environmental influences can be considered alongside clearly independent, biologically determined, credible and sound genetic influences, these studies are inescapably circular. Proxy indicators of a genetic contribution to the risk of experiencing psychosis such as the presence of an afflicted first degree relative cannot be entirely independent of their environmental, familial or social consequences. Thus, until or unless they can employ truly independent measures of any genetic influence there might be, these studies suffer because they may well be simply exploring contributions to the risk of experiencing psychosis arising from a range of related environmental, familial and social factors.

To summarise

There is strong and reliable evidence that the risk of troublesome psychotic experiences is significantly higher among people who have one or more first-degree relatives that have suffered similar experiences, but that is where the certainty comes to an end. Conventionally, and supported by evidence from twin and adoption studies this has been assumed to reflect a 'genetic' contribution to the risk, and indeed early in the twentieth century this assumption was responsible for some very brutal approaches to the business of reducing that risk. Technologically advanced searches for that genetic contribution, in the form of identifiable configurations of DNA associated with the risk of experiencing psychosis, appear to have run into the sand. Furthermore, the notion of fixed and rigidly transmissible genes, which has underpinned broader understandings of what 'inheritability' means is proving to be a gross over-simplification. Strings of DNA might carry the blueprint of an individual's biology, but whether or not, and how, they operate are contextually determined. 'Nature' and 'Nurture' are not independently interacting contributors ... to anything, and indeed it is quite possible that a parent's life experiences might have an enduring effect upon how their offspring's DNA functions; upon their offspring's biology. Attempts to discriminate between genetic and environmental contributions to the clearly observable fact that 'madness runs in families' oversimplify the complex and intimate relationships between 'genes' and the 'environment'. A better understanding of why 'madness runs in families' is going to depend upon refreshed insights into what constitutes 'madness' and what constitutes (or does not) a healthily conducive family. Historically, progress with the latter has been hindered by unhelpfully critical judgements suggesting that parents, and in particular mothers, might be held responsible for their offspring suffering troublesome psychotic experiences. Nevertheless, there is evidence that certain features of the family's configuration and habits *are* associated with an enhanced risk of that happening. However, although they are relevant influences, individual parents should not be held responsible for socio-economic circumstances, others' prejudices and additional features of the social and material world they inhabit, and which powerfully and undoubtedly influence families' configurations and habits. In considering how the environment impacts upon mental health, that scion of developmental psychology and psychiatry, Michael Rutter once wrote:

> ... there is a need for a better understanding of the kinds of environmental influences that have major risk effects. The evidence so far suggests that these include restrictions on the possibility of developing intense selective social relationships (as with institutional rearing), severe disruptions in the security of such relationships (as with neglect, rejection and scapegoating), life events that carry a long-term threat to such relationships (as with humiliating experiences, personal rebuffs or rejections), and social ethos or group influences of a maladaptive kind (as with antisocial peer groups or malfunctioning social peer groups or malfunctioning schools). Also, however, the overall quality of adult-child interaction and communication has been shown to matter.
>
> (Rutter 2005, p. 5)

This makes considerable intuitive sense but conducting the research that will unlock these secrets, and acting upon its findings, will require a readiness to intrude into the privacy of family life that has yet to be fully welcomed; indeed, it has been resisted. The last few decades' foray into a search for the 'Schizophrenia Gene' might well be understood, in part, as a displacement in response to that resistance. Perhaps the time has come to recognise this and acknowledge the fact that some families, under some circumstances can be unwittingly, harmfully toxic. Intriguingly, this is one of the lessons that systemic and related approaches to therapy are uncovering. They also present a need to address such circumstances with more sensitivity than Fromm-Reichmann and her adherents displayed.

References

Alegría-Torres, J. A., Baccarelli, A. and Bollati, V. (2011) 'Epigenetics and lifestyle', *Epigenomics*, Vol. 3, No. 3, pp. 267–277.

Dalgard, O. S. and Kringlen, E. (1976) 'A Norwegian Twin Study of Criminality', *The British Journal of Criminology*, Vol. 16, No. 3, pp. 213–232.

Fisher, H. L., McGuffin, P., Boydell, J., Fearon, P., Craig, T. K., Dazzan, P., Morgan, K., Doody, G. A., Jones, P. B., Leff, J., Murray, R. M. and Morgan, C. (2014) 'Interplay Between Childhood Physical Abuse and Familial Risk in the Onset of Psychotic Disorders', *Schizophrenia Bulletin*, Vol. 40, No. 6, pp. 1443–1451.

Fosse, R., Joseph, J. and Richardson, K. (2015) 'A critical assessment of the equal-environment assumption of the twin method for schizophrenia', *Frontiers in Psychiatry*, Vol. 6, No. 62. doi:10.3389/fpsyt.2015.00062.

Frank, G. H. (1965) 'The Role of the Family in the Development of Psychopathology', *Psychological Bulletin*, Vol. 64, No. 3, pp. 191–205.

Franklin, T. B., Russig, H., Weiss, I. C., Gräff, J., Linder, N., Michalon, A., Vizi, S. and Mansuy, M. (2010) 'Epigenetic Transmission of the Impact of Early Stress Across Generations', *Society of Biological Psychiatry*, Vol. 68, pp. 408–415.

Fromm-Reichmann, F. (1948) 'Notes on the Development of Treatment of Schizophrenics by Psychoanalytic Psychotherapy', *Psychiatry*, Vol. 11, No. 3, pp. 263–273.

Gottesman, I. I., McGuffin, P. and Farmer, A. E. (1987) 'Clinical Genetics as Clues to the "Real" Genetics of Schizophrenia (A Decade of Modest Gains While Playing for Time) ', *Schizophrenia Bulletin*, Vol. 13, No. 1, pp. 23–47.

Grech, A., van Os, J. and GROUP Investigators (2017) 'Evidence That the Urban Environment Moderates the Level of Familial Clustering of Positive Psychotic Symptoms', *Schizophrenia Bulletin*, Vol. 43, No. 2, pp. 325–331.

Harrington, A. (2012) 'The art of medicine: The fall of the schizophrenogenic mother', *Perspectives*, Vol. 379, pp. 1292–1293.

Jacob, T. (1975) 'Family Interaction in Disturbed and Normal Families: A Methodological and Substantive Review', *Psychological Bulletin*, Vol. 82, No. 1, pp. 33–65.

Kasanin, J., Knight, E. and Sage, P. (1934) 'The Parent-Child Relationship in Schizophrenia', *The Journal of Nervous and Mental Disease*, Vol. 79, No. 3, pp. 249–263.

Kendler, K. S. and Diehl, S. R. (1993) 'The Genetics of Schizophrenia: A Current, Genetic-Epidemiologic Perspective', *Schizophrenia Bulletin*, Vol. 19, No. 2, pp. 261–285.

Kety, S. S. and Ingraham, L. J. (1992) 'Genetic Transmission and Improved Diagnosis of Schizophrenia from Pedigrees of Adoptees', *Journal of Psychiatric Research*, Vol. 26, No. 4, pp. 247–255.

Konings, M., Bak, M., Hanssen, M., van Os, J. and Krabbendam, L. (2006) 'Validity and reliability of the CAPE: a self-report instrument for the measurement of psychotic experiences in the general population', *Acta Psychiatrica Scandinavica*, Vol. 114, pp. 55–61.

Lam, M., Chen, C.-Y., Li, Z., Martin, A. R., Bryois, J., Ma, X., Gaspar, H., Ikeda, M., Benyamin, B., Brown, B. C., Liu, R., Zhou, W., Guan, L., Kamatani, Y., Kim, S.-W., Kubo, M., Kusumawardhani, A., Li, C.-M., Ma, H., Periyasamy, S., Takahashi, A., Xu, Z., Yu, H., Zhu, F., Schizophrenia Working Group of the Psychiatric Genomics Consortium, Indonesia Schizophrenia Consortium, Genetic REsearch on schizophreniA neTwork-China and The Netherlands (GREATCN),

Chen, W. J., Faraone, S., Glatt, S. J., He, L., Hyman, S. E., Hwu, H.-G., McCarroll, S. A., Neale, B. M., Sklar, P., Wildenauer, D. B., Yu, X., Zhang, D., Mowry, B. J., Lee, J., Holmans, P., Xu, S., Sullivan, P. F., Ripke, S., O'Donovan, M. C, Daly, M. J., Qin, S., Sham, P., Iwata, N., Hong, K. S., Schwab, S. G., Yue, W, Tsuang, M., Liu, J., Ma, X., Kahn, R. S., Shi, Y., Huang, H. (2019) 'Comparative genetic architectures of schizophrenia in East Asian and European populations', *Nature Genetics*, Vol. 51, No. 12, pp. 1670–1678.

Llewellyn, J., Southey, J. and Thompson, S. (2020) Alpha History. https://alphahistory.com/nazigermany/nazi-eugenics/ (accessed October 2022).

Lewis, J. M., Beavers, W. R., Gosset, J. T. and Phillips, V. A. (1976) *No Single Thread. Psychological Health in Family Systems.* New York: Brunner/Mazel.

Loehlin, J. C. (1978) 'Identical twins reared apart and other routes to the same direction'. In W. Nance, G. Allen and P. Parisi (Eds.) *Twin Research, Part A: Psychology and Methodology.* New York, NY: Allan R. Liss, pp. 69–77.

Mariaselvam, C. M., Wu, C.-L., Boukouaci, W., Richard, J.-R., Barau, C., Le Corvoisier, P., OPTiMiSE Study Group, Dazzan, P., Egerton, A., Pollak, T. A., McGuire, P., Rujescu, D., Jamain, S., Leboyer, M. and Tamouza, R. (2021) 'The Complement C4 Genetic Diversity in First Episode Psychosis of the OPTiMiSE Cohort', *Schizophrenia Bulletin Open.* doi:10.1093/schizbullopen/sgab003.

National Heart, Blood and Lung Institute (2022) 'What Causes Cystic Fibrosis?' https://www.nhlbi.nih.gov/health/cystic-fibrosis/causes (accessed October 2022).

Pedersen, C. B. and Mortensen, P. B. (2006) 'Urbanization and traffic related exposures as risk factors for Schizophrenia', *BMC Psychiatry*, Vol. 6, No. 2. doi:10.1186/1471-244X-6-2..

Rutter, M. (2005) 'How the environment affects mental health', *British Journal of Psychiatry*, Vol. 186, pp. 4–6.

Scarr, S. and Carter-Saltzman, L. (1979) 'Twin method: defense of a critical assumption', *Behavioural Genetics*, Vol. 9, No. 6, pp. 527–542.

Schizophrenia Working Group of the Psychiatric Genomics Consortium (2014) 'Biological insights from 108 schizophrenia-associated genetic loci', *Nature*, Vol. 511, pp. 421–427.

Sekar, A., Bialas, A. R., de Rivera, H., Davis, A., Hammond, T. R., Kamitaki, N., Tooley, K., Presumey, J., Baum, M., Van Doren, V., Genovese, G., Rose, S. A., Handsaker, R. E., Schizophrenia Working Group of the Psychiatric Genomics Consortium, Daly, M. J., Carroll, M. C., Stevens, B. and McCarroll, S. A. (2016) 'Schizophrenia risk from complex variation of complement component 4', *Nature*, Vol. 530, No. 7589, pp. 177–183.

Sharma, I., Pandit, B., Pathak, A. and Sharma, R. (2013) 'Hinduism, marriage and mental illness', *Indian Journal of Psychiatry*, Vol. 55 (suppl 2) pp. S243–S249.

Shevlin, M., McElroy, E., Christoffersen, M. N., Elklit, A., Hyland, P. and Murphy, J. (2016) 'Social, familial and psychological risk factors for psychosis: A birth cohort study using the Danish Registry System', *Psychosis*, Vol. 8, No. 2, pp. 95–105.

Tienari, P., Lahti, I., Sorri, A., Naarala, M., Moring, J., Wahlberg, K.-E. and Wynne, L. C. (1987) 'The Finnish Adoptive Family Study of Schizophrenia', *Journal of Psychiatric Research*, Vol. 21, No. 4, pp. 437–445.

Tienari, P., Wynne, L. C., Moring, J., Lahti, I., Naarala, M., Sorri, A., Wahlberg, K.-E., Saarento, O., Seitamaa, M., Kaleva, M. and Läksy, K. (1994) 'The Finnish

Adoptive Family Study of Schizophrenia Implications for Family Research', *British Journal of Psychiatry*, Vol. 164, No. 23, pp. 20–26.

Tienari, P., Wynne, L. C., Moring, J., Läksy, K., Nieminen, P., Sorri, A., Lahti, I., Wahlberg, K.-E., Naarala, M., Kurki-Suonio, K., Saarento, O., Koistinen, P., Tarvainen, T., Hakko, H. and Miettunen, J. (2000) 'Finnish adoptive family study: sample selection and adoptee DSM-III-R diagnoses', *Acta Psychiatrica Scandinavica*, Vol. 101, pp. 433–443.

Tienari, P., Wynne, L. C., Sorri, A., Lahti, I., Läksy, K., Moring, J., Naarala, M., Nieminen, P. and Wahlberg, K.-E. (2004) 'Genotype-environment interaction in schizophrenia-spectrum disorder: Long-term follow-up study of Finnish adoptees', *British Journal of Psychiatry*, Vol. 184, pp. 216–222.

Van Os, J., Pedersen, C. B. and Mortensen, P. B. (2004) 'Confirmation of Synergy Between Urbanicity and Familial Liability in the Causation of Psychosis', *American Journal of Psychiatry*, Vol. 161, pp. 2312–2314.

Yehuda, R., Daskalakis, N. P., Bierer, L. M., Bader, H. N., Klengel, T., Holsboer, F. and Binder, E. B. (2016) 'Holocaust Exposure Induced Intergenerational Effects on FKBP5 Methylation', *Biological Psychiatry*, Vol. 80, pp. 372–380.

5

ETHNICITY, MIGRATION, AND TROUBLING PSYCHOTIC EXPERIENCES

In 1988 Glynn Harrison and his colleagues published striking findings. The rate at which a 'diagnosis' of Schizophrenia was being made among people of Afro-Caribbean origin living in Nottingham was considerably higher than in the general population (Harrison et al. 1988). 'Cases' arose at a rate of 29.1 per 10,000 population amongst younger people of Afro-Caribbean origin and 19.7 per 10,000 population amongst thirty- to forty-four-year-olds. Comparable rates were 2.2 and 1.6 per 10,000 population in the general population. This was not the first time such figures had come to light, but Harrison and his colleagues went to particular trouble to ensure that experiences of psychosis classified as 'Schizophrenia' fulfilled well-defined criteria and did not, for instance, include unusual forms and presentations. However psychosis might be understood, these findings indicated a clear and substantial difference between the frequency of such experiences amongst a minority sub-population (in this case identified by ethnicity), and the wider population.

Although earlier surveys of European migrants into the United States (Ödegaard 1932; Malzberg 1955) had resulted in comparable findings amongst minority sub-populations from a different set of ethnic backgrounds, and Cochrane (1977) had found higher rates of admission to a psychiatric hospital (for all reasons) amongst migrants to England from Ireland, Scotland and Poland, Harrison's paper sparked considerable interest. Do these differences reflect an inheritable, racially related vulnerability? Do they reflect a propensity to migrate among the more vulnerable? Do they reflect the socially stressful consequences of migration? Do they reflect 'institutional racism'? Do they reflect other less immediately obvious consequences of having migrated, or of belonging to a minority sub-population? Given the political sensitivity of such questions considerable investment has gone into attempting to answer them. Partly in response to this Cantor-Graae and Selten (2005) carried out a meta-analysis of data from eighteen independent studies exploring rates of psychosis amongst migrant

DOI: 10.4324/9780429059094-6

populations that had been published between 1977 and 2003. The majority of these concerned migrants from erstwhile colonies, and their descendants. Twelve of the studies concerned immigrants into the United Kingdom from Africa, the Caribbean or the Indian sub-continent. Two concerned migrants into the Netherlands from Surinam and the Dutch Antilles. One concerned migrants into Australia from a variety of European countries, one concerned migrants from Turkey and Morocco into the Netherlands and two concerned migrants into Sweden and Denmark from a variety of sources.

Migrants into the United Kingdom from erstwhile colonies

Rwegellera (1977) identified everyone of West African or West Indian origin living in Camberwell, South London, who had been in contact with psychiatric services between the beginning of 1965 and the end of 1968. All were first generation migrants in that they were recorded as having been born in West Africa, the West Indies or Guyana. 'Psychiatric contact' was inferred on the basis of admission to a psychiatric or mental hospital, attending a psychiatric outpatient department, being seen by a psychiatrist in a general hospital or at home as a domiciliary visit, admission to a 'mental sub-normality hospital', or having been seen by a psychiatric social worker. At the time clinical information about individuals who had experienced such contact was held as the Camberwell Psychiatric Case Register, from which it was possible to obtain a psychiatric 'diagnosis'. The troubling experience of psychosis was inferred on the basis of that having been Schizophrenia or Schizo-affective psychosis. The size of the West African/West Indian population in Camberwell was estimated by extrapolation from the 1961 census. Amongst those born in West Africa there were twelve instances of 'Schizophrenia' or 'Schizo-affective Psychosis', twenty-five among those born in the West Indies, and sixty-six among those born in the United Kingdom. As incidence rates; instances per 1,000 population, these figures were computed as 4.18, 0.92 and 0.12.

Dean and colleagues (1981) considered data from first hospital admissions' records during 1976 across South Eastern England. Information about place of birth was available in 91%. Migrants were made up, largely, of those born in the West Indies, Africa (mainly ethnic Asians from Uganda), and those born in India or Pakistan. The population structure was extrapolated from the 1971 census with adjustments for known numbers of immigrants. 'Diagnosis' was taken from hospital records. If the experience of troubling psychosis is inferred from a 'diagnosis' of Schizophrenia, of Depressive Psychosis or of Other Psychosis, then seventy-one individuals born in the West Indies were admitted to hospital for this reason, for the first time, during 1976. The expected number, given no systematic difference between them and the wider population would have been twenty. Comparable numbers for those of Indian origin were forty-six and twenty-five, those of Pakistani origin twenty-one and 23.5, and those of 'Ugandan Asian' origin sixty and 19.4.

McGovern and Cope (1987) conducted a similar investigation of first admissions to a psychiatric hospital in Birmingham. Individuals of Caribbean origin were considered and an attempt was made to capture data that distinguished between 'first' and 'second' generation migrants, the former being people who had likely migrated as adults and the latter those who were born in the United Kingdom or who had likely migrated as children and grown up in the United Kingdom. The population structure was based upon estimates from the 1981 census with additional extrapolations. Ethnicity was assumed to be the same as the head of household, where the subject was not themselves head of household, and this contributed to the estimate of the 'second generation migrant' population when the head of household had been born in the Caribbean. An estimate of the 'second generation migrant' population that were themselves head of household was obtained by extrapolation from other surveys and sources. On the basis of these estimates the population at risk was considered to be made up of 105,620 'white' males, 94,920 'white' females, 5,600 male and 5,180 female 'first generation migrants', and 2,580 male and 2,580 female 'second generation migrants'. Reasons for admission were derived from case notes and classified as 'Schizophrenia/Paranoid Psychosis', 'Affective Disorder', 'Cannabis Psychosis' and 'Other diagnoses'. Because they had likely migrated as children (during the peak years of 1955–64) and grown up in the United Kingdom those aged sixteen to twenty-nine were considered 'second generation migrants' even though their place of birth was registered as having been in the Caribbean, along with those who were registered as having been born in the United Kingdom. Among male 'white' and 'second generation migrant' sixteen to twenty-nine-year-olds, the annual rates of admission with a recorded 'diagnosis' of Schizophrenia/Paranoid Psychosis, per 100,000 population were 20.5 and 138 respectively. Among young females they were seven and ninety-eight. Among older male 'whites' and 'first generation' migrants they were 9.8 and 49.3, and amongst older females they were 13.3 and 52.8.

Cochrane and Bal (1987) analysed data concerning all recorded 186,000 admissions to a psychiatric hospital in England during 1981. These data included the place of birth, which was used as a proxy indicator of migrant status. As an exploration of the effects of ethnicity that approach had imperfections; place of birth would not reflect ethnicity among Caucasians born outside England, or among second generation migrants, but this was an opportunity to study a large sample and explore the effects of migration *per se*. Among males born in England, the rate of first admission to hospital with a 'diagnosis' of Schizophrenia and/or Paranoia was nine per 100,000 population; among males born in the Caribbean it was thirty-nine, among males born in Ireland it was eighteen, among males born in India it was eleven and among males born in Pakistan it was nineteen. Among females, the comparable figures were nine, thirty-five, twenty-two, eighteen and twelve.

Castle and colleagues (1991) were stimulated by the fact that rates of 'Schizophrenia' in South London appeared not to have fallen during the years between the mid-1960s and the mid-1980s in the way that they had elsewhere in the country. They explored the possibility that this was because of a rise in the proportion of the population who were migrants, particularly from the Caribbean. Census data for Camberwell showed that the proportion of the population born in the West Indies increased from 2.5% in 1961, to 4.9% in 1971, and 6.6% in 1981. If information about heads of household were taken into account, then the proportion of migrants from the Caribbean ('first' and 'second' generation) living in Camberwell could be estimated to have risen from 2.5% in 1961 to as high as 11.5% in 1981. Stringent diagnostic criteria were applied to all available records of individuals identified from the Camberwell Cumulative Psychiatric Case Register as having received a 'diagnosis' of Schizophrenic Psychosis, Paraphrenia or another form of Non-organic (functional) Psychosis. This procedure identified some 500 instances of 'Schizophrenia'. There was no evidence of a fall in frequency over the period in question but there was clear evidence of higher rates amongst those identified as born in the Caribbean or, in 1981, likely 'second generation' migrants. On the basis of 1965–1969 case records, Schizophrenia was 'diagnosed' at a rate of 46.7 individuals of Caribbean origin per 100,000 population, in contrast to a rate of 8.8 per 100,000 amongst those of British origin. Comparable figures for the period 1980–1984 were 57.6 and 9.7, by which time the size of the Afro-Caribbean population in that part of London had increased nearly five-fold.

Thomas and colleagues conducted a similar study in Manchester (Thomas et al. 1993). Acute admissions records from the beginning of 1984 to the end of 1986 were examined, and age, place of birth, ethnicity and 'diagnosis' (ICD-9 criteria) were extracted. Ethnicity was considered as 'White', 'Afro-Caribbean', or 'Asian', and among non-whites migrations status was defined as either first or second generation on the basis of ethnicity, place of birth and information about the head of household if that was someone other than the subject. Younger (sixteen- to twenty-nine-year-old) 'White' and second generation 'Asian' subjects were admitted to hospital and acquired a 'diagnosis' of Schizophrenia at a rate of thirty-five persons per 100,000 population, compared with 320 per 100,000 population among 'Afro-Caribbean' second generation migrants of the same age range; nearly ten times more frequently than their 'White' or second generation migrant 'Asian' peers.

Van Os and colleagues were able to use 1991 census data. This was the first UK census to include comprehensive data on the ethnic composition of the general population. It provided an early opportunity to accurately assess the incidence of both 'Schizophrenia' and 'Other Psychoses' across ethnic groups unhindered by the need to make indirect estimates of the underlying

94

population structure (Van Os et al. 1996). Once again, the population of Camberwell was the focus. First admissions aged sixteen and over receiving a discharge 'diagnosis' of Schizophrenic Psychosis or Other Non-organic (functional) Psychosis between 1988 and 1992 were identified from the Maudsley/Bethlem Royal Hospital admissions index. Their case notes were systematically scrutinised, and diagnostic criteria for 'Schizophrenia' and 'Non-organic psychosis' were applied. This resulted in 110 'cases' of functional psychosis, of which seventy-nine fulfilled criteria for a 'diagnosis' of Schizophrenia. This investigation did not focus upon migration, per se, but the availability of high-quality population data concerning ethnicity did allow more reliable comparisons between groups and a focus upon associations with ethnicity. Overall, there were twenty-two 'cases' from amongst the Afro-Caribbean population; the expected number, had there been no systematic differences from the 'White' population would have been 7.2. Amongst 'other Africans' the comparable figures were 23 and 5.5. In other words, the rate of first admission amongst both groups of ethnically defined 'Black' subjects was between three and four times greater than their Caucasian counterparts.

In 1997 Harrison and colleagues published further findings from Nottingham which also took advantage of more accurate population structure data provided by the 1991 census, and of the availability of a well-defined catchment (Harrison et al. 1997). Over a twenty-four-month period (1992–1994) every instance of potential psychosis making first contact with mental health services in Nottingham was identified. This included all service contacts, including first hospital admissions. Potential instances of troubling psychosis were followed up with a more detailed assessment. This included standardised and reviewed diagnostic interviews and rating scales, and a personal history including information from informants that could establish whether one or both parents were born in the Caribbean, and other aspects of genealogy. The experience of psychosis was inferred in two ways; a standardised 'diagnosis' of Schizophrenia conforming to ICD-10 (1994) criteria, and a wider definition of having experienced psychosis on the basis of a broader range of ICD-10 criteria. This approach identified 168 instances of broadly defined troubling psychosis: 124 were of European origin; thirty-two were first- or second-generation Afro-Caribbean migrants; three were African in origin and nine were south Asian. Only those with a personal or family history of migration from the Caribbean were considered in the analysis. Fifty-seven instances of narrowly defined schizophrenia were identified, of which eleven were from an Afro-Caribbean background. Taking into account the 1991 census data, these figures mean that new instances of broadly defined functional psychosis were occurring at a rate of 174 per 100,000 population per year among those of an Afro-Caribbean background, in comparison to a rate of eighteen per 100,000 population per year among the rest of the population. Comparable figures for narrowly defined Schizophrenia were sixty and six. Once again, there was evidence of a clearly increased risk of experiencing troubling psychosis amongst those from an Afro-Caribbean background, whether as a 'first', 'second' or later generation migrant.

Bhugra and colleagues (1997) also studied migrants into London from erstwhile British colonies and their descendants. Service contacts aged between eighteen and sixty-four who had lived for at least six months in the west London district of Ealing, where, at the time, those of an Asian ethnic background made up 19% of the population, or in the south east districts of Southwark and Lambeth where the Afro-Caribbean population made up 13% of the population were screened for the occurrence of a first experience of psychosis. Subjects were sought among those who had made first contact with general practitioners, community psychiatric nurses, prison services, private hospitals, outpatient and in-patient services, domiciliary consultants, and emergency services. The screening instrument used was one which casts a wide net and subjects were considered 'positive' if there was a suggestion of them having had at least one overt psychotic experience or two suggestive experiences. 'Positive' subjects were invited to undergo a more detailed 'diagnostic' assessment. Where possible corroborating evidence was obtained from a nearest relative, and ethnicity was determined on the basis of self-report. No attempt was made to distinguish between 'first' or subsequent generation migrants. The initial screening identified forty-six 'Whites', forty-six 'Afro-Caribbeans' and thirty-one 'Asians' who had probably experienced psychosis. The more detailed assessment of these subjects resulted in thirty-eight 'Whites', thirty-eight 'Afro-Caribbeans' and twenty-four 'Asians' whose experiences of psychosis fulfilled diagnostic criteria for a broad definition of Schizophrenia. On the basis of the 1991 census data, these figures translate into rates at which troubling experiences of psychosis (as inferred from a 'diagnosis' of broadly defined Schizophrenia) occurred at the rate of fifty-nine per 100,000 population among 'Afro-Caribbeans', thirty per 100,000 population among 'Whites' and thirty-six per 100,000 population among 'Asians'. Younger male 'Afro-Caribbeans' had a much higher rate of 147 per 100,000 population, whereas among younger 'White' males the rate was seventy-five per 100,000 population. Among male Asians of the same age the rate was only twenty-six per 100,000 population.

Goater and colleagues (1999) were able to follow up subjects at one and five years after recruitment. All those aged between sixteen and fifty-nine, resident in the catchment area of a north London psychiatric hospital, and who had made first contact with mental health services between the beginning of July 1991 and the end of June 1992 were screened for the possibility of a significant psychotic experience. Those that screened 'positive' were interviewed in more detail with a view to establishing 'diagnosis' on the basis of ICD-9 (1979) and DSM-III (1980) criteria. This was reported as either Schizophrenia or the broader definition of Non-affective Psychosis. Ethnicity was established on the basis of self-report, and reported as 'White', 'Black',

'Asian' or 'Other'. No attempt was made to distinguish between first and second or subsequent generation migrants. Where possible subjects and informants were reviewed again after one and five years. At the time of initial screening ninety-three subjects (thirty-nine 'White', thirty-eight 'Black', eleven 'Asian' and five 'Other') were considered to have experienced psychosis. Of these sixty-two fitted diagnostic criteria for broadly defined Non-Affective Functional Psychosis (twenty-four 'White', twenty-seven 'Black', eight 'Asian' and three 'Other') and thirty-eight for more narrowly defined Schizophrenia (fifteen 'White', fourteen 'Black', seven 'Asian' and two 'Other'). On the basis of 1991 census data, these reflect rates of first occurrence of broadly defined Non-Affective Functional Psychosis of twenty, eighty-seven, sixty-nine and fifty-eight per 100,000 among 'Whites', 'Blacks', 'Asians' and 'Other ethnic groups' respectively. For instances of more narrowly defined Schizophrenia comparable figures were twelve, forty-six, sixty and thirty-nine. These ethnicity-associated differences were stable across the five-year follow-up period. 'Black' subjects were more likely to be formally detained in hospital, brought to hospital by the police or forcibly given a tranquillizing injection than any of the other ethnically defined groups.

Migrants into the Netherlands from erstwhile colonies, and elsewhere

Cantor-Graae and Selten's (2005) meta-analysis included three reports of the incidence of psychosis among immigrants into the Netherlands by the same team of investigators who considered data from differing sources (Selten and Sijben 1994, Selten et al. 1997, 2001).

There are similarities and differences between mass immigration into the Netherlands and into the United Kingdom. Surinam is what was once a Dutch plantation colony on the north eastern coast of South America. It obtained political independence from Holland in 1975, but during the years leading up to this a significant part of the population migrated to the Netherlands in order to escape economic hardship and uncertainty. These migrants were from a mixture of racial backgrounds; indigenous South American stock, decedents of the trans-Atlantic slave trade and those with origins in indentured labourers brought from Indonesia by Dutch colonists. The Dutch Antilles were Caribbean colonies with greater similarity to the British Caribbean colonies, but migration from there to the Netherlands occurred somewhat later than migration to the UK from erstwhile British Caribbean colonies; not until the later 1980s.

Holland also includes significant sub-populations with their origins in Turkey and Morocco. These migrations occurred as two waves, each officially sanctioned and encouraged as a response to labour shortages. The first was during the late 1960s and the second, during the later 1970s. These migrants did not come from a former colony, were perhaps more 'European' before migrating than their colonial counterparts, and were recruited more actively in order to make up short-falls in lower waged parts of the economy. Selten and colleagues' findings suggest that these differences may be associated with different risks of troublesome psychotic experiences after migration.

The first report (Selten and Sijben 1994) is of routine data collected across the Dutch healthcare system. This includes a record of each admission to a psychiatric hospital that gives the diagnostic classification assigned by an admitting psychiatrist, place of birth and basic demographic variables such as age and gender. Records referring to admissions during 1990 were considered and census data were available to provide information about the underlying population structure. Among twenty- to thirty-nine-year-olds born in the Netherlands, the rate of first admission with a 'diagnosis' of Schizophrenia was fifty-one per 100,000 population and the rate of first admission with a 'diagnosis' of Other non-organic functional psychosis was forty per 100,000. Among twenty- to thirty-nine-year-olds born in Surinam comparable rates were 259 and 115, among those born in the Antilles rates were 247 and 120, among those born in Turkey twenty-nine and forty-one, and among those born in Morocco, 173 and 112.

The second analysis of data from the Netherlands (Selten et al. 1997) considered data from the same sources, but from over a longer period; 1983–1992. Three classes of 'patient' were considered; those with a 'diagnosis' of Broad Schizophrenia on the basis of ICD-9 (1979) criteria, those with a 'diagnosis' of Restricted Schizophrenia by the same criteria, and those with clear evidence of a relatively prolonged and disabling condition on the basis of there having been more than one admission during the period studied. This approach effectively surveyed 30.7 million males between the ages of fifteen and thirty-nine, and 29.5 million females of the same age. These populations included 11,659 individuals with a first experience of troublesome psychosis that was classified as Broad Schizophrenia, 5,448 from among them who were classified as Restricted Schizophrenia and 4,684 from among these who were considered to be suffering a relatively prolonged and disabling condition. Males in the Broad Schizophrenia category and registered as having been born in the Netherlands occurred at a rate of 22.3 per 100,000 population, males registered as having been born in Surinam at a rate of 101.8 per 100,000 and males registered as having been born in the Dutch Antilles, 107.7. For females in the Broad Schizophrenia category comparable figures were 13.9, 40.4, and 44.7. For males in the Restricted Schizophrenia category they were 11.9, 61.9 and 60.7, and for females 5.4, 19.4 and 17.8. Males born in the Netherlands and considered to have a relatively prolonged and disabling condition were present at a rate of 9.3 per 100,000 population, males born in Surinam at a rate of 49.3 and males born in the Dutch Antilles, 42.8. Comparable figures for female subjects were 5.0, 16.5 and 10.

The third Dutch survey included in Cantor-Graae and Selten's meta-analysis considered the fifteen- to fifty-four-year-old population of The

Hague (Selten et al. 2001). It was designed in an attempt to overcome some of the shortcomings of routinely collected clinical data such as mis-diagnosis or differential thresholds for admission. An effort was made to interview all of that age range who had lawfully lived in The Hague for at least six months, and who had made first contact with a physician on account of troubling psychotic or potentially psychotic experiences between the beginning of April 1997 and the beginning of April 1998. Detailed 'diagnostic' interviews resulted in 177 'cases' where troublesome psychotic experiences were or had been certainly present and four in which they were highly likely; 126 were male and fifty-five female. This approach also provided information that was collected in other ways, such as the status of individuals registered as having been born in the Netherlands but of immigrant descent. Among those born in the Netherlands, troublesome psychotic experiences inferred by a 'diagnostic' interview that identified this, occurred for the first time at a rate of 21.8 individuals per 100,000 population; among those born in Surinam or of Surinamese descent it was 52.3, among those born in the Antilles or of Antillean descent it was 54.5. Among those born in Turkey or of Turkish descent the rate was 26.2 per 100,000 population, among those born in Morocco or of Moroccan descent 104.6 and among those born in other locations outside the Netherlands or descended from them, 39.2. Broadly, these differences were present among first- and second-generation migrants, even when considered separately. These differences were also present in relation to instances where diagnostic criteria had indicated a 'diagnosis' of Schizophrenia.

Other migrant populations

Zolkowska and colleagues (2001) sought 'cases' among the immigrant population of Malmö, Sweden's third largest city. Malmö has a sizeable immigrant population from a range of overseas sources including Iraq, Iran, Serbia, Denmark, Hungary and Poland. Advantage was taken of the facts that it had but one centralised psychiatric treatment facility, and that there were reliable and detailed data concerning the background population. Instances of first admission to hospital between the beginning of April 1997 and the end of March 1998 were identified, as were all instances of first contact with outpatient psychiatric services for the same reasons between the beginning of January and the end of December 1998. On the basis of case-note information each was classified as 'Schizophrenia', 'Schizophreniform Disorder' or 'Non-Affective Functional Psychosis'. Individuals who were not registered residents were excluded. The status of 'immigrant' was conferred on those identified as foreign-born and of non-Swedish parentage on the basis of information from the Malmö Municipal Person Registry which contained, by law, up to date records of; place of birth, parentage, country of citizenship, and arrival date in Sweden for foreign-born residents. This process revealed fifty-six separate individuals who had likely experienced troubling psychosis for the first time during the period of study. Of these thirty-four were born in Sweden, and twenty-two were 'first generation' migrants. These amount to rates of first contact with mental health services on account of psychosis of 21.9 per 100,000 population among the native born, and forty-four instances among the 'immigrants'.

Cantor-Graae and colleagues (2003) published an analysis of data from the Danish Civil Registration System which was able to provide information concerning everyone resident in Denmark by their fifteenth birthday; some 21.4 million persons at the time. Enforced by law, this includes country of birth, maternal and paternal country of birth, and emigrations and immigrations to and from other countries. This information was linked to the Danish Psychiatric Central Register which contained data on all admissions to Danish psychiatric in-patient facilities since April 1969 and psychiatric out-patient visits since 1995. 'Diagnosis' was recorded on the basis of ICD-8 (1968) criteria until December 1993. Thereafter ICD-10 criteria were used. The experience of troubling psychosis was inferred on the basis of having been classified as fulfilling diagnostic criteria for 'Schizophrenia' in the course of an admission to hospital or a series of outpatient consultations. The period studied was from the beginning of April 1970 or the subject's fifteenth birthday (whichever came later) to the first recorded experience of psychosis, death, or the end of December 1998 (whichever came first). This process revealed 10,244 instances in which an inferred experience of troublesome psychosis had occurred for the first time during the study period. Of these, 8,648 were of individuals who had been born in Denmark to Danish parents, and amounts to a baseline rate of 30.59 per 100,000 population-based person years. Migrants were from a range of backgrounds but with the sole exception of those born in Denmark to non-Danish parents of undefined origin, all migrant groups had higher rates of experiencing psychosis. These ranged from 65.5 per 100,000 population-based person years amongst migrants from North America to 117.8 per 100,000 population-based person years amongst migrants from Africa and 126.5 amongst migrants from Australia.

Meta-analysis

As outlined earlier, where studies or data sets consider comparable phenomena they can be brought together in an attempt to draw out findings that they hold in common, or to balance research that has come to one conclusion with research that has come to another. Convention holds that this is the most convincing form of medical or psychological data analysis. Credible meta-analysis does however narrow the field in that included studies have to share certain core features. In the case of Cantor-Graae and Selten's 2005 meta-analysis of studies investigating the relationships between migration and the experience of psychosis, these were that included studies reported 'Schizophrenia' incidence rates for one or more migrant groups. This requires information about the proportions of the studied population which fall into those migrant groups, and that the publication provided information allowing mathematical corrections to be made that would take differing age ranges into account. These limits the analysis to instances of a particular manifestation of psychotic experiences, but without that limitation a number of studies might have been included that could not have been compared with one another. Where there was clear evidence of significant overlap between the populations reported in different publications, only one was chosen. For practical reasons the authors also restricted their search to English language, peer reviewed, scientific journals. The eighteen studies that are each briefly outlined above are the result of this search and related processes of selection. Notably all eighteen are of migrants into countries which would be considered 'developed' and where the native population is largely Caucasian.

Where it was not already provided, data from each of the studies were transformed to give a measure of 'relative risk' for each of the reported migrant groups. What this means is that a number was calculated reflecting the ratio between the rate at which 'Schizophrenia' might arise amongst members of any one migrant group and the rate at which it might arise amongst members of the native population. Thus, a relative risk of two would reflect a twofold difference in rates, of three a threefold difference, and so on. For any one set of comparisons these relative risks were combined and the credibility of an overall relative risk was expressed as its confidence interval. In total the available data provided fifty independent measures of relative risk if all reported groups of 'first' and 'second' generation migrants are considered. This analysis resulted in a mean, or average relative risk of 2.9 and confidence limits were such that this is a highly credible statistic. In other words, taking all the available data into account, immigrants were nearly three time more likely to be 'diagnosed' as suffering Schizophrenia than their indigenous peers. There were forty measures of relative risk that pertained to comparisons between 'first generation' migrants and the native population, and combined, these amounted to an overall relative risk of 2.7. There were only seven sets of data that allowed analysis of the relative risk among 'second generation' migrants, but this amounted to 4.5 with a credible range of confidence limits. There were sixteen sets of data that allowed relative risk to be calculated among migrants from countries where the majority of the population is Caucasian, and sixteen that allowed the same among migrants from countries where the majority of the population is 'Black'. The former resulted in an overall relative risk of 2.3 and for the latter, of 4.8.

Though these must remain headline figures, they are convincing evidence of an association between migrant status and the risk of 'Schizophrenia'. Cantor-Graae and colleagues' meta-analysis has since been replicated by

101

ETHNICITY, MIGRATION AND PSYCHOSIS

another (Bourgue et al. 2011) and comparable findings have come from further case register studies (e.g. Coid et al. 2008). Basing evidence of troubling experiences of psychosis upon a 'diagnosis' derived from reviewing case records is clearly imperfect, as is the attribution of migrant status to population statistics, but these studies and their meta-analytic synthesis leave no doubt that there is an association between migration and the likelihood of troubling psychotic experiences, that this association is not limited to 'first generation' migrants but is also seen among those of migrant stock who have been born and raised in the 'host' country, and that the strength of the association is influenced by racial background or skin colour.

Relatively similar rates of 'Schizophrenia' across a wide range of indigenous populations (Jablensky et al. 1992), increased relative risk among migrants of the same racial background as the 'host' country, and higher relative risk among 'second generation' migrants than amongst 'first generation' migrants of the same racial background are strong evidence that these are not racially mediated genetic effects. Similarly, high levels of relative risk among some groups of 'second generation' migrants make it highly unlikely that high rates among migrants reflect vulnerability amongst those who choose to migrate or that the direct effects of migration are responsible. These striking and robust findings have to be taken as evidence of something else that is at play, that influences the risk of acquiring a 'diagnosis' of Schizophrenia, or another psychotic disorder, and is not a vulnerability, either genetic or psychological that is located exclusively in the individual. More recent epidemiology offers some pointers towards what that could be.

Ethnic density

Social scientists have long considered the processes and consequences of cultural conflict and admixture (see, for instance, Park 1928). One of the findings from Faris and Dunham's (1939) classic Chicago study was that although white people generally had lower psychiatric first admission rates than black people, this did not hold for the primarily black area of the city. In this area white people were found to have unusually high admission rates and black people were found to have unusually low rates. The highest admission rates amongst black people were found among those who lived in less deprived parts of the city where, numerically, they were a smaller proportion of the population. As far as white people were concerned, this could be explained by selection or drift, whereby the less able or less socially graced tended to move to or live in less privileged districts, but that could not explain the parallel findings among black people. To live in more privileged surroundings could only have been a desirable goal, more readily achieved by the more able, but likely to result in a life more strongly overshadowed by the experiences of being of minority ethnic status. In 1993 David Halpern suggested that the high rates of mental health difficulties found amongst migrant populations might possibly, in part, reflect the psychological consequences of living as an ethnic or racial minority. Thus, rates would be higher in social environments where the minority was a particularly small one, and lower in social environments where minority status was 'buffered' by the availability of an ethnically compatible sub-group, the so-called 'ethnic density' hypothesis (Halpern 1993). There had been some empirical support for this, such as relatively low rates amongst French Canadians, and Greek and Italian migrants to America and to Australia during earlier parts of the twentieth century, where they tended to form their own communities (Mintz and Schwartz 1964; Rabkin 1979; Krupinski 1984), but it had not been established in the UK Afro-Caribbean and Asian populations that have been the subject of more recent interest (Cochrane and Bal 1988).

As population-based data have become more detailed, it has become possible to investigate this more thoroughly. Boydell and colleagues (2001) explored the possibility that the incidence of 'Schizophrenia' among people from non-white ethnic minorities would be greater in neighbourhoods where they constitute a smaller proportion of the total population, than in neighbourhoods that were more predominantly non-white. The Camberwell case register was scrutinised for 'cases' that presented with probable experiences of troubling psychosis during the period between 1988 and 1997. This judgement was made on the basis of case records that fulfilled diagnostic criteria for a broad definition of 'Schizophrenia'. Ethnicity was attributed on the basis of recorded self-report, or where that was not available, any record there was of skin colour, place of birth or parents' places of birth. 'Cases' were then classified as either 'White' or 'Non-white'. This process identified 222 instances of first contact with mental health services on account of troubling psychotic experiences, as inferred by a retrospective 'diagnosis' of Schizophrenia. Ninety-six were 'White' and 126 were 'Non-white'.

For electoral purposes Camberwell is divided into fifteen wards, each with a population of around 10,000. Census data for 1991 were used to estimate the population structure of each ward, and these wards were grouped on the basis of ethnic density; those with the lowest proportion of ethnic minority residents (8%–22%), those of middle rank (23%–28.1%), and those with the highest proportion (28.2%–57%). The relative risk (as opposed to there being no difference in rates on account of ethnic status or place of residence) of a 'Non-white' person coming into contact with mental health services on account of psychosis was 4.4 among those living in wards with the lowest proportion of ethnic minority residents, 3.63 among those living in wards with an intermediate proportion of ethnic minority residents and 2.38 among those living in wards with the highest proportion of ethnic minority residents. A similar association between the ethnic density of the place of residence and the risk of experiencing psychosis has also been established from Dutch data and from a further study of South London residents (Veling et al. 2008; Kirkbride et al.. 2007). An obvious explanation of these findings is that

103

living among others of a similar cultural and/or racial background somehow protects against the increased risk of being identified as someone suffering 'Schizophrenia' or another form of psychotic disorder.

That possibility was explicitly explored by Das-Munshi and colleagues (2012). They made use of data from the Ethnic Minorities Psychiatric Illness Rates in the Community (EMPIRIC) survey. This was a nationally representative survey of 7,009 English adults undertaken in 2000. Of these 4,281 were traced and interviewed, seeking information about the experience of psychosis, ethnicity, place of birth, occupationally defined social class, social support, educational achievement and experiences of racism, discrimination and chronic strains and difficulties. Demographic characteristics of subjects' places of residence were taken from census data reported at 'middle super middle super output area level'; an administrative area with a minimum population of 5,000 and a mean population of approximately 7,200.

An experience of psychosis was identified on the basis of answers to questions framed as the Psychosis Screening Questionnaire (Bebbington and Narayani 1995). This explores the experience of auditory hallucinations, persecutory delusions, hypomania, a feeling that 'something strange' is going on that others might find hard to believe and thought interference over the previous year. Overall, 8% of the sample endorsed one or more of these experiences to the interviewer's satisfaction ('White British' 6%, 'Irish' 8%, 'Black Caribbean' 12%, 'Bangladeshi' 5%, 'Indian' 9%, 'Pakistani' 10%). These data added to previous reports of an association between lower ethnic density and a higher probability of experiencing psychosis across all ethnic minority groups, but there were differences in the strength of the association between ethnic minorities. There were associations between the risk of experiencing psychosis and recent experiences of racism, discrimination in the workplace, social support and reports of one or more chronic strains, and there were associations between several of these individual experiences and ethnic density. Although areas where the density of an ethnic minority was relatively high tended to be more deprived, the presence of a higher proportion of the population from an ethnic minority appeared to 'protect' subjects from the association between chronic strains and difficulties, and the risk of troubling psychotic experiences, and this appeared to be mediated through higher levels of interpersonal support. These are robust findings in that the same authors conducted a meta-analysis confirming them across a range of mental health difficulties, countries, settings and ethnicities (Becares et al. 2018). They point to complex interactions, in that the risk of being troubled by psychotic experiences seems to be influenced by individual-based factors such as the status of 'migrant', belonging to an ethnic minority, racial background *per se*, education, and occupation; by context, such as the proportion of the population from the same background living in the immediate neighbourhood, and deprivation indices of that neighbourhood, and interactions between them. Although quantitative, epidemiological approaches have established these relationships now beyond reasonable doubt, it is challenging to see how more of the same will enable a fuller understanding of their meaning.

There is relatively little qualitative research in this area. One study of subjects resident in an area of north London (Whitley et al. 2006) identified four ways in which the experience of being of an ethnic minority might jeopardise psychological well-being, and therefore potentially enhance the risk of experiencing psychosis. Subjects identifying themselves as of an ethnic minority reported perceived exclusion from local social groups and networks. They would travel to other parts of London to socialise with compatriots rather than taking part in more local activities. There were a number of accounts of direct physical intimidation and finally, sadly, reports of explicit racism. These are barely surprising findings but their connections to the experience of psychosis and other forms of mental health difficulty are there and justify closer attention.

To summarise

More recent epidemiology that is focused upon associations between ethnicity and the experience of troubling psychosis has cleared away the misconception that the widely documented high rates of psychosis among ethnic minorities reflect biologically determined racial characteristics. There are strong associations between the risk of being identified as someone suffering a psychotic disorder, and an individual or family background of migration, irrespective of ethnicity. These associations are trans-generational in that they persist in migrants' offspring even though they will have grown up in the country of residence, and so it is hard to attribute such associations to the consequences of an individual's direct experiences of migration. Where it has been studied, ethnic density appears to offer some protection from the risk of troublesome psychotic disorder. Communities in which the proportion of residents of an ethnic minority is relatively small have a higher rate of troubling psychotic experiences among those of that ethnic minority, than in communities where the proportion of residents of that ethnic minority is higher. Intuitively, communities in which the proportion of residents of an ethnic minority is relatively small offer limited opportunities to exercise, express and inhabit ethnically familiar habits of relationship, family life and world-view; opportunities that would be more readily available in a community that included more like-minded people of a similar heritage. The history of migration reflects this. From earlier times to the present-day migrants have tended to form their own communities as a way of affirming their identity. Obvious examples include the Jewish diaspora of the Middle Ages and earlier, Italian, Irish, French, German and Scandinavian migrants to the Americas, which were otherwise, culturally, largely 'English' colonies in the north and 'Spanish' colonies in the south. Sub-cultural groupings exist even within ethnically dominant populations, as is so vividly illustrated by aspects of the English class hierarchy, where the expression 'Not PLU' (People Like Us) can still be heard used by some who heavily invest their identity in member-ship of the 'higher' echelons. Identity extends beyond an interaction with the immediate here and now. 'Who am I?' can only be answered with reference to family background, not uncommonly by several generations, and educational and other developmental experiences, and answers to that question are rela-tional. Most mundane answers to 'Who am I?' are usually answers to 'Which groupings do I belong to?', or even 'Who am I not?'. Migration into a situation of ethnic minority status brings these questions into sharper focus, and overt racial characteristics such as skin colour can make their own, additional contributions to such concerns.

Formal, quantitative research attempting to address embarrassing questions about the frequency with which 'Black' people are identified as suffering a psy-chotic disorder, being detained in hospital and being coerced into receiving anti-psychotic medication has brought our understanding of the interactions between ethnicity, migration and community to a point at which these issues come to the fore. Systematically derived, 'hard' numerical data, suggest that being able to access and make use of a like-minded community affords some people protec-tion from what would otherwise be an enhanced risk of mental health problems, and that being unable to access or make use of such a community can enhance that risk. Communities in which an ethnic minority is relatively well represented will offer a different set of potential human interactions in response to someone hearing voices or puzzled by strange beliefs and their immediate associates, from communities in which the same ethnic minority is poorly represented. Those of an ethnic minority in communities that differ in this way may have differing levels of trust and appreciation of authorities and institutional healthcare facil-ities, for good or ill. Those living in a community where their ethnic background is well represented are more likely to experience their social context as convivial and supportive than those who experience themselves as living among strangers. These undeniably high rates of 'Schizophrenia' and related 'diagnoses' among migrants and ethnic minorities raise many questions, but one must be to con-sider the parts differing patterns of human interaction and the meanings they generate play in determining differing responses and reactions to relevant psychological phenomena and behaviours.

References

Bebbington, P. and Nayani, T. (1995) 'The Psychosis Screening Questionnaire', *International Journal of Methods in Psychiatric Research*, Vol. 5, pp. 11–19.

Bécares, L., Dewey, M. E. and Das-Munshi, J. (2018) 'Ethnic density effects for adult mental health: systematic review and meta-analysis of international studies', *Psychological Medicine*, Vol. 48, pp. 2054–2072.

Bhugra, D., Leff, J., Mallett, R., Der, G., Corridan, B. and Rudge, S. (1997) 'Inci-dence and outcome of schizophrenia in Whites, African-Caribbeans and Asians in London', *Psychological Medicine*, Vol. 27, pp. 791–798.

Bourque, F., van der Ven, E. and Malla, A. (2011) 'A meta-analysis of the risk for psychotic disorders among first- and second-generation immigrants', *Psychological Medicine*, Vol. 41, pp. 897–910.

Boydell, J., van Os, J., McKenzie, K., Allardyce, J., Goel, R., McCreadie, R. G. and Murray, R. M. (2001) 'Incidence of schizophrenia in ethnic minorities in London: ecological study into interactions with environment', *British Medical Journal*, Vol. 323, pp. 1–4.

Cantor-Graae, E., Pedersen, C. B., McNeil, T. F. and Mortensen, P. B. (2003) 'Migration as a risk factor for schizophrenia: a Danish population-based cohort study', *British Journal of Psychiatry*, Vol. 182, pp. 117–122.

Cantor-Graae, E. and Selten, J.-P. (2005) 'Schizophrenia and Migration: A Meta-Analysis and Review', *American Journal of Psychiatry*, Vol. 162, pp. 12–24.

Castle, D., Wessely, S., Der, G. and Murray, R. M. (1991) 'The Incidence of Operationally Defined Schizophrenia in Camberwell, 1965–84', *British Journal of Psychiatry*, Vol. 159, pp. 790–794.

Cochrane, R. (1977) 'Mental Illness in Immigrants to England and Wales: An Analysis of Mental Hospital Admissions, 1971', *Social Psychiatry*, Vol. 12, pp. 25–35.

Cochrane, R. and Bal, S. S. (1987) 'Migration and schizophrenia: an examination of five hypotheses', *Social Psychiatry*, Vol. 22, pp. 181–191.

Cochrane, R. and Bal, S. S. (1988) 'Ethnic Density is Unrelated to Incidence of Schizophrenia', *British Journal of Psychiatry*, Vol. 153, pp. 363–366.

Coid, J. W., Kirkbride, J. B., Barker, D., Cowden, F., Stamps, R., Yang, M. and Jones, P. B. (2008) 'Raised Incidence Rates of All Psychoses Among Migrant Groups', *Archives of General Psychiatry*, Vol. 65, No. 11, pp. 1250–1258.

Das-Munshi, J., Bécares, L., Boydell, J. E., Dewey, M. E., Morgan, C., Stansfeld, S. A. and Prince, M. J. (2012) 'Ethnic density as a buffer for psychotic experiences: findings from a national survey (EMPIRIC)', *The British Journal of Psychiatry*, Vol. 201, pp. 282–290.

Dean, G., Walsh, D., Downing, H. and Shelley, E. (1981) 'First Admissions of Native-Born and Immigrants to Psychiatric Hospitals in South-East England 1976', *British Journal of Psychiatry*, Vol. 139, pp. 506–512.

Faris, R. E. L. and Dunham, H. W. (1939) *Mental disorders in urban areas: an ecological study of schizophrenia and other psychoses*. Chicago: University of Chicago Press.

Goater, N., King, M., Cole, E., Leavey, G., Johnson-Sabine, E., Blizard, R. and Hoar, A. (1999) 'Ethnicity and outcome of psychosis', *British Journal of Psychiatry*, Vol. 175, pp. 34–42.

Halpern, D. (1993) 'Minorities and Mental Health', *Social Science & Medicine*, Vol. 36, No. 5, pp. 597–607.

Harrison, G., Owens, D., Holton, A., Neilson, D. and Boot, D. (1988) 'A prospective study of severe mental disorder in Afro-Caribbean patients', *Psychological Medicine*, Vol. 18, pp. 643–657.

Harrison, G., Glazebrook, C., Brewin, J., Cantwell, R., Dalkin, T., Fox, R., Jones, P. and Medley, I. (1997) 'Increased incidence of psychotic disorders in migrants from the Caribbean to the United Kingdom', *Psychological Medicine*, Vol. 27, pp. 799–806.

Jablensky, A., Sartorius, N., Ernberg, G., Anker, M., Korten, A., Cooper, J., Day, R. and Bertelsen, A. (1992) 'Schizophrenia: Manifestations, incidence and course in different cultures A World Health Organization Ten-Country Study', *Psychological Medicine. Monograph Supplement*, Vol. 20, pp. 1–97.

Kirkbride, J. B., Morgan, C., Fearon, P., Dazzan, P., Murray, R. M. and Jones, P. B. (2007) 'Neighbourhood-level effects on psychoses: re-examining the role of context', *Psychological Medicine*, Vol. 37, pp. 1413–1425.

Krupinski, J. (1984) 'Changing Patterns of Migration to Australia and Their Influence on the Health of Migrants', *Social Science & Medicine*, Vol. 18, No. 11, pp. 927–937.

Malzberg, B. (1955) 'Trends of Mental Disease in New York State, 1920–1950', *Proceedings of the American Philosophical Society*, Vol. 99, No. 3, pp. 174–183.

McGovern, D. and Cope, R. V. (1987) 'First psychiatric admission rates of first and second generation Afro Caribbeans', *Social Psychiatry*, Vol. 22, pp. 139–149.

Mintz, N. L. and Schwartz, D. T. (1964) 'Urban Ecology and Psychosis: Community Factors in the Incidence of Schizophrenia and Manic-Depression Among Italians in Greater Boston', *International Journal of Social Psychiatry*, Vol. 10, No. 2, pp. 101–118.

Ödegaard, O. (1932) 'Emigration and insanity', *Acta Psychiatrica et Neurologica Scandinavica. Supplementum*, Vol. 4, pp. 1–206.

Park, R. E. (1928) 'Human Migration and the Marginal Man', *American Journal of Sociology*, Vol. 33, No. 6, pp. 881–893.

Rabkin, J. G. (1979) 'Ethnic density and psychiatric hospitalization: hazards of minority status', *American Journal of Psychiatry*, Vol. 136, No. 12, pp. 1562–1566.

Rwegellera, G. G. C. (1977) 'Psychiatric morbidity among West Africans and West Indians living in London', *Psychological Medicine*, Vol. 7, pp. 317–329.

Selten, J. P. and Sijben, N. (1994) 'First admission rates for schizophrenia in immigrants to the Netherlands: The Dutch national register', *Social Psychiatry and Psychiatric Epidemiology*, Vol. 29, pp. 71–77.

Selten, J.-P., Slaets, J. P. J. and Kahn, R. S. (1997) 'Schizophrenia in Surinamese and Dutch Antillean immigrants to The Netherlands: evidence of an increased incidence', *Psychological Medicine*, Vol. 27, pp. 807–811.

Selten, J.-P., Veen, N., Feller, W., Blom, J. D., Schols, D., Camoenië, W., Oolders, J., van der Velden, M., Hoek, H. W., Vladár Rivero, V. M., van der Graaf, Y. and Kahn, R. (2001) 'Incidence of psychotic disorders in immigrant groups to The Netherlands', *British Journal of Psychiatry*, Vol. 178, pp. 367–372.

Thomas, C. S., Stone, K., Osborn, M., Thomas, P. F. and Fisher, M. (1993) 'Psychiatric Morbidity and Compulsory Admission Among UK-Born Europeans, Afro-Caribbeans and Asians in Central Manchester', *British Journal of Psychiatry*, Vol. 163, pp. 91–99.

Van Os, J., Castle, D. J., Takei, N., Der, G. and Murray, R. M. (1996) 'Psychotic illness in ethnic minorities: clarification from the 1991 census', *Psychological Medicine*, Vol. 26, pp. 203–208.

Veling, W., Susser, E., van Os, J., Mackenbach, J. P., Selten, J.-P. and Hoek, H. W. (2008) 'Ethnic Density of Neighborhoods and Incidence of Psychotic Disorders Among Immigrants', *American Journal of Psychiatry*, Vol. 165, pp. 66–73.

Whitley, R., Prince, M., Mckenzie, K. and Stewart, R. (2006) 'Exploring the Ethnic Density Effect: A Qualitative Study of a London Electoral Ward', *International Journal of Social Psychiatry*, Vol. 52, No. 4, pp. 376–391.

Zolkowska, K., Cantor-Graae, E. and McNeil, T. F. (2001) 'Increased rates of psychosis among immigrants to Sweden: is migration a risk factor for psychosis? ', *Psychological Medicine*, Vol. 31, pp. 669–678.

6

LIVING IN THE CITY

In the majority of cases, the onset of psychotic symptoms can be traced to the years immediately after puberty and into early adult life (see for instance Jones 2013, where the bulk of 'cases' had an onset aged between sixteen and thirty-six). Place of birth and early life is a significant contributor to this risk. Although Georg Simmel posited interactions between the occurrence of 'madness' and late nineteenth century urban life (Levine 1971), the first more modern account of this is Faris and Dunham's (Faris and Dunham 1939) Chicago study. The geographic origins of 34,864 so called 'mental disorder cases' who were admitted to four state hospitals and eight private sanitoriums in Chicago during the period 1922–1934 were identified. There was a close relationship between rates of admission and the ecological structure of the city. What were described as 'disorganised' areas near the centre of the city were responsible for 'cases' at the rate of more than 362 per 100,000 population. Through gradations this fell to around fifty-five 'cases' per 100,000 population amongst those living in more affluent residential suburbs. This association held for those classified as 'Schizophrenic', but not for those classified as 'Manic-depressive'.

For many years this was understood as a consequence of social drift; individuals with mental health difficulties were considered impaired and less capable, and as a result 'drifted' down the social scale and into living in less salubrious circumstances. That was in spite of further data obtained by Hollingshead and Redlich (1958) in New Haven CT and New England during the 1950s. They identified clear class (as defined at the time by occupation and income) differences across the backgrounds of 847 cases of 'Schizophrenia'. Of the 658 who were not from recently immigrating families, twenty-seven were born into social classes I and II, and 551 were born into social classes IV and V. In 778 cases they were able to establish whether or not the individual had drifted from their social origins. In thirty-two instances they had … upwards. Ten had drifted downwards and 736 were considered to have remained in essentially the same social class into which they had been born. Nevertheless, it has taken several decades for 'social drift' to lose its place as the leading explanation for associations between social class

DOI: 10.4324/9780429059094-7

and environments of residence, and the occurrence of troubling psychotic experiences. In more recent years there has been a proliferation of larger scaled studies and more sophisticated methodologies that clearly associate growing up and/or living in an urban environment with an increased risk of subsequently being troubled by psychosis. A frequently cited example is the meta-analysis by Vassos and colleagues (Vassos et al. 2012) who combined findings from four high quality studies that were able to provide sufficient quantitative data.

Lewis and colleagues (1992a) were able to link data obtained in the course of military conscription concerning 95% of the Swedish male population aged eighteen to nineteen in 1969–1970 with data from the Swedish National Register of Psychiatric Care. This allowed them to associate conscripts' answers to 'Where did you live mostly when you were growing up?' with information about admission to a psychiatric hospital over the period between 1969 and 1983 (when the register was closed). Places where conscripts had grown up were categorised as cities; Greater Stockholm, Göteborg or Malmö, another town of more than 50,000 population, a town of less than 50,000 population, or 'in the country'. The experience of troublesome psychosis was recorded on the basis of admission to hospital and acquiring a 'diagnosis' of either Schizophrenia or Other Psychosis. Thirty-four subjects were deemed to have such a diagnosis at the time of conscription, and information about where they had grown up was missing for 1,231. Having excluded these 1,255 subjects, the study reflects findings from 49,191 individuals. Of these 268 were admitted to hospital and acquired a 'diagnosis' of Schizophrenia at least once during the follow-up period, and 267 acquiring a 'diagnosis' of Other Psychosis. The rates at which these cases first presented, per 100,000 person-years were 51.4, 43.2, 39.8 and 31.2 for those growing up in cities, large towns, smaller towns and the country respectively among those acquiring a 'diagnosis' of Schizophrenia, and 47.9, 44.7, 35.3 and 35.7 respectively among those acquiring a 'diagnosis' of Other Psychosis. Those growing up in cities did have a higher rate of cannabis use but statistically controlling for this did not completely remove the relationship between place of growing up and subsequent experiences of psychosis. Furthermore, these figures offer what might be understood as a 'dose response relationship', in that the more densely populated the place of growing up became, the greater the risk of subsequently experiencing troubling psychosis.

Marcelis and colleagues (1998) conducted a similar analysis in the Netherlands. All live births recorded between 1942 and 1978 in any of the 646 Dutch municipalities were followed up through the National Psychiatric Case Register for first psychiatric admission on account of psychosis between 1970 and 1992. The experience of psychosis was inferred from records of having been first discharged from hospital with a 'diagnosis' of Schizophrenia, whether narrowly or broadly defined, Affective Psychosis or Other Psychosis, on the basis of ICD-9 (1979) criteria. Altogether this amounted to 42,115 'cases'.

Population density of the place of birth was derived from the Central Bureau of Statistics' ratings, and collapsed to three levels; fewer than 500 addresses per square kilometre, more than 1,500 addresses per square kilometre and those lying between (500–1500 addresses per square kilometre). The cumulative incidence; 'cases per 1000 population' of 'broadly defined Schizophrenia' (which includes those otherwise categorised as 'narrowly defined Schizophrenia') was 1.3 amongst those born in the least densely populated municipalities, 1.5 amongst those born in the intermediately populated municipalities and 2.3 amongst those born in the most densely populated municipalities. Comparable figures for 'narrowly defined Schizophrenia' were 0.4, 0.5 and 0.8; for 'Affective Psychosis' 1.0, 1.1 and 1.4, and for 'Other Psychosis', 1.2, 1.3 and 1.8. Again, there is evidence of a dose response relationship, and in this case the probability of experiencing troublesome psychosis, having been born in a densely populated municipality, is some two times what it would have been if born in a less populated region.

Harrison and colleagues (2003) considered data obtained by linking the Swedish Medical Birth Registry (MBR), the Population and Housing Censuses of 1970 and 1990, and the Swedish Inpatient Discharge Register (up to December 1997). This captured 69,6025 subjects. The experience of psychosis was inferred on the basis of a hospital admission between 1989 and 1997 when a 'diagnosis' of Schizophrenia or another Non-affective, non-drug related psychosis based upon ICD criteria had been applied. Place of birth was coded as one of three categories: main cities (Stockholm, Gotenborg and Malmo) and their suburbs; large and medium size cities (population > 20,000) and municipalities where >40% of the population was employed in the industrial sector regardless of size or had a population of > 15,000; and municipalities in rural areas with a population of < 15,000 or sparsely populated countryside.

Three hundred and sixty-three (0.05%) subjects were admitted to hospital with a 'diagnosis' of Schizophrenia at least once during the period in question, and 590 (0.08%) were admitted with a 'diagnosis' of Non-affective, non-schizophrenic psychosis. Once again there was evidence of a dose response relationship between the degree of urbanicity at the place of birth and the risk of troubling experiences of psychosis later in life, either in a form that had attracted a 'diagnosis' of Schizophrenia, or in another Non-affective, non-drug related form.

Mortensen and colleagues (1999) made use of Danish population and case-registers. They used data from the Danish Civil Registration System to obtain a large and representative set of data concerning children born to Danish women between April 1968 and December 1993, thus identifying place of birth. These data were then linked to the Danish Psychiatric Central Register which contained data concerning all admissions to Danish psychiatric inpatient facilities. A troubling experience of psychosis was inferred from the occurrence of an admission to a psychiatric hospital for reasons that were

111

classified as a 'diagnosis' of Schizophrenia on the basis of ICD-8 or ICD-9 criteria. This identified 2,669 individuals across a population of 1.75 million. The relative risk of such experiences (as compared with having been born in a rural location) was 2.4 amongst those born in central Copenhagen, 1.6 amongst those born in its suburbs or in a provincial city with a population of more than 100,000 and 1.24 amongst those born in a provincial town with a population of more than 10,000. This dose response relationship was still apparent after statistically controlling for the effects of having a parent or a sibling who had also acquired a 'diagnosis' of Schizophrenia.

In a further analysis of data from Danish population and case-registers Pedersen and Mortensen (2001) were able to extend these findings to include outpatient contacts that resulted in a 'diagnosis' of Schizophrenia, and use a more detailed classification of population densities. Neither of these improvements in the analysis made a significant difference to their findings, which in this case ranged from a place-of-birth related relative risk of acquiring a 'diagnosis' of Schizophrenia (compared with having been born in a rural environment) of 2.3 amongst those born in central Copenhagen through 1.5 among those born in more densely populated suburban area, to 1.09 amongst those born in municipalities where between a third and a half of the population live in built up areas.

Meta-analysis

Vassos and colleagues (2012) chose these particular studies because they provided reliable, comparable, quantitative data that allowed the pooling of findings from all categories of 'urbanicity'. They derived an 'urbanicity index'. Each of the studies had compared the incidence rate of 'Schizophrenia' between at least three differing levels of 'urbanicity'. Furthermore, in order to definitively rule out bias due to the selective migration of people who had or were experiencing psychosis, and to narrow the analysis to exploration of the possibility that 'urbanicity' exerts its effects before the occurrence of troublesome psychotic experiences, studies were restricted to those which gave data from early life; at birth or before the age of fifteen. In order to avoid inaccuracies in the measurement of the at-risk population from which cases were drawn, included studies were also restricted to those where the at-risk population was a fully representative cohort, such as con-scripts or a birth register, and where 'cases' were identified from a fully representative national register. These stringent criteria allowed a definitive test of the association between growing up in an 'urban' environment and the risk of subsequently being troubled by psychotic experiences which has yet to be improved upon.

Data from Mortensen et al. (1999) and Petersen and Mortensen (2001) were combined with further Danish data, and so there were four data sets which together amount to some 23,600 'cases' detected over the course of more than 53 million person-years. For each study 'urbanicity' was considered to range from 0 to 1 between the least 'urban' or most 'rural', to the most 'urban', and least 'rural'. For each study incidence rates at each level of 'urbanicity' were standardised as an incidence rate ratio, by comparing them with the incidence rate at the lowest level of 'urbanicity' in each study, which was set at 1. This allowed comparisons between, and the combination of, data across the studies. Similarities were considerable. There was a clear dose response relationship between the degree to which the environment in which individuals had grown up was 'urban' and their subsequent risk of troubling psychotic experiences. Those growing up in the most 'urban' environments were more than twice as likely to experience psychosis later in life than those growing up in the most 'rural' environments.

These are convincing findings. An obvious limitation is that they are based on contemporary, North West European populations, but comparable data have emerged from studies in China, Brazil, India and Africa (Coid et al. 2018; Andrade et al 2011; Ganguli 2000; Gureji et al. 2010). Clearly, growing up and living in a large city substantially increases the risk of subsequently being troubled by psychotic experiences, but what none of this research is able to do, so far, is help explain why. Though quantitatively robust, the Northern European studies simply explored the possibility of a relationship between population density of the locality of growing up, and the relative risk of troubling psychotic experiences. The Asian, African, Indian and South American studies and related data from elsewhere are all compounded by the consequences of mass migration from differing forms of rural self-sufficiency into rapidly growing and materially heterogenous large conurbations. The two sources of data are not necessarily comparable, but both include myriad factors that might influence the risk of experiencing psychosis in different combinations and to differing degrees. These could be atmospheric pollution from industrial sources or traffic, noise, light, access to toxic drugs and alcohol, social and material deprivation, social fragmentation, ethnic tensions, isolation, separation from family ties, and more. Research that might begin to unpick why city life makes a significant contribution to the risk of experiencing psychosis is only just beginning, though the projection that more than two thirds of the world's population will be 'urbanised' by 2050 makes that a pressing task. Considering the data concerning the relatively simple example of air pollution illustrates how complex that will be.

Atmospheric pollution

Growing concerns about environmental degradation have re-focused attention on air pollution as one of the more important, adverse, material consequences of urbanisation (World Health Organisation 2021). Earlier concerns related to the consequences of coal-fired domestic heating and other activities, which were largely responsible for the 'smogs' of the 1950s and 1960s, and which had such serious effects upon health that they led to legislation prohibiting the widespread use of coal fires in densely populated places (HMSO 1968). Latterly attention has shifted to the polluting effects of diesel and petrol engines as a result of their emitting particulate matter and nitrogen oxides. There are now formalised associations between long-term exposure to these pollutants and reduced life expectancy, mainly due to cardiovascular and respiratory diseases and lung cancer, and between short-term exposure and other health impacts, including effects on lung function, exacerbations of asthma, increases in respiratory and cardiovascular hospital admissions and mortality (Lim et al.. 2021). Evidence that fine particulate matter presumed to have come from vehicle engines can be found in the human brain, and experimental evidence that it can cause inflammation of the nervous system, oxidative stress, activation of microglial cells, protein condensation, and cerebro-vascular barrier disorders (e.g. Kim et al.. 2020) has led to a search for associations between exposure to atmospheric pollutants and mental health difficulties. One review (Attademo et al.. 2017) found thirteen reports in which a one or more of a wide range of atmospheric pollutants, ranging from lead to fine particulate matter, were associated with the experience of troublesome psychosis, as identified by a 'diagnosis' of Schizophrenia.

An early contribution to this literature was an exploration of the association between presumed traffic related exposure and the risk of acquiring a 'diagnosis of' Schizophrenia (Pedersen and Mortensen 2006). Danish population registers were used to identify the geographical distance from place of residence to the nearest major road during childhood for 1.89 million people who were born between 1956 and 1983 and who were still alive at their fifteenth birthday. 65.7% were living between 100 and 1,000 m from the nearest major road at the time of their fifteenth birthday; 18.5% were living closer and 16.1% were living further away. The Danish Psychiatric Central Register recorded a subsequent 'diagnosis' of Schizophrenia in 10,755. When compared with those living more than 2000 m from a major road at the age of fifteen, those growing up between 500 and 1,000 m from one were 1.3 times more likely to acquire a 'diagnosis' of Schizophrenia later in life.

Living close to a major road might well be associated with higher exposure to atmospheric pollution than living far from one, but it is also likely to be associated with other features of 'urbanicity' such as population density and greater socio-economic inequalities. Where there are many cars, there are also, generally, a lot of people. Thus, in themselves, these associations do not necessarily point to an independent link between atmospheric pollution and the occurrence of psychotic experiences. When the data were statistically adjusted for the degree of urbanicity, as in 'Capital', 'Capital suburb', 'Provincial city' 'Provincial town' or 'Rural area', the association between growing up near a major road and the risk of subsequently experiencing psychosis

114

was lost. As far as these data were concerned, it seemed that it was growing up in an urban environment (as Vassos and colleagues (2012) identified) *per se*, that enhanced the risk of subsequent troubling psychotic experiences, and that living close to a major road was merely one aspect of that experience.

So-called 'Big Data' have been employed. Kahn and colleagues (2019) acquired and explored US data from the IBM Health MarketScan Commercial Claims and Encounters Database. This records, and details healthcare contacts in the course of accounting insurance payments, and from this they considered data concerning some 151 million unique individuals on behalf of whom claims had been made during 2003–2013. This yielded some 7 million 'cases' of Depression, 0.9 million 'cases' of Bipolar Disorder, 0.4 million 'cases' of Schizophrenia and 0.17 million 'cases' of Personality Disorder that could be traced to their county of residence. These locations were stratified by Environment Protection Agency data concerning: i) air quality; an index reflecting measurements of eighty-seven pollutants, ii) water quality; an index reflecting analysis of eighty water quality indicators, iii) land quality; an index constructed by the analysis of twenty-six land quality indicators, and iv) built environment quality; an index derived from analysis of fourteen indicators such as the amount of vehicular traffic, access to public transport and pedestrian safety. Prevailing weather was also considered in terms of the mean number of 'good weather days', where at least four hours in the day were between 18 °C and 27°C, and humidity was between 6.71% and 10%, and 'bad weather days', where for four or more hours the temperature was less than -5°C or more than 35°C. The statistical modelling used to investigate all these potential interactions with the occurrence of a 'diagnosis' also included county level data concerning population density, median income, ethnic and racial composition, and the percentages of uninsured and insured populations. Thus, the data set was large and comprehensive, including much more than just measures of atmospheric pollution.

Perhaps unsurprisingly counties' ethnic composition had a strong association with recorded diagnoses. Rates of 'Major Depression' and 'Bipolar Disorder' were strongly associated with higher proportions of White Non-Hispanic residents, whereas rates of 'Schizophrenia', and less so, rates of 'Bipolar Disorder' were associated with higher proportions of Black Non-Hispanic residents. Of the environmental measures, poorer air quality was associated with higher rates of 'Bipolar Disorder', the mean number of 'good weather days' was associated with lower rates of 'Bipolar Disorder', and poorer land quality was associated with higher rates of 'Personality Disorder'. There were systematic associations between rates of all four diagnostic categories and population density, especially so for 'Bipolar Disorder' and 'Schizophrenia', but no significant associations between any of them and any of the other socio-demographic variables that were included. Notably, there was no association between air quality and the troublesome experience of psychosis insofar as a 'diagnosis' of Schizophrenia reflected that. In other words, this application of 'big data' did not reveal an association between the experience of psychosis and living with higher levels of atmospheric pollution, though it did confirm Vassos et al's conclusions, of an association between the risk of psychotic experiences and population density.

Antonsen and colleagues (2020) were able to obtain better quality (i.e. higher resolution) estimates of atmospheric pollution; daily estimates of atmospheric pollution quality across 1 x 1 km squares of Denmark in terms of nitrogen oxides and particulate matter concentrations. Danish population records and medical records were used to explore the relationship between exposure to atmospheric pollutants during childhood and the risk of troubling subsequent psychotic experiences, inferred from a recorded 'diagnosis' of Schizophrenia. 230,844 individuals were identified who had been born in Denmark between 1980 and 1984, both of whose parents had also been born in Denmark and for whom their places of residence from birth to the age of ten were known. A 'diagnosis' of Schizophrenia on the basis of ICD criteria was identified from case records in 2,189 instances. Thus, it was possible to relate exposure to direct estimates of atmospheric pollution during childhood to the risk of subsequently acquiring a 'diagnosis' of Schizophrenia. Growing up in a locality where the mean daily level of atmospheric NO_2 was 26.5 or more $\mu g/m^3$ was associated with a risk of subsequently acquiring a 'diagnosis' of Schizophrenia 1.62 higher than amongst those growing up in a locality where the mean level of atmospheric NO_2 was 14.5 $\mu g/m^3$ or less. The association with estimated total levels of all nitrogen oxides was similar, but there were no statistically significant effects attributable to levels of particulate matter. These data were also considered in relation to the 'urbanicity' of where subjects had lived, in terms of: in the 'Capital' (Copenhagen), 'Capital suburbs', a 'Provincial city', a 'Provincial town' or in a 'Rural area'. When these distinctions were taken into account the strength of the association between levels of atmospheric pollution and the risk of experiencing psychosis remained, but it was attenuated.

In England and Wales, Newbury and colleagues (2019) were able to take advantage of a carefully recruited longitudinal study; the Environmental Risk (E-Risk) Longitudinal Twin Study which has followed 1,116 twin pairs (2,232 children) born in those countries during 1994 and 1995. This report was based upon 2,036 who were interviewed at the age of eighteen and provided information about troubling psychotic experiences between then and the age of twelve. 623 had had at least one such experience on the basis of answers to seven questions exploring the experience of 'hallucinations' and 'delusions', such as 'Have you ever thought you were being watched, followed, or spied on?' and 'Do you hear voices that others cannot?', and six questions exploring unusual experiences such as 'People or places I know seem different' and 'My thinking is unusual or frightening'.

Pollution exposure was estimated by associating participants' residential address and two other locations where they reported spending much of their time, with air quality modelling data for 2012. This was based upon the local-scale Community Multiscale Air Quality (CMAQ-urban) Modelling System, which uses a road traffic emissions inventory to model UK air quality down to individual streets. It gives hourly estimates of pollutants on a 20×20 m grid, thus providing address-by-address resolution. Individual exposures were estimated as the mean level across their one, two or three habitual locations. Registered pollutants included NO_2, NOx (all oxides of nitrogen), and fine and coarser particulate matter ($PM_{2.5}$ and PM_{10}; particulate matter with aerodynamic diameters of < 2.5μm and <10μm respectively), all of which are regulated by UK environmental standards. A level of 'urbanicity' applicable to the time of the investigation and derived from census data was assigned to each participant as 'rural', 'intermediate'; urban cities and towns, or 'urban'; minor/major conurbations. Other variables which could conceivably influence the risk of experiencing psychosis and which are established features of the cohort's family and contextual data were included in analyses; namely family socioeconomic status (on the basis of mean income and parental occupation), family psychiatric history, maternal psychosis, childhood psychotic symptoms, adolescent smoking, cannabis use, alcohol dependence, neighbourhood socioeconomic status (on the basis of census data), neighbourhood crime (on the basis of police data), and neighbourhood social conditions (on the basis of a questionnaire exploring neighbourhood social cohesion and neighbourhood social disorder sent to other residents of the same locality when the cohort was twelve years old).

Analysis focused on comparisons between those exposed to the highest levels of atmospheric pollution and those exposed to the least, and this revealed strong associations between atmospheric pollution and the risk of adolescent psychotic experiences. These were much more closely attributable to NO_2 and NO_x than they were to levels of particulate matter. In this case the associations were not significantly altered by the inclusion of neighbourhood factors, family history or even adolescent drug and alcohol misuse.

Similarly high-resolution air pollution data have also been used to consider the relationship between levels of NO_2, NOx, Ozone (O_3), $PM_{2.5}$ and PM_{10}, and mental health difficulties in two London-based studies, though neither of these focused specifically upon the experience of psychosis. In the first (Bakolis et al. 2021), the homes of 1,698 adults living in 1,075 households in South East London between 2008 and 2013 were linked to 20 x 20 m resolution average air pollution concentrations of those pollutants. The experience of so-called common mental health difficulties was assessed using the Revised Clinical Interview Schedule (Lewis et al. 1992b) and physical symptoms indicative of mental distress using the Patient Health Questionnaire subscale (Kroenke et al. 2002) on two occasions; between 2008 and 2010, and between 2011 and 2013. The possibility of psychotic experiences was explored during the first survey using the Psychosis Screening Questionnaire (Bebbington and Nayani 1995). There were associations between estimated

117

levels of NO_2, NOx and $PM_{2.5}$, and symptoms of common mental health difficulty and physical symptoms indicative of mental distress, that were stable across time, i.e., among the 754 interviewees who did not move address between the two surveys. These associations were not attenuated by adjustments for age, sex, socio-economic status, ethnicity, alcohol consumption, physical activity and estimated traffic noise. The earlier survey also found a single, cross-sectional association between troubling psychotic experiences and PM_{10} exposure.

Newbury and colleagues (2021) have also explored associations between the level of mental health service use and exposure to atmospheric pollutants, following a first presentation with psychotic experiences (identified as a recorded 'diagnosis' of Psychotic Disorder) or with depression and/or anxiety (identified as a recorded 'diagnosis' of Mood Disorder). 13,887 individuals who first presented to a South London mental health service over a five-year period and whose place of residence could be linked to air quality modelling data were identified. Clinical records allowed estimates of acute and less acute care over short and medium periods of time following first contact. Acute care was inferred from the occurrence of an admission to a psychiatric in-patient unit or involvement of an intensive home treatment team, and acute service use was quantified as the number of days spent in hospital and/or in receipt of intensive home treatment over the first one, and the first seven years following initial contact. Less acute care was inferred from records of community mental health service contact and quantified as the number of distinct face-to-face attended appointments and/or clinic visits, again over the first one and first seven years following initial presentation.

The amounts of acute and less acute care over both short and medium periods of time since first contact were all associated with estimated levels of NO_2, NOx, $PM_{2.5}$ and PM_{10} exposure. These associations were stronger for the two estimates of nitrogen oxides than they were for those of particulate matter. When data were adjusted for the possible effects of gender, ethnicity, age, marital status, population density, deprivation, ethnic density and social fragmentation these associations remained but they were weakened in relation to acute care. These are more robust findings but as they point specifically to the possibility that NO_2 and NO_x are implicated, they also point specifically to road traffic, which is the major source of atmospheric pollution by these gases in residential settings. Although it is clearly a significant feature of urban environments, road traffic has direct effects which might in themselves influence the probability of troubling psychotic experiences independently of the fumes they generate, such as noise and light pollution which have been linked to sleep disturbances, 'stress' and cognitive impairments. It is also associated with congestion and, at a micro-geographic level, with impoverishment of the natural environment. Within urban environments high levels of traffic density are generally associated with less popular residential settings, and therefore with more deprived and disadvantaged communities.

118

Poor air quality is undoubtedly a feature of city life and there is firm evidence that it has an adverse effect upon health. There is also evidence that some pollutants find their way into the human brain and experimental evidence of associations between some pollutants and tissue damage. A search for associations between atmospheric pollution and the development of mental health difficulties is warranted. However, what these investigations have so far revealed, is how complex these relationships appear to be. The association between levels of 'urbanicity' and the risk of experiencing psychosis is robust but attempts to narrow that down to the effects of atmospheric pollution reveal how difficult it is to identify what it is about city living that enhances the risk of experiencing psychosis. Vassos' (2012) definitive meta-analysis was of fully representative data that reliably detected experiences of psychosis among people who had grown up in environments readily classified as 'rural' 'urban' or 'intermediate', and although their overall conclusions are widely accepted, they leave many unanswered questions about the relevant and potentially causative features of 'urbanicity'. In their attempt to tie this down to the effects of atmospheric pollution from road traffic Pedersen and Mortensen (2001) were able to identify an association between the risk of experiencing psychosis and the distance between home and the nearest major road. However, when these data were adjusted for the effects of 'urbanicity', the association was lost. Living close to a major road is only one of many socio-environmental features of what might considered 'urbanicity', and adjusting the analysis to take this into account even as bluntly as 'Capital', 'Capital suburb', 'Provincial city' 'Provincial town' or 'Rural area' appeared to overwhelm the apparent effects of road traffic.

Kahn and colleague's (2019) attempt to use 'big data' doesn't really add anything useful. Of necessity, estimates of atmospheric pollution across the whole of the US were at county level and therefore of relatively low resolution. 'Case' detection was by way of a health insurance database which was less than an ideal, fully representative sample, and certainly would not have included all of the most deprived and disadvantaged who are less likely to have health insurance. The analysis did confirm other established findings, of associations between the risk of troubling experiences of psychosis and ethnicity, and with population density, but there was no association between that risk and estimates of atmospheric pollution. There was an association between the risk of acquiring a 'diagnosis' of Bipolar Disorder and exposure to atmospheric pollutants but whether this is robust, what it means and whether it actually reflects differing habits of classification are unclear.

Antonsen and colleague's (2020) analysis was of data from the same Danish sources reported on alongside the US 'big data', and it came to similar conclusions; there was a relationship between exposure to atmospheric pollutants during childhood and the risk of experiencing psychosis later in life. These data included higher resolution (1 x 1 km squares) estimates of pollution, and they were also adjusted for the effects of 'urbanicity' in terms of 'Capital', 'Capital suburbs', 'Provincial city', 'Provincial town' or 'Rural area'. On this occasion the association remained significant when the adjustment was made, but the association between childhood exposure to pollution and the risk of troubling psychotic experiences was weakened.

The three UK studies (Newbury et al. 2019, 2021; Bakolis et al. 2021) were able to use even higher resolution pollution estimates (20 x 20 m squares). One explored the occurrence of psychotic experiences in young people recruited from across England and Wales. A weakness here is that these were twin pairs, where other concordant experiences might have influenced outcomes. Nevertheless, this study did identify an association between psychotic experiences and that more fine-grained approach to estimates of pollution across a range of population densities. The other two were confined to South London and were less specifically focused upon psychotic experiences, but they bring an important finding into view. Both used data drawn from catchments extending from south central London to its inner suburbs, all of which would be considered 'Capital' or 'Capital suburb' by the definitions used in analysis of the Danish data and, indeed, Vassos' meta-analysis. Nevertheless, this more geographically fine-grained atmospheric pollution data was able to detect associations between exposure, or location of residence, and the risk of experiencing mental health difficulties at a finer level of geographic detail. In other words, even within what broader definitions would identify as urban areas there are geographically identifiable variations in the risk of experiencing mental health difficulties. It is unlikely that these variations are entirely due to differences in atmospheric pollution. When Pedersen and Mortensen's (2001) association between living close to a major road and the risk of experiencing psychosis was corrected for 'urbanicity', the association was lost, suggesting that in this case levels of atmospheric pollution simply reflected the more composite phenomenon, 'urbanicity'. Adjusting Antonsen et al.'s (2020) more direct and more detailed estimates of atmospheric pollution for levels of 'urbanicity' weakened their association with the risk of troubling psychotic experiences. Correcting associations found in the Environmental Risk (E-Risk) Longitudinal Twin Study data for socioeconomic status, crime statistics and the findings of a neighbourhood survey conducted six years earlier did not influence it, but neither did more firmly established associations such as family history of psychosis or adolescent cannabis use. Similarly, the South East London study concerning a full range of mental health difficulties was not sensitive to the established risks of gender, ethnicity, socioeconomic status or alcohol consumption, whereas the South West London association between atmospheric pollution and mental health service use was sensitive to adjustment for population density, deprivation index and ethnic density.

It would appear there is an association between living or growing up in environments that entail exposure to atmospheric pollution, in particular levels of nitrogen oxides attributable to motor vehicles, and the risk of a range of 'mental health difficulties', including troubling psychotic experiences. However, the epidemiology leading to this conclusion also points to the possibility of geographic variations in that risk *within* what would be considered 'urban' environments. Such variations are also sensitive to a variety of other measures, in particular features of the social environment such as population density and deprivation index, which also vary *within* any one more broadly defined urban location. Insofar as any direct effects of atmospheric pollution might be expected to result in detectable evidence of altered brain morphology, the absence of such evidence, to date (Frissen et al. 2017), makes it unlikely that atmospheric pollution *per se* explains these finergrained geographic variations in the risk of troubling psychotic experiences. Thus, although the study of associations between exposure to poor air quality has provided evidence of geographically fine-grained variations in the risk of troublesome psychotic experiences *within* an urban environment, it has not advanced an understanding of exactly what it is about 'urbanicity' that so clearly increases that risk. What it does do is suggest that the answer to such questions is going to depend upon closer and more detailed scrutiny of how city lives are conducted.

This is barely an advance on Faris and Dunham's (1939) findings from Chicago in the 1930s. 'Schizophrenia' was concentrated in the central city area which they described as more socially 'chaotic', and reference was made to poorer living conditions and the possible effects of a materially toxic environment. It is now clear that city living generates an increased risk of troubling psychotic experiences rather than the observation of increased rates being a result of less 'able' people migrating to cities, but the relative contributions of material and social influences remain unclear and of the latter, little definitive progress has been made beyond Faris and Dunham's (and indeed Georg Simmel's even earlier) hypothesis, that poor social relations increase the risk of mental disorder. An abiding difficulty has been the challenge of dissecting apart differing features of 'poor social relations'. These are not necessarily peculiar to city life and they overlap with the effects of ethnicity, migration and adverse social experiences more generally, but however they are conceptualised and measured, they are possibly more commonly and more intensely experienced in an urban environment.

Recognising the potential for interaction between conventional indicators of disadvantage, Goodman and colleagues (2017) explored intersections between the effects of socio-economic status, ethnicity and migration status. They used a sophisticated approach to socio-economic status which combined income, occupation, housing and educational attainment. Ethnicity was self-reported and migration status a reflection of how long subjects had been resident in the country. Latent class analysis was used to relate these variables and their interactions to psychological well-being as quantified using the Revised Clinical Interview Schedule (CIS-R) (Lewis et al, 1992b). Participants were 1,052 residents of South East London. The socio-economic indicators identified six groups of varying privilege and disadvantage, and among them the economically inactive group with multiple levels of disadvantage were most likely to have a mental health difficulty. Ethnicity and migration status enhanced this contrast, with migrant and economically inactive, and White British and economically inactive groups both at highest risk.

The same inner London survey has also been used to consider the relationship between ethnic minority status and several reflections of mental health difficulties (Schofield et al. 2016), and the effects and nature of differing social networks and available social support (Smyth et al. 2015). Ethnic minority status was defined in three ways; by ethnicity, by household status and by occupational social class. Being Black in an area where this was less common (less than 10% neighbourhood) was associated with an increased risk of troublesome psychotic experiences and of attempted suicide. Living alone where less than 10% neighbourhood did so was also associated with an increased risk of troublesome psychotic experiences, and occupying a disadvantaged social class in a neighbourhood where less than 10% did was associated with an increased risk of attempted suicide.

Social networks were quantified in terms of reported contacts with people (face to face or by phone) in a typical week, and characterised as the family social network or the friends' social network (close friends, neighbours, other acquaintances or members of same group or club). Social support was quantified on the basis of whether or not participants felt they had someone to lend them money to pay bills or help them get along; help with an emergency (minor or health emergency); talk to when something was bothering them or when they felt lonely and wanted company, or make them feel good, loved or cared for. Ethnic minority groups reported larger family networks but less perceived support. Older individuals, migrant groups and participants from less privileged socioeconomic circumstances reported smaller networks and less support, and perceived support and network size emerged as protective factors for common mental disorder, personality dysfunction and psychotic experiences. Unsurprisingly, among those recovering from an episode of mental distress, individuals who were able to access appropriate network resources reported better outcomes than those who did not, but this appears to extend beyond simple transactional experiences into a wider sphere, reflecting the quality of experienced relationship with relevant social structures such as professional support (Perry and Pescosolido 2015).

Wickham and colleagues (2014) reviewed data collected in the course of the 2007 Adult Psychiatric Morbidity Survey, a cross-sectional dataset including 7,353 individuals recruited from across England which included screening for the experience of troubling psychosis. Their social environment was defined in terms of the index of multiple deprivation, a measure of social and economic deprivation based upon neighbourhood levels of income; employment; health and disability; education, skills and training; barriers to housing and services; living environment; and crime, data which had been collected between 1997 and 2003. Measures were also made of participants' experiences of stress in the course of tasks at home and at work; of social support from family and friends such as whether family and friends did things to make them happy, made them feel loved, could be relied on no matter what, would see that they were taken care of no matter what, accepted them just the way they are, made them feel an important part of their lives, and gave them support and encouragement; and discrimination in terms of the extent to which they had experienced being unfairly treated on account of skin colour/ethnicity, sex, religious beliefs, age, mental health, other health problems or disability, or sexual orientation. Predictably participants' neighbourhood index of multiple deprivation was significantly associated with the risk of experiencing psychosis, but in addition, social support estimated in this way, significantly protected the more deprived.

Such effects have been detected even within groupings already known to be at higher risk of mental health difficulties. Mama and colleagues (2016) explored psychosocial mediators of the association between social environment and mental health in African American adults. 1,467 African American men and women completed questionnaires providing information about their social environment, stress, depressive symptoms, experiences of racial discrimination and their mental health which was measured in general terms: vitality, social functioning, role limitations due to emotional problems, psychological distress and psychological well-being. Experienced low social status in the community and low social support were associated with poor mental health and with greater perceived stress, depressive symptoms, and perceived racial discrimination. In other words, the relationship between the social environment and mental ill-health could be 'unpicked' to a degree, by considering more detailed aspects of individuals' relational environments.

If social disadvantage, however conceptualised, is a significant contributor to the risk of developing a psychotic disorder, then it is possible its effects will be cumulative. Stilo and colleagues (2017) considered this possibility using information collected from 332 'patients' and 301 'control subjects' recruited in South London. 'Patients' were individuals between the ages of eighteen and sixty-four who had presented to mental health services with an experience of psychosis for the first time and in whom that experience had been confirmed by the use of a screening questionnaire, and 'control subjects' were drawn from a random sample of people living in the same locations. Longer term social disadvantage was identified as separation from, or death of a parent before the age of seventeen, and/or other significant changes in family arrangements before that age, and adult social disadvantage was identified in terms of living status (alone, alone with children, with relatives, with others), relationship status (single, divorced, widowed; married or steady relationship), employment, housing status and income. Across all of these domains, 'cases' were more likely to report social disadvantage than the 'control subjects', they were twice as likely have had a parent die, and three times more likely to have experienced a long-term parental separation. They were also more likely to report two or more indicators of adult social disadvantage. When the timing of these was taken into account there was evidence of additive and cumulative effects.

These and related empirical studies all converge on the same point. The risk of developing a psychotic disorder or another form of 'mental ill-health' is increased in association with evidence of social vicissitude, variously defined and measured. The robust observation that these risks are increased as a result of growing up or living in an urban environment is likely due to the fact that various forms of social vicissitude are either more likely or more intensely experienced in such contexts than elsewhere. An interesting investigation exploring the possibility that urban environments were less likely to harbour pro-social behaviour revealed no effect of either urbanicity or population density on people's willingness to help a stranger. Instead, it was the neighbourhood level of deprivation that was most closely associated with helping behaviour, with help being offered less frequently in more deprived neighbourhoods (Zwirner and Raihani 2020).

To summarise

How the clearly apparent social forces contributing to an association between city life and the risk of troubling experiences of psychosis might be conceptualised and researched remains elusive, and the literature reflects that: social fragmentation, social isolation and social inequality (Van Os 2004; Morgan et al. 2008; Zammit et al. 2010), social 'defeat' (Selten and Cantor-Graae 2005), social capital (De Silva et al. 2005; Krabbendam and van Os 2005; Kim 2008; Ehsan and De Silva 2015; Zhu et al. 2019), neighbourhood composition (Kirkbride et al. 2007; March et al. 2008), social coherence and social stress (Lederbogen et al. 2013), social adversity and deprivation (Heinz et al. 2013), familial influences specific to the urban environment (March and Susser 2006), and discrimination in contexts such as China where this is structurally condoned (i.e. the *hukou* system, in which migrants into the city from rural areas have formally restricted access to housing, education and other forms of community support) (Li and Rose 2017). There is a strong signal here, but understanding what it reflects is going to require an altered conceptual framework. There is a need to exploit approaches, such as ethnography, that can move beyond associations between measurably convenient but contextually restricted phenomena such as 'social capital' or 'deprivation' and the occurrence of troubling psychotic experiences which conventional epidemiology has been able to provide (Manning 2019; Rose et al. 2022). Rapid urbanisation, especially in so-called developing countries demands rapidly developing understanding of its health implications, in all respects. On the other hand, that imperative is an opportunity. However conceptualised, an understanding of the social forces contributing to higher rates of mental health difficulty, especially the risk of troubling psychotic experiences, that are found in the city must, also, contribute to an improved understanding of how they occur more widely, and how they might be prevented. Acquiring that understanding is going to involve digging deeper and in greater detail into what these epidemiologically identified constructs; 'social capital', 'social coherence', 'neighbourhood composition', 'social fragmentation' and more, actually reflect at an individual and relational level. One of the things all of these have in common is that they reflect, in one way or another, differing patterns of human interaction. Might differing forms or quantities of social capital, social coherence, neighbourhood composition or social fragmentation also result in differing patterns of human interaction, with differing implications for how psychotic experiences are understood, and for how statutory arrangements for responding to them might be viewed?

References

Andrade, L. H., Wang, Y.-P., Andreoni, S., Silveira, C. M., Alexandrino-Silva, C., Siu, E. R., Nishimura, R., Anthony, J. C., Gattaz, W. F., Kessler, R. C. and Viana, M. C. (2012) 'Mental Disorders in Megacities: Findings from the São Paulo Megacity Mental Health Survey, Brazil', *PLoS ONE*, Vol. 7, No. 2. doi:10.1371/journal.pone.0031879.

Antonsen, S., Mok, P. L. H., Webb, R. T., Mortensen, P. B., McGrath, J. J., Agerbo, E., Brandt, J., Geels, C., Christensen, J. H. and Pedersen, C. B. (2020) 'Exposure to air pollution during childhood and risk of developing schizophrenia: a national cohort study', *Lancet Planet Health*, Vol. 4, pp. e64–e73.

Attademo, L., Bernardini, F., Garinella, R. and Compton, M. T. (2017) 'Environmental pollution and risk of psychotic disorders: A review of the science to date', *Schizophrenia Research*, Vol. 181, pp. 55–59.

Bakolis, I., Hammoud, R., Stewart, R., Beevers, S., Dajnak, D., MacCrimmon, S., Broadbent, M., Pritchard, M., Shiode, N., Fecht, D., Gulliver, J., Hotopf, M., Hatch, S. L. and Mudway, I. S. (2021) 'Mental health consequences of urban air pollution: prospective population-based longitudinal survey', *Social Psychiatry and Psychiatric Epidemiology*, Vol. 56, pp. 1587–1599.

Bebbington, P. and Nayani, T. (1995) 'The Psychosis Screening Questionnaire', *International Journal of Methods in Psychiatric Research*, Vol. 5, pp. 11–19.

Coid, J. W., Hu, J., Kallis, C., Ping, Y., Zhang, J., Hu, Y., Zhang, T., Gonzalez, R., Ullrich, S., Jones, P. B. and Kirkbride, J. B. (2018) 'Urban Birth, Urban Living, and Work Migrancy: Differential Effects on Psychotic Experiences Among Young Chinese Men', *Schizophrenia Bulletin*, Vol. 44, No. 5, pp. 1123–1132.

De Silva, M. J., McKenzie, K., Harpham, T. and Huttly, S. R. A. (2005) 'Social capital and mental illness: a systematic review', *Journal of Epidemiology and Community Health*, Vol. 59, pp. 619–627.

Ehsan, A. M. and De Silva, M. J. (2015) 'Social capital and common mental disorder: a systematic review', *Journal of Epidemiology and Community Health*. doi:10.1136/jech-2015-205868.

Faris, R. E. L. and Dunham, H. W. (1939) *Mental disorders in urban areas: an ecological study of schizophrenia and other psychoses*. Chicago: University of Chicago Press.

Frissen, A., van Os, J., Lieverse, R., Habets, P., Gronenschild, E., Marcelis, M. and Genetic Risk and Outcome in Psychosis (G.R.O.U.P.) (2017) 'No Evidence of Association between Childhood Urban Environment and Cortical Thinning in Psychotic Disorder', *PLoS ONE*, Vol. 12, No. 1. doi:10.1371/journal.pone.0166651.

Ganguli, H. C. (2000) 'Epidemiological Findings on Prevalence of Mental Disorder in India', *Indian Journal of Psychiatry*, Vol. 42, No. 1, pp. 14–20.

Goodman, M. L., Serag, H., Keiser, P. K., Gitari, S. and Raimer, B. G. (2017) 'Relative social standing and suicide ideation among Kenyan males: the interpersonal theory of suicide in context', *Social Psychiatry and Psychiatric Epidemiology*, Vol. 52, pp. 1307–1316.

Gureje, O., Olowosegun, O., Adebayo, K. and Stein, D. J. (2010) 'The prevalence and profile of non-affective psychosis in the Nigerian Survey of Mental Health and Wellbeing', *World Psychiatry*, Vol. 9, pp. 50–55.

Harrison, G., Fouskakis, D., Rasmussen, F., Tynelius, P., Sipos, A. and Gunnell, D. (2003) 'Association between psychotic disorder and urban place of birth is not mediated by obstetric complications or childhood socio-economic position: a cohort study', *Psychological Medicine*, Vol. 33, pp. 723–731.

Heinz, A., Deserno, L. and Reininghaus, U. (2013) 'Urbanicity, social adversity and psychosis', *World Psychiatry*, Vol. 12, pp. 187–197.

HMSO (1968) Clean Air Act 1968. HMSO: London.

Hollingshead, A. B. and Redlich, F. C. (1958) *Social Class and Mental Illness: A Community Study*. New York, NY: John Wiley.

Jones, P. B. (2013) 'Adult mental health disorders and their age at onset', *British Journal of Psychiatry*, Vol. 202, pp. s5–s10.

Khan, A., Plana-Ripoll, O., Antonsen, S., Brandt, J., Geels, C., Landecker, H., Sullivan, P. F., Pedersen, C. B. and Rzhetsky, A. (2019) 'Environmental pollution is associated with increased risk of psychiatric disorders in the US and Denmark', *PLOS Biology*, Vol. 17, No. 8. doi:10.1371/journal.pbio.3000353.

Kim, D. (2008) 'Blues from the Neighborhood? Neighborhood Characteristics and Depression', *Epidemiologic Reviews*, Vol. 30, pp. 101–117.

Kim, H., Kim, W.-H., Kim, Y.-Y. and Park, H.-Y. (2020) 'Air Pollution and Central Nervous System Disease: A Review of the Impact of Fine Particulate Matter on Neurological Disorders', *Frontiers in Public Health*, Vol. 8. doi:10.3389/fpubh.2020.575330.

Kirkbride, J. B., Morgan, C., Fearon, P., Dazzan, P., Murray, R. M. and Jones, P. B. (2007) 'Neighbourhood-level effects on psychoses: re-examining the role of context', *Psychological Medicine*, Vol. 37, pp. 1413–1425.

Krabbendam, L. and van Os, J. (2005) 'Schizophrenia and Urbanicity: A Major Environmental Influence-Conditional on Genetic Risk', *Schizophrenia Bulletin*, Vol. 31, No. 4, pp. 795–799.

Kroenke, K., Spitzer, R. L. and Williams, J. B. W. (2002) 'The PHQ-15: Validity of a New Measure for Evaluating the Severity of Somatic Symptoms', *Psychosomatic Medicine*, Vol. 64, pp. 258–266.

Lederbogen, F., Haddad, L. and Meyer-Lindenberg, A. (2013) 'Urban social stress be Risk factor for mental disorders. The case of schizophrenia', *Environmental Pollution*, Vol. 183, pp. 2–6.

Levine, D. (1971) *The Metropolis and Mental Life. in Simmel: On Individuality and Social Forms*. Chicago: Chicago University Press.

Lewis, G., David, A., Andréassen, S. and Allebeck P. (1992a) 'Schizophrenia and City Life', *Lancet*, Vol. 340, pp. 137–140.

Lewis, G., Pelosi, A. J., Araya, R. and Dunn, G. (1992b) 'Measuring psychiatric disorder in the community: a standardized assessment for use by lay interviewers', *Psychological Medicine*, Vol. 22, pp. 465–486.

Li, J. and Rose, N. (2017) 'Urban social exclusion and mental health of China's rural-urban migrants – A review and call for research', *Health & Place*, Vol. 48, pp. 20–30.

Lim, S., Holliday, L., Barratt, B., Griffiths, C. J. and Mudway, I. S. (2021) 'Assessing the exposure and hazard of diesel exhaust in professional drivers: a review of the current state of knowledge', *Air Quality, Atmosphere & Health*, Vol. 14, pp. 1681–1695.

Mama, S. K., Li, Y., Basen-Engquist, K., Lee, R. E., Thompson, D., Wetter, D. W., Nguyen, N. T., Reitzel, L. R. and McNeill, L. H. (2016) 'Psychological Mechanisms Linking the Social Environment to Mental Health in African Americans', *PLoS ONE*, Vol. 11, No, 4. doi:10.1371/journal.pone.0154035.

Manning, N. (2019) 'Sociology, biology and mechanisms in urban mental health', *Social Theory and Health*, Vol. 17, pp. 1–22.

Marcelis, M., Navarro-Mateu, F., Murray, R., Selten, J.-P. and van Os, J. (1998) 'Urbanization and psychosis: a study of 1942–1978 birth cohorts in The Netherlands', *Psychological Medicine*, Vol. 28, pp. 871–879.

March, D. and Susser, E. (2006) 'Invited Commentary: Taking the Search for Causes of Schizophrenia to a Different Level', *American Journal of Epidemiology*, Vol. 163, No. 11, pp. 979–981.

March, D., Hatch, S. L., Morgan, C., Kirkbride, J. B., Bresnahan, M., Fearon, P. and Susser, E. (2008) 'Psychosis and Place', *Epidemiologic Reviews*, Vol. 30, pp. 84–100.

Morgan, C., Kirkbride, J., Hutchinson, G., Craig, T., Morgan, K., Dazzan, P., Boydell, J., Doody, G. A., Jones, P. B., Murray, R. M., Leff, J. and Fearron, P. (2008) 'Cumulative social disadvantage, ethnicity and first-episode psychosis: a case-control study', *Psychological Medicine*, Vol. 38, pp. 1701–1715.

Mortensen, P. B., Pedersen, C. B., Westergaard, T., Wohlfahrt, J., Ewald, H., Mors, O., Andersen, P. K. and Melbye, M. (1999) 'Effects of Family History and Place and Season of Birth on the Risk of Schizophrenia', *The New England Journal of Medicine*, Vol. 340, No. 8, pp. 603–608.

Newbury, J. B., Arseneault, L., Beevers, S., Kitwiroon, N., Roberts, S., Pariante, C. M., Kelly, F. J. and Fisher, H. L. (2019) 'Association of Air Pollution Exposure With Psychotic Experiences During Adolescence', *JAMA Psychiatry*, Vol. 76, No. 6, pp. 614–623.

Newbury, J. B., Stewart, R., Fisher, H. L., Beevers, S., Dajnak, D., Broadbent, M., Pritchard, M., Shiode, N., Heslin, M., Hammoud, R., Hotopf, M., Hatch, S. L., Mudway, I. S. and Bakolis, I. (2021) 'Association between air pollution exposure and mental health service use among individuals with first presentations of psychotic and mood disorders: retrospective cohort study', *The British Journal of Psychiatry*, Vol. 219, pp. 678–685.

Pedersen, C. B. and Mortensen, P. B. (2001) 'Family history, place and season of birth as risk factors for schizophrenia in Denmark: a replication and reanalysis', *British Journal of Psychiatry*, Vol. 179, pp. 46–52.

Pedersen, C. B. and Mortensen, P. B. (2006) 'Urbanization and traffic related exposures as risk factors for Schizophrenia', *BMC Psychiatry*, Vol. 6, No. 2. doi:10.1186/1471-244X-6-2.

Perry, B. L. and Pescosolido, B. A. (2015) 'Social network activation: The role of health discussion partners in recovery from mental illness', *Social Science & Medicine*, Vol. 125, pp. 116–128.

Rose, N., Birk, R. and Manning, N. (2022) 'Towards Neuroecosociality: Mental Health in Adversity', *Theory Culture & Society*, Vol. 39, pp. 121–144.

Schofield, P., Das-Munshi, J., Bécares, L., Morgan, C., Bhavsar, V., Hotopf, M. and Hatch, S. L. (2016) 'Minority status and mental distress: a comparison of group density effects', *Psychological Medicine*, Vol. 46, pp. 3051–3059.

Selten, J.-P. and Cantor-Graae, E. (2005) 'Social defeat: risk factor for schizophrenia? ', *British Journal of Psychiatry*, Vol. 187, pp. 101–102.

Smyth, N., Siriwardhana, C., Hotopf, M. and Hatch, S. L. (2015) 'Social networks, social support and psychiatric symptoms: social determinants and associations within a multicultural community population', *Social Psychiatry and Psychiatric Epidemiology*, Vol. 50, pp. 1111–1120.

Stilo, S. A., Gayer-Anderson, C., Beards, S., Hubbard, K., Onyejiaka, A., Keraite, A., Borges, S., Mondelli, V., Dazzan, P., Pariante, C., Di Forti, M., Murray, R. M. and Morgan, C. (2017) 'Further evidence of a cumulative effect of social disadvantage on risk of psychosis', *Psychological Medicine*, Vol. 47, pp. 913–924.

Van Os, J. (2004) 'Does the urban environment cause psychosis? ', *British Journal of Psychiatry*, Vol. 184, pp. 287–288.

Vassos, E., Pedersen, C. B., Murray, R. M., Collier, D. A. and Lewis, C. M. (2012) 'Meta-Analysis of the Association of Urbanicity With Schizophrenia', *Schizophrenia Bulletin*, Vol. 38, No. 6, pp. 1118–1123.

Wickham, S., Taylor, P., Shevlin, M. and Bentall, R. P. (2014) 'The Impact of Social Deprivation on Paranoia, Hallucinations, Mania and Depression: The Role of Discrimination Social Support, Stress and Trust', *PLoS ONE*, Vol. 9, No. 8. doi:10.1371/journal.pone.0105140.

World Health Organization (1979) Manual of the International Classification of Diseases, Ninth Revision (ICD-9). Geneva: WHO.

World Health Organization (2021) 'Ambient (Outdoor) Air Pollution'. https://www.who.int/news-room/fact-sheets/detail/ambient-(outdoor)-air-quality-and-health (accessed October 2022).

Zammit, S., Lewis, G., Rasbash, J., Dalman, C., Gustafsson, J.-E. and Allebeck, P. (2010) 'Individuals, Schools, and Neighborhood: A Multilevel Longitudinal Study of Variation in Incidence of Psychotic Disorders', *Archives of General Psychiatry*, Vol. 67, No. 9, pp. 914–922.

Zhu, Y., Gao, J., Nie, X., Dai, J. and Fu, H. (2019) 'Associations of individual social capital with subjective well-being and mental health among migrants: a survey from five cities in China', *International Health*, Vol. 11, No. 1, pp. s64–s71.

Zwirner, E. and Raihani, N. (2020) 'Neighbourhood wealth, not urbanicity, predicts prosociality towards strangers', *Proceedings of the Royal Society B: Biological Sciences*, Vol. 287. doi:10.1098/rspb.2020.1359.

7

LIFE'S UPS AND DOWNS

The notion of a connection between intense emotion and psychological breakdown is so engrained in everyday discourse, literature and expectations, that it has its own place in our language: 'This is driving me crazy', 'You are driving me up the wall', 'If that doesn't stop, I'll go mad', and more. These expressions convey the view that there is a limit to how much intense feeling (good or bad) can be accommodated before there is a breakdown, and indeed that is how it often is. Circumstances generating strong emotions can also lead to tears, anger, panic, dismay or any one of a longer list of disruptive reactions. There is a breakdown in the ability to deal with what is happening in a more composed manner. Overt distress dominates the situation, and priority is usually given to addressing the immediate needs of someone who has become overwhelmed in one of these ways. This is usually accepted as a feature of everyday life, and provided the disturbance is not too prolonged or too disruptive, most social contexts can accommodate such an outburst without ascribing it to an 'illness', or evidence of more enduring incompetence. Whether the same might be the case when the disruption takes the form of incomprehensible beliefs, intense suspicion, voice-hearing or persistently disruptive behaviour generally associated with a 'diagnosis' of Schizophrenia or another form of psychotic disorder is much less certain, even though everyday expressions include 'driving me crazy' or 'going mad because of it'.

Expressed Emotion

Although the research did not explicitly focus upon the possible effects of either acute psychological trauma or accumulated distress, truly empirical investigations of psycho-social phenomena that might influence the course and consequences of troubling psychotic experiences can best be dated from George Brown's Medical Research Council Social Psychiatry Unit exploration of the relational environment in the homes to which male 'Schizophrenics' were discharged as the large asylums began to be closed down during the early 1960s.

DOI: 10.4324/9780429059094-8

In one seminal study (Brown et al. 1962), 128 men with a 'diagnosis' of Schizophrenia were followed-up for a year after leaving hospital. The severity of their symptoms was assessed just before discharge. Of these, 101 were seen at home with their relatives two weeks after discharge and assessed in relation to the amount of 'expressed emotion' shown between them. Consistent with the psychodynamic background against which this research was conducted, it was hypothesised that the person's behaviour would deteriorate if they returned to a home in which strongly expressed emotion, hostility, or dominating behaviour was shown towards them by a member of the family. It was further hypothesised that even if the person returned to such a home, relapse could be avoided if the degree of personal contact with the family was limited.

A family interview was conducted some two weeks after discharge from hospital. It involved, as a minimum, the person and his 'key relative', who was usually either their mother or their wife, and on the surface, it explored matters such as the man's behaviour since leaving hospital, plans for the future and other issues that might arise. Covertly, during this interview, the two interviewers rated what they observed as familial 'Emotional Involvement' across five dimensions: Emotion Expressed by the Key Relative towards the Patient; Hostility Expressed by the Key Relative towards the Patient; Dominant or Directive Behaviour by the Key Relative towards the Patient; Emotion Expressed by the Patient towards the Key Relative, and Hostility Expressed by the Patient towards the Key Relative and Other Members of the Family who were present at the Interview. There were clear findings. Higher levels of 'Emotional Involvement', later termed 'Expressed Emotion' were robustly associated with a higher risk of deterioration and readmission irrespective of the person's clinical condition at the time of discharge, and among those whose clinical condition was towards the more 'severe' end of the spectrum and the home was a source of relatively high 'Expressed Emotion', less time in the company of the key relative reduced the risk of deterioration and readmission. Trials of family intervention based upon these findings later showed that relapse rates and readmissions could be reduced by addressing levels of critical comment and hostility (Leff et al. 1990).

Subsequent research has done little to weaken these conclusions, indeed their relevance has, if anything, broadened. A major review (Hooley 2007) concluded that high levels of expressed emotion predict relapse, not only in individuals with a 'diagnosis' of Schizophrenia, but also amongst those with 'diagnoses' of Mood Disorder, Eating Disorder, Post Traumatic Stress Disorder, and Substance Abuse, and expressed emotion emerges as an independent predictor of relapse even when clinical factors in patients are considered and are statistically controlled for (ibid). It is both an indicator of relatives' reactions to behaviour and characteristics, and an indicator of relatives' own relational characteristics (Haidl et al. 2018). Interventions that improve family communication and problem-solving skills tend to lower levels of expressed emotion, improve the family environment and reduce the rate of relapse across several conditions (Eisler et al. 2000; Miklowitz et al. 2003). There is little doubt that high levels of expressed emotion have a toxic effect upon most who are susceptible to mental health difficulties, not least amongst those who experience psychosis.

Life events

Expressed Emotion is not the only way in which potentially harmful emotional distress has been conceptualised. Although the investigators were initially interested in the possibility that the onset of tuberculosis and other physical illnesses might be associated with changes in social status (Rahe et al. 1964), the Social Readjustment Rating Scale (Holmes and Rahe 1967) and subsequent derivatives that have emerged from this work have proved central in exploring how psycho-social challenges can influence the intensity and nature of psychological distress and the occurrence of 'psychiatric symptoms' and 'diagnoses'.

In its original form the Social Readjustment Rating Scale is a hierarchically organised set of forty-three potential social challenges ranging from the most potent, in terms of their assumed potential for psychological disruption, such as death of a spouse, through less disturbing, such as foreclosure on a loan, to relatively minor challenges such as minimal violations of the law. This hierarchic approach has enabled a quantitative approach to 'life events' and indirectly, to the needs for social readjustment they might impose. Over the years the scale has been revised and refined and a number of variants have emerged, but all respect the same underpinning framework. Past life events can be detected from within subjects' recollections and personal histories. These can be set in time and to some degree their likely intensity can be rated, and temporal associations with the onset or otherwise of psychological difficulties can be identified.

Beards and colleagues (2013) conducted a review and meta-analysis of data relating the experience of troubling psychosis to the occurrence of life events or imposed social readjustment obtained in this way. A subsequent review and meta-analysis of associations between life events and the risk of troubling psychotic experiences was published by Kraan and colleagues (2015), but this did not distinguish between traumatic childhood experiences and life events later in life. Beards and colleagues identified sixteen studies published between 1968 and 2012 which had explored whether or not adverse life events directly and independently lead to experiences of psychosis. Attention was given to methodological quality in relation to selection bias, sample size, how life events had been identified and recorded, how the experience of psychosis was detected and recorded, and whether or not confounding variables such as drug and/or alcohol misuse were taken into account. Studies that did not rate positively in these respects were not included in the sixteen chosen for meta-analysis.

Of the chosen studies, eleven were of 'clinical' samples; five of subjects coming to medical attention either as a result of a first experience of troubling psychosis or as a result of a re-occurrence, and six were of subjects coming to medical attention exclusively after a first experience of psychosis. Five considered associations between adult life events and the experience of psychosis in the general population.

Studies investigating associations between adult life events and troubling experiences of psychosis in mixed, first-episode and re-occurrence subjects

Arguably, the cornerstone of this research is Brown and Birley's 1968 study. This was an early application of the approach to identifying and characterising life events in the weeks leading up to the onset of psychological difficulties which developed into the Life Events and Difficulties Schedule (LEDS) (Brown and Harris 1978). It consolidated the value of the approach. Furthermore, it was a case-controlled study in which findings from a sample of fifty subjects who were experiencing psychosis were compared with a substantial (325) population of unaffected community controls.

A semi-structured interview explored the occurrence of events which might, on common-sense grounds, result in emotional disturbance. These included role change such as leaving school or a job change, role changes amongst close relatives or household members such as a husband not working because of a strike, or a family wedding; major changes in health such as admission to hospital or the development of an illness thought to be serious; similar changes, including death, amongst close relatives or household members (and family pets), changes of residence or other marked changes in contact with close relatives or household members, warnings of such changes, significant goal achievements or disappointments, and other striking turns such as the arrest of a close relative, or witnessing a serious road accident. The timing of such an event was established, and it was only considered if this could be done reliably. Efforts were made to characterise how independent events were, in other words, to what extent they were clearly imposed upon the subject and therefore independent of any changes that might, conceivably, be due to changes in their condition. Only events that were either clearly or possibly independent in these terms were taken into account. Happenings were considered if they occurred within a period of thirteen weeks before the onset of psychosis (or before the interview amongst the control subjects).

'Cases' were selected from the records of hospital admissions among subjects who had conformed to diagnostic criteria for 'Schizophrenia' (forty-five), 'Schizo-affective Disorder' (four) and 'Mixed Affective Disorder with paranoid ideas' (one), on the basis of a mental state examination carried out shortly after admission. Thirty-seven had developed troublesome psychotic experiences against a psychosis-free background, and thirteen had experienced a

132

striking increase in the intensity of pre-existing psychotic experiences. Control subjects were recruited from local (South London) employers: 115 clerical workers, sixty skilled factory workers, 148 semi or unskilled factory workers and fifty-four building labourers, resulting in 325 full data sets of 'control' data. The only significant differences between the 'cases' and the 'controls' were that the former were less likely to be married and more likely to be living either alone or in the parental home. Among control subjects the proportion experiencing at least one independent life event was relatively stable at around 15% across the four three-week periods leading up to the date of interview. Among those who had developed troublesome psychotic experiences, the proportion experiencing such a life event was similar during the earlier weeks of the studied period but rose to 46% in the final three weeks before the onset of psychotic difficulties.

Canton and Fraccon (1985) compared the rate of life events among fifty-four 'cases' classified as suffering Schizophrenia with an equal number of control subjects. The 'cases' were patients admitted to an Italian psychiatric inpatient unit. Twenty-four had been admitted following their first experience of psychosis, and thirty were experiencing a recurrence. All were classified as 'Schizophrenic' on the basis of DSM III (1980) criteria. Control subjects were fifty-four individuals drawn from a medical screening programme matched to the 'cases' by age, gender, marital status and social class.

Paykel & Mangen's Interview for Recent Life Events (Paykel 1997) was used to explore life events during the six months prior to admission among the 'cases', or the six months prior to interview amongst the control subjects. This is a sixty-four-item semi-structured interview, which classifies each event by context; work, education, financial standing, health, mourning, emigration, courtship, legal problems, social, family and marital relations, by consequence; entrance or exit, desirable or undesirable, and whether or not it was considered controllable or uncontrollable. Overall, 61% 'cases' experienced two or more life events during the six months leading up to the onset or recurrence of psychotic experiences, in contrast to 7% control subjects. These differences appeared around the contexts of work, health and family relations, and those developing troublesome psychotic experiences for the first time appeared to experience more intense life events than those whose psychotic experiences had recurred.

Al Khani and colleagues (1986) explored the possibility of associations between life events and the onset of psychotic experiences amongst residents of the Najd region of Saudi Arabia. The Najd is a largely desert region which includes the Saudi capital, Riyadh. At the time it was considered a very traditional society attempting to reconcile rapid changes in material circumstances with strict adherence to Islamic values and practices. Thus, at the time it was considered a very different culture from that of the 'developed' world where previous such research had been conducted, particularly in relation to family life and the role of women. Patients were selected from outpatient clinics serving the region. An Arabic translation of the Present State Examination (Wing et al. 1974) was used to classify and identify recent psychotic experiences and ICD-9 criteria were applied to determine whether or not these fulfilled a 'diagnosis' of Schizophrenia. This resulted in forty-eight 'cases' providing data suitable for analysis. Sixty-two 'control' subjects were drawn from among employees at King Saud University, school employees, residents of a village in the centre of the Najd, and by approaching those who accompanied patients attending non-psychiatric out-patient clinics.

Life events were detected using the (unpublished) WHO Life Events Schedule which embodies a list of seventy specified events embedded in a structured interview. This establishes a narrative account of their timing and quality, rates the impact of the most significant four and allows for the classification of events as independent or uncontrollable, controllable but possible independent or controllable and probably dependent (quite possibly due to changes in the subject's mental state). Only events falling into the first two categories were considered in the analysis.

The results were equivocal. Although the frequency of life events during the six months before the onset of psychotic experiences among the 'cases' was higher than amongst the 'controls' during the six months prior to the interview, this was not statistically significant across the whole sample. On the other hand, the rate of life events in the months leading up to the onset of psychotic experiences among married women was significantly higher than their control peers. The authors drew attention to distinctive women's roles and the possibility that strict adherence to Islamic customs might have contributed to these differences from findings in what were, at the time, more secular and industrialised cultures.

In 1987 Bruce Dohrenwend and colleagues (1987) reported on a body of work which was then underway in Israel and New York. The New York project included an investigation of associations between the occurrence of life events and either the onset or sharp intensification of psychotic experiences. Sixty-six 'cases' of 'Schizophrenic disorder' were identified among the clientele of the New York State Psychiatric Institute and the Columbia Presbyterian Medical Centre. 'Diagnosis' was based upon DSM-III criteria exercised in relation to clinical records and unstructured clinical interviews by formally trained psychiatrists. Twenty-one subjects were recruited in the context of their first experience of psychosis; the remaining forty-five were recruited in the context of a relapse involving either the recurrence of psychotic experiences or their abrupt intensification. This process of clinical screening also identified 122 'cases' of major depression. 197 'control' subjects were recruited from a community sample.

Recent life events were classified as: 'Fateful loss events'; unwanted events other than physical illness or injury that occurred beyond the control or potential control of the subject such as the death of a child or spouse, being unable to get treatment for an illness or injury, loss of housing through fire, flood or other disaster, 'Physical Illness or Injury'; events that might exhaust the individual physically or were experienced as life threatening, or 'Non-fateful loss events'; events likely to lead to losses of network support such as divorce, imprisonment, retirement, stopping working for an extended period, or breaking up with a friend. Cases with a 'diagnosis' of Depression, but not those with a 'diagnosis' of Schizophrenia, had experienced more Fateful Loss events than the control subjects. Both 'patient' groups had experienced more Physical Illness or Injury events than the controls and the same was true for Non-fateful events.

This work also measured the extent, and to some degree the quality, of social networks. The 'Schizophrenic' and the 'Depressed' subjects both had smaller and less extensive social networks, and fewer social confidants than the control subjects, and in most cases these differences were more pronounced in relation to the 'Schizophrenic' subjects. 'Schizophrenic' subjects were also more likely to report having been in trouble with law enforcement agencies in adolescence. Overall 'Schizophrenic' subjects showed observable signs of prior poorer social integration than either the control subjects or their 'Depressed' counterparts.

Bebbington and colleagues (1993) compared the occurrence of life events in the months leading up to the onset of psychotic experiences among ninety-seven affected individuals, with the pattern of life events among a control population of 207. DSM criteria were used to identify subjects, and the Life Events and Difficulties Scale was used to identify and classify relevant events. Efforts were made to determine the chronological relationship between events and the onset of psychotic experiences, the severity of events and their 'independence'. Independent events were those where there was no logical possibility of an association between the subject's behaviour and the event, such as the sudden death of a loved one, and possibly independent events were those where such an association was judged to be unlikely. Non-independent events were not included in the analysis. Severity was rated 1–4 on the basis of the threat an average person would experience in response to the event. In the analysis scores 1 and 2 (marked and moderate) were considered as 'severe', and 3 (mild). Events rated 4 (no threat) were not included. Severe and 'independent' events occurred in 33 (34%) 'patients' during the three months before the onset of psychotic experiences. Over the same period severe and 'independent or possibly independent' events occurred in 51 (53%) 'patients' but only 21 (10%) controls. There were less striking differences between groups in the rates of less severe events.

Studies investigating associations between adult life events and troubling experiences of psychosis in first-episode samples

Day and colleagues (1987) reported on data from the WHO Collaborative Project on the Determinants of Outcome of Severe Mental Disorders

(DOSMeD, Jablensky et al. 1992). These data concerned 386 newly present-ing instances of troublesome psychosis amongst the populations of centres in four 'developing' countries; two in India, one in Nigeria and one in Colom-bia (250 cases), and the populations of centres in five 'developed' countries (136 cases); two in the USA, and one in each of Czechoslovakia, Denmark and Japan. Subjects' experiences were classified on the basis of ICD-9 (1979) criteria as 'definitely', 'probably', 'possibly', or 'doubtfully' reflecting 'Schizophrenia', with some 83% falling into the first two categories.

Life events during the three months preceding the onset of psychotic experiences were identified by semi-structured interview with the subject and their close informants. Considerable investment went into developing a schedule and a rating manual sufficiently reliable and yet sufficiently flexible to embrace the range of cultures recruited into DOSMeD. Interviewers identified relevant life events, and their timing in relation to the onset of psychotic experiences. They classified each event in terms of its likely impact and its relationship to the subject's 'illness'. Impact was rated by estimating the degree of change events imposed upon the subject, and relationship to their 'illness' was an estimate of the likelihood (or otherwise) that the event was a consequence of developing difficulties. Events could range from the truly independent, such as the unexpected death of a relative, to the possibly consequential, such as an arrest for vagrancy which might have occurred during the onset of psychotic experiences.

Associations between life events and the development of psychotic experi-ences were considered on the basis of timing. In six of the nine centres, the proportion of subjects experiencing the impact of a life event during the two weeks immediately before the onset of psychotic experiences was significantly higher than the proportion experiencing the impact of a life event between three and twelve weeks prior to the onset of psychotic experiences. Excep-tions were in data from the two American centres, where numbers were small, and the Nigerian centre. Across the other six centres 43% subjects reported at least one life event during the two weeks immediately before the onset of psychotic experiences. In contrast only 12% reported one during the eleventh and twelfth weeks before the onset of psychosis.

The following year Gureje and Adewunmi (1988) published a case control series from Nigeria. They compared the experiences of forty-two subjects experiencing psychosis for the first time (on the basis of Research Diagnostic Criteria for Schizophrenia (Spitzer et al. 1975)) with those of forty-two 'control' subjects matched for age, gender, marital status and social class. Paykel's Life Event Schedule (Paykel et al. 1969) was used. This is a thirty-three-item semi-structured interview which identifies discrete and recogni-sable experiences that can be easily dated and about which their circum-stances can clarified by subjects and their close informants. It allows events to be classified as; 'independent': an event over which the subject had no control, 'possibly independent': an event within the subject's control but which, in the circumstances in which it occurred, could not be attributed to their condition, or 'probably dependent': an event that was likely to have occurred as a consequence of their condition. In this study the onset of troublesome psychotic experiences was not preceded by a significant life event. Across the whole sample, 67% control subjects and 52% patients experienced an 'independent' or 'possibly independent' life event within six months before the onset of psychotic experiences, or the date of interview in the case of control subjects. Only 7% 'patients' experienced one within a month of experiencing psychosis, as opposed to 24% controls experiencing one within a month of the interview.

Chakraborty and colleagues (2007) collected data from patients attending an Indian tertiary care psychiatric training and research institute. Their specific interest was in the possibility of differential effects of life events upon the development of psychosis and the development of 'Mania'. Eighteen subjects identified as experiencing 'Acute and/or transient psychotic disorder', and twenty subjects identified as experiencing 'Mania' were recruited. These classifications were based upon the opinions of the treating psychiatric teams who were not involved in the study, and who followed ICD-10 (1994) Diagnostic and Research Criteria.

The role of life events was explored using the Presumptive Stressful Life Events Scale (Singh et al. 1983). This is a fifty-one-item scale developed for use in Indian populations focusing upon events generally considered stressful in an Indian context, such as death of spouse, loss of job, marriage, theft, monetary loss, loss in agriculture, or substance related problems in the family. Ratings were made on the basis of semi structured interviews verified by reliable key informants, and included classifying life events as 'desirable', 'undesirable' or 'ambiguous', and for each of these, whether or not they were 'impersonal, in other words beyond the subject's control, or 'personal'. Those subsequently experiencing troubling psychosis rather than 'mania' had a significantly higher rate of undesirable events during the preceding two weeks, and significantly higher rates of impersonal events six months, three months and two weeks beforehand.

Faravelli and colleagues (2007) conducted a wide-ranging community-based study of psychiatric disorders among a cohort representative of adults in an Italian town. 2,363 subjects were interviewed by their own general practitioner using a screening instrument. 613 subjects reported experiences that could be construed as mental health difficulties of some sort, and at further interview nine of these were considered to be experiencing psychosis on the basis of the Florence Psychiatric Interview (Faravelli et al. 2001). Their experience of life events during the preceding year was compared with that of 123 randomly selected population controls using the Life Events and Difficulties Schedule (LEDS) (Brown and Harris 1978). Irrespective of 'diagnosis', 35.8% of the Italian sample who fulfilled criteria for any form of psychiatric disorder had experienced significant life events in the year before its onset, in comparison to

12% of the controls. Unfortunately, this study included only nine instances of troublesome psychotic experiences. Although three of these were life-event positive, this was too few for them to have any statistical meaning.

Raune and colleagues (2009) also used the LEDS. In their study interest focused upon the possibility of events and difficulties clustering immediately before onset. Newly developing instances of troublesome psychotic experience on the basis of ICD-10 criteria were identified. These included forty-one subjects in whom difficulties with psychotic experiences had begun within the previous twelve months, and whose onset could be dated to within a week. Comparisons were made with control subjects recruited into two earlier studies (Bebbington et al. 1981; Harris et al. 1987). This comparison revealed a higher rate of significant life events among those experiencing psychosis in the year leading up to onset, but there was little proximity in time. During the three months prior to the onset of psychotic experiences 34.1% 'cases' experienced independent threat events of at least moderate severity in contrast to 13.5% controls (Bebbington et al. data), whilst during the preceding nine months comparable proportions were 41.5% and 19.7% respectively. Comparisons with the Harris et al. data were 34.1% 'cases' and 2.9% controls experiencing intrusive events of at least moderate severity during the final three months, and 33.6% and 8.8% respectively during the preceding nine months.

Mondelli and colleagues (2010) were primarily concerned with whether or not there are detectable abnormalities of cortisol secretion amongst subjects experiencing psychosis for the first time. Cortisol is a 'stress' hormone, and it is possible that it's aberrant release during difficult times might contribute to the disturbance. Fifty 'cases' who were experiencing psychosis for the first time were compared with thirty-six volunteer control subjects. Information concerning stressful life events in the preceding six months was obtained using the Brief Life Events Questionnaire (Brugha and Cragg 1990) which assesses the number and emotional impact of stressors such as illness or injury, bereavement, financial disruption or relationship difficulties. Perceived stress during the preceding month was measured using a ten-item self-report scale; the Perceived Stress Scale (Cohen and Williamson 1988). Measures of cortisol secretion were also made. By these measures the 'cases' had a mean rate of 2.3 life events during the six months prior to the onset of psychosis, compared with a mean rate of 0.7 among the controls. There were abnormalities of cortisol secretion amongst some of the 'cases' but those data did not relate these to measures of perceived stress.

Studies investigating associations between adult life events and troubling psychotic experiences in general population samples

Beards and colleagues identified five cross sectional studies in which the occurrence of troubling psychotic experiences in the adult general population had been related to life events.

Vinokur and Selzer (1975) investigated associations between the experience of challenging life events and a range of psychological difficulties in 1,059 male truck drivers who had been recruited through official channels; licence renewal and traffic offences (774) and mandatory treatment for alcohol difficulties (285). Life events during the preceding year were identified by self-report using the Holmes and Rahe (1967) Social Readjustment Rating Scale, and a variety of self-report measures were used to identify levels of depression, suicidal thinking, paranoid experiences, aggression, anxiety, tension and distress. For each subject a self-rated score of pressure and adjustment due to life events was calculated on the basis of Social Readjustment Rating Scale responses, and this was further subdivided into 'desirable' and 'undesirable' events scores. There were strong correlations between all of these scores and the self-reported experiences of psychological distress, including the experience of paranoid thinking, with the exception of 'desirable' life event scores amongst the alcohol treatment group.

Johns and colleagues (2004) reported an analysis of associations between the occurrence of troubling psychotic experiences and a range of potential causes including cannabis and alcohol misuse, victimisation, recent stressful life events, lower intellectual ability and neurotic symptoms. Data were drawn from 8,580 adult subjects who had taken part in the 2000 British National Survey of Psychiatric Morbidity. The Psychosis Screening Questionnaire (Bebbington and Nayani 1995) was used to screen for the experience of psychosis during the past year. This explores the experience of mania, thought insertion, paranoia, strange experiences and hallucinations. Four criteria were considered likely indicative of psychotic experiences: a self-reported diagnosis or symptoms suggestive of psychotic disorder on the basis of responses to the Psychosis Screening Questionnaire; taking anti-psychotic medication; a history of taking anti-psychotic medication, or a history of admission to a psychiatric hospital or ward. Respondents who met one or more of these screening criteria were followed up using the Schedules for Clinical Assessment in Neuropsychiatry (SCAN). In cases where this follow up was not possible the status of 'probable psychosis' was assigned to those who scored positively on two or more of the screening criteria. Particular attention was given to the experience of paranoid thoughts and to the experience of hallucinations.

Life events in the six-month period prior to interview were identified using a modified version of the List of Threatening Experiences (Brugha et al. 1985). Candidate life events were: being the victim of serious illness, injury or assault; serious illness, injury or assault of a close relative; death of a close relative; death of a close friend/other relative; separation or divorce; serious problem with a close friend, neighbour or relative; job loss; unemployed/seeking work for more one month; major financial crisis; problem with police and/or court appearance, or something valued lost or stolen. The experience of victimisation was recorded in response to questions exploring bullying, violence at work, violence in the home, sexual abuse, being expelled from school, running away from school, running away from home, or being homeless. 8520 subjects were included in the final analysis, of whom 2,136 reported at least one significant life event in the preceding six months and 2,437 reported victimisation during the same period. 478 reported more than one experience of psychosis during the preceding year. There was a statistically significant association between the probability of reporting either a significant life event or victimisation, and the probability of reporting a psychotic experience.

Jenkins and colleagues (2010) reported a survey of 899 adults drawn randomly from two districts of Dar es Salaam. Again, the Psychosis Screening Questionnaire was used to screen for psychotic experiences during the previous year, but there was no follow up clinical interview. Respondents were given a list of eighteen different stressful life events, and asked to say which, if any, they had experienced in the past six months. The list included relationship problems, employment, financial crises and experiences of victimisation. Life event scores were grouped into 'none', 'one' and 'two or more' life events. Information about social networks was obtained through questions about the number of friends or relatives whom informants felt close to: adults who lived with the respondent and to whom they felt close; relatives living elsewhere to whom they felt close, and friends or acquaintances living elsewhere who informants would describe as close or good friends. Results were grouped 'none to three', 'four to eight' and 'nine or more', and coded as 'severe', 'moderate' or 'no' lack of social support. Thirty-five (3.9%) respondents reported one or more psychotic experiences during the period in question, and of these twenty-three (66%) reported one or more significant life events during the preceding six months. This compares with 323 (37%) of the asymptomatic respondents. Nineteen (54%) reported severe or moderate lack of social support.

van Nierop and colleagues (2012) explored the prevalence and associations of self-reported psychotic experiences in a Dutch population. The report in question was part of the second Netherlands Mental Health Survey and Incidence Study, a longitudinal study of the prevalence, incidence, course, and consequences of psychiatric disorders. A screening interview explored the lifetime experience of psychosis in 6,646 subjects. It involved rating the occurrence of twenty psychotic experiences across their lifetime as 'yes,' 'no,' 'don't know,' or 'refuse', and when such an experience was endorsed, further rated in terms of frequency, how distressing it was, and what impact it had on their lives. At this interview information was also collected concerning physical health, life events, treatment seeking, and childhood trauma. Psychotic experiences were considered secondary if all endorsed items were thought to be caused by use of drugs, alcohol or physical illness.

Individuals who endorsed at least one lifetime psychotic experience (1,078 out of 6646 participants) were contacted for a telephone interview with an experienced clinician. Data were obtained from 792 such clinical assessments, which were based on the Structured Clinical Interview for DSM (Spitzer et al. 1992). This confirmed the occurrence of 'true' psychotic experiences in 384 (6%) total sample. Of these 249 (66%) reported negative life events in the preceding year, as opposed to 48% who were not considered to have experienced psychosis.

Lataster and colleagues (2012) reported on data from the Early Developmental Stages of Psychopathology (EDSP) Study. This collected data on the prevalence, incidence, risk factors, comorbidity, and course of mental disorders in a random, representative population sample of German adolescents and young adults from the population of Munich and its twenty-nine counties. The sample was randomly drawn in 1994 to reflect all those born between 1 June 1970 and 31 May 1981. This longitudinal design provided data concerning 3,021 individuals fourteen to twenty-four years old at baseline, 2,548 some three and a half years later, and 2,210 some five years after that. Screening for the experience of psychosis was conducted using the Munich-Composite International Diagnostic Interview (Wittchen et al. 1998), which was based upon the Composite International Diagnostic Interview using additional probes administered by trained clinical interviewers. The experience of recent life events during the period between the first and second assessment was explored using the Munich Interview for the Assessment of Life Events and Conditions (Wittchen et al. 1989). This instrument is a three-step interview procedure for assessing recent adversity through recognition rather than free recall. It uses a list of eighty-four very detailed and specific descriptions of positive and negative life events encompassing eleven dimensions which include school and education, family, social contacts, professional activities and living circumstances. A life chart was used to identify anchor events and the date of their occurrence. Subjects were then interviewed about the content, timing, and context of these events, and finally probes were used to identify any additional events that had not already been identified.

There were complete data concerning 1,722 subjects who had not reported psychotic experiences at the first or second assessment, and of these 170 (9.9%) reported one or more experience of psychosis during the period between the second and third assessment. These subjects reported an average of 7.49 negative life events during that period, compared with an average of 5.98 among those who did not report developing psychotic experiences during that period.

Meta-analysis

Beards and colleagues have drawn these sixteen studies together (Beards et al. 2013). They reflected upon the fact that sixteen methodologically robust studies of 'whether or not difficult circumstance drive you mad' over forty-

141

four years is surprisingly few. Nevertheless, the evidence they offer is fairly consistent. Fourteen of the sixteen reported an increased likelihood of psychotic experiences following one or more significant life events. This ranged from twice (Raune et al. 2009) to eight (Canton and Fraccon 1985) times more likely among the 'clinical' samples, and from twice (Johns et al. 2004) to seven (Jenkins et al. 2010) times more likely among the population surveys. Three of the sixteen publications (Day et al. 1987; Chakraborty et al. 2007; Vinokur and Selzer 1975) were unable to provide the numbers of subjects exposed to, and not exposed to life events. The remaining thirteen were suitable for inclusion into a formal meta-analysis which yielded an overall odds ratio of 3.19, with 95% confidence intervals of 2.15 to 4.75. In other words, taking all of these available data into account, the likelihood of troublesome psychotic experiences is reliably three times greater following a significant life event than it would otherwise have been.

Accumulated distress

Expressed emotion and life events have both proved to be amenable to relatively clear operational definition. As a result, it has been possible to identify and, to some degree measure them. This has allowed quantitative assessment and subsequent meta-analysis of collected findings. All of this is less so in relation to what might be identified as 'accumulated distress', which refers to the effects of a wide range of longer standing and more persistent difficulties. The early epidemiology (e.g. Burr 1903; Faris and Dunham 1939; Hollingshead and Redlich 1958) established an association not only between urban life and the risk of experiencing psychosis, but also with the conditions of everyday life. That remains a firm finding, but unravelling it further represents a conceptual and methodological challenge.

The ÆSOP cohort of 390 'cases' at the first onset of psychotic experiences, and 391 geographically matched 'controls' in three English locations has repeatedly and reliably confirmed differences between 'cases' and 'controls' across a range of socio-demographic measures. 'Cases' were defined on the basis of ICD-10 (1994) criteria for 'First episode psychosis'. In one analysis (Morgan et al. 2008) 'cases' were three-and-a-half times more likely to have left school without qualifications than 'controls', four times more likely to be currently unemployed, nearly three times more likely to have been unemployed for more than a year, more than two-and-a-half times more likely to be living in rented accommodation, nearly twice as likely to have moved home within the previous six months, three times more likely to be living alone (and twice as likely to have been doing so for more than a year), more than three times more likely to be single and never having been in a long-term relationship, more than four-and-a-half times less likely to be in contact with a friend more than weekly and seven-and-a-half times less likely to have a confidant. In addition, there were clear interactions between these 'disadvantages'. The greater the number of 'disadvantages' the stronger the relationship between disadvantage and 'case/control' status. There were similar findings from an analysis of subjects who had psychosis-like experiences but did not fulfil ICD diagnostic criteria (Morgan et al. 2009), and further analyses exploring interactions that might be relevant to the effects of unemployment (Reininghaus et al. 2008) and interactions between adverse childhood experiences and adult indicators of disadvantage (Morgan et al. 2009).

There are similar findings from other settings (e.g. Pignon et al. 2021). A range of socio-environmental 'disadvantages' are clearly associated with the risk of troublesome psychotic experiences but it is unclear what this means. On the one hand there is evidence of social decline among young people prior to the onset of symptoms that resulted in a 'diagnosis' of Schizophrenia (Jones et al. 1993), and so these associations could, after all, reflect this though that is unlikely given their breadth and strength. On the other hand, these associations are between socio-environmental *situations* rather than directly with their psychological consequences. Intuitively, all of them could result in 'stress', but that leaves 'stress' itself broadly and poorly defined. Although having left school without qualifications, living alone and being unemployed can all be considered social disadvantages, how any or all of them might increase the risk of troubling psychotic experiences remains unclear without closer attention to the details of their psychological consequences.

Momentary assessment

With this in mind, investigators have attempted to understand more about the implications of detailed day-to-day experiences (Smyth and Stone 2003). The advent of digital technology has facilitated this. Characteristically subjects keep a paper or smartphone diary, and are alerted at semi-random intervals of about ninety minutes, several times during the day. When prompted they enter information about current and most recently past experiences. Investigations focused upon the effects of 'stress', commonly under the name of the Experience Sampling Method, have structured responses around the most recent notable event; 'Think about the most important event since the last beep. This event was...', and a rating is provided, perhaps on a scale from 'very unpleasant' to 'very pleasant', and ratings are also provided of subjects' mood; how 'cheerful', 'relaxed', 'insecure', 'anxious', 'irritated', or 'down' they are feeling, whether they are putatively experiencing psychosis, as in; 'I feel suspicious' or 'I am afraid of losing control', whether or not their thoughts are pleasant or otherwise, whether or not they feel tired, what they are doing, how engaged they are with it and whether or not they are alone.

Insofar as people comply and respond authentically, such techniques provide fine-grained information about associations between circumstances, which may or may not be 'stressful', associated feelings, and their consequences, including whether or not they are associated with psychotic experiences. In this way a bridge can be built between socio-environmental circumstances and their psychological concomitants. They promise a new chapter in the search for insights into how social and material circumstances might influence the likelihood of troubling psychotic experiences. Intriguingly, what seems to be emerging is that this is a complex set of interactions. One example is a summary of such studies published by Klippel and colleagues (2018). By combining six previous studies, they were able to compare data from 244 'control' subjects, 165 first degree relatives of people who were experiencing psychosis and 245 'psychotic patients'. An everyday 'stress' was identified on the basis of an unpleasant 'most recent event', and mathematical modelling was used to determine ways in which this was followed by changes in mood, putative psychotic experiences, pleasant or unpleasant thoughts, tiredness or activity, and whether or not they were alone. Perhaps unsurprisingly, following a 'stressful' event, the various elements of subjects' feelings; irritability, cheerfulness, anxiety, insecurity, whether feeling relaxed or down, all changed in concert, as did the possibility of putative psychotic experiences, subjects' level of activity and their experience of pleasant or unpleasant thoughts. The orchestration of these changes; the pattern of their interactions, differed between 'controls', relatives, and those with psychotic experiences. Among those with experiences of psychosis higher levels of minor everyday 'stress' did lead to greater levels of suspiciousness and a sense of losing control, but this was not an isolated phenomenon. These subjects also had tighter associations among other elements of their feelings, and between them and putative experiences of psychosis. By exploring experiences at this fine level of detail, it seems to emerge that if and when 'stress' is followed by, or enhances the risk of, troubling psychotic experiences, the association reflects a complex interaction. 'Stress' might well disturb feelings but it does so in different ways in different people under different circumstances, and in ways that have differing effects upon the risk of troubling psychotic experiences.

To summarise

Beards and colleagues' meta-analysis drew together sixteen methodologically robust studies exploring the association between the likelihood of troubling psychotic experiences and the occurrence of one or more significant and conceivably traumatic life events. These studies involved several hundreds of 'cases' and controls from a wide range of populations and contexts. The statistically significant conclusion was that a troubling psychotic experience is some three times more likely following a significant life event than in its absence. Accumulating distress has proved more difficult to define, measure and investigate quantitatively but there is no doubt that living under disadvantaged circumstances is associated with an increased risk of disturbing psychotic experiences.

The life events data are robust and conclusive but they are limited by varying ways of defining and detecting 'life events'. The combined studies used several different schedules and differing approaches to the timings of life events and psychotic experiences. Furthermore, of necessity, life events are detected retrospectively. Thus, although they have been debated and explored in detail for more than fifty years, although they have considerable face validity, and although they are clearly associated with the onset of many forms of mental health difficulty, exactly what a life event is, and is not, remains a matter of circular definition. Certain, usually adverse, experiences are clearly associated with the experience of psychosis, but it raises more questions than answers to assume that, say, the death of a spouse, bankruptcy or a life-changing injury are in some way comparable.

'Living under disadvantaged circumstances' is equally difficult to pin down more precisely. Here the research has identified associations between the risk of troubling psychotic experiences and various combinations of: unfinished education, unemployment, insecure accommodation, relationship status and social isolation. These are all quantitatively identifiable socio-economic phenomena, and their association with the risk of troubling psychotic experiences makes a strong case for policies that might mitigate them. However, in and of themselves they offer little more than; 'living under disadvantaged circumstances increases the likelihood of troubling psychotic experiences' When viewed in the round, the life events and accumulated distress findings establish robust associations between the risk of psychotic experiences and adverse circumstances, but that is where the trail runs cold. What is it about adverse circumstances that leads to this? What data there are from more detailed experience sampling get inside this a little. Psychotic experiences are indeed more likely following a 'stressful' experience, but what is and what is not experienced as stressful, and how 'stress' itself impacts, differs between those who subsequently experience psychosis and those who do not. This line of research is very much in its infancy, but it points to the need for more detailed information about individuals' reactions to adversity, others' interactions with them under such circumstances and how and with what consequences meaning is generated in the course of such interactions.

References

Al Khani, M. A. F., Bebbington, P. E., Watson, J. P. and House, F. (1986) 'Life Events and Schizophrenia: A Saudi Arabian Study', *British Journal of Psychiatry*, Vol. 148, pp. 12–22.

Beards, S., Gayer-Anderson, C., Borges, S., Dewey, M. E., Fisher, H. L. and Morgan, C. (2013) 'Life Events and Psychosis: A Review and Meta-analysis', *Schizophrenia Bulletin*, Vol. 39, No. 4, pp. 740–747.

Bebbington, P., Hurry, J., Tennant, C., Sturt, E. and Wing, J. K. (1981) 'Epidemiology of mental disorders in Camberwell', *Psychological Medicine*, Vol. 11, pp. 561–579.

Bebbington, P. and Nayani, T. (1995) 'The Psychosis Screening Questionnaire', *International Journal of Methods in Psychiatric Research*, Vol. 5, pp. 11–19.

Bebbington, P., Wilkins, S., Jones, P., Foerster, A., Murray, R., Toone, B. and Lewis, S. (1993) 'Life Events and Psychosis: Initial Results from the Camberwell Collaborative Psychosis Study', *British Journal of Psychiatry*, Vol. 162, pp. 72–79.

Brown, G. W. and Birley, J. L. T. (1968) 'Crises and Life Changes and the Onset of Schizophrenia', *Journal of Health and Social Behavior*, Vol. 9, No. 3, pp. 203–214.

Brown, G. W. and Harris, T. (1978) *Social Origins of Depression: A study of psychiatric disorder in women*. London: Tavistock.

Brown, G. W., Monck, E. M., Carstairs, G. M. and Wing, J. K. (1962) 'Influence of Family Life on the Course of Schizophrenic Illness', *British Journal of Preventive and Social Medicine*, Vol. 16, No. 2, pp. 55–68.

Brugha, T., Bebbington, P., Tennant, C. and Hurry, J. (1985) 'The List of Threatening Experiences: a subset of 12 life event categories with considerable long-term contextual threat', *Psychological Medicine*, Vol. 15, pp. 189–194.

Brugha, T. S. and Cragg, D. (1990) 'The List of Threatening Experiences: the reliability and validity of a brief life events questionnaire', *Acta Psychiatrica Scandinavica*, Vol. 82, pp. 77–81.

Burr, R. H. (1903) 'A Statistical Study of Patients Admitted at the Connecticut Hospital for Insane from the Years 1868 to 1901', *Publications of the American Statistical Association*, Vol. 8, No. 62, pp. 305–343.

Canton, G. and Fraccon, I. G. (1985) 'Life Events and Schizophrenia. A Replication', *Acta Psychiatrica Scandinavica*, Vol. 71, pp. 211–216.

Chakraborty, R., Chatterjee, A., Choudhary, S., Singh, A. and Chakraborty, P. K. (2007) 'Life Events in Acute and Transient Psychosis – A Comparison with Mania', *German Journal of Psychiatry*, Vol. 10, pp. 36–40.

Cohen, S. and Williamson, G. (1988) 'Perceived Stress in a Probability Sample of the United States'. In S. Spacapan and S. Oskamp (Eds.) *The Social Psychology of Health: Claremont Symposium on Applied Social Psychology*. Newbury Park, CA: Sage, pp. 31–67.

Day, R., Nielsen, J. A., Korten, A., Ernberg, G., Dube, K. C., Gebhart, J., Jablensky, A., Leon, C., Marsella, A., Olatawura, M., Sartorius, N., Strömgren, E., Takahashi, R., Wig, N. and Wynne, L. C. (1987) 'Stressful life events preceding the acute onset of schizophrenia: A cross-national study from the World Health Organization', *Culture, Medicine and Psychiatry*, Vol. 11, pp. 123–205.

Dohrenwend, B. P., Levav, I., Shrout, P. E., Link, B. G., Skodol, A. E. and Martin, J. L. (1987) 'Life Stress and Psychopathology: Progress on Research Begun with Barbara Snell Dohrenwend', *American Journal of Community Psychology*, Vol. 15, No. 6, pp. 677–715.

Eisler, I., Dare, C., Hodes, M., Russell, G., Dodge, E. and Le Grange, D. (2000) 'Family Therapy for Adolescent Anorexia Nervosa: The Results of a Controlled Comparison of Two Family Interventions', *Journal of Child Psychology and Psychiatry*, Vol. 41, No. 6, pp. 727–736.

Faravelli, C., Bartolozzi, D., Cimminiello, L., Cecchi, C., Cosci, F., D'Adamo, D., Di Matteo, C., Di Primio, C., Fabbri, C., Lo Iacono, B., Paionni, A., Perone, A., Rosi, S., Alessandra Scarpato, M., Serena, A. and Taberna, A. (2001) 'The Florence

146

Psychiatric Interview', *International Journal of Methods in Psychiatric Research*, Vol. 10, pp. 157–171.

Faravelli, C., Catena, M., Scarpato, A. and Ricca, V. (2007) 'Epidemiology of Life Events', *Psychotherapy and Psychosomatics*, Vol. 76, No. 6, pp. 361–368.

Faris, R. E. L. and Dunham, H. W. (1939). *Mental disorders in urban areas: an ecological study of schizophrenia and other psychoses*. Chicago: University of Chicago Press.

Gureje, O. and Adewunmi, A. (1988) 'Life Events and Schizophrenia in Nigerians: A Controlled Investigation', *British Journal of Psychiatry*, Vol. 153, pp. 367–375.

Haidl, T., Rosen, M., Schultze-Lutter, F., Nieman, D., Eggers, S., Heinimaa, M., Juckel, G., Heinz, A., Morrison, A., Linszen, D., Salokangas, R., Klosterkötter, J., Birchwood, M., Patterson, P. and Ruhrmann, S. (2018) 'Expressed emotion as a predictor of the first psychotic episode – Results of the European prediction of psychosis study', *Schizophrenia Research*, Vol. 199, pp. 346–352.

Harris T. (1987) 'Recent developments in the study of life events in relation to psychiatric and physical disorders'. In B. Cooper (Ed.) *Psychiatric Epidemiology*. London: Croom-Helm, pp. 81–103.

Hollingshead, A. B. and Redlich, F. C. (1958) *Social Class and Mental Illness: A Community Study*. New York, NY: John Wiley.

Holmes, T. H. and Rahe, R. H. (1967) 'The Social Readjustment Rating Scale', *Journal of Psychosomatic Research*, Vol. 11, pp. 213–218.

Hooley, J. M. (2007) 'Expressed Emotion and Relapse of Psychopathology', *The Annual Review of Clinical Psychology*, Vol. 3, pp. 329–352.

Jablensky, A., Sartorius, N., Ernberg, G., Anker, M., Korten, A., Cooper, J. E., Day, R. and Bertelsen, A. (1992) 'Schizophrenia: Manifestations, Incidence and Course in Different Cultures. A World Health Organization Ten-Country Study', *Psychological Medicine Monograph Supplement*, Vol. 20, pp. 1–97.

Jenkins, R., Mbatia, J., Singleton, N. and White, B. (2010) 'Prevalence of Psychotic Symptoms and Their Risk Factors in Urban Tanzania', *International Journal of Environmental Research and Public Health*, Vol. 7, pp. 2514–2525.

Johns, L. C., Cannon, M., Singleton, N., Murray, R. M., Farrell, M., Brugha, T., Bebbington, P., Jenkins, R. and Meltzer, H. (2004) 'Prevalence and correlates of self-reported psychotic symptoms in the British population', *British Journal of Psychiatry*, Vol. 185, pp. 298–305.

Jones, P. B., Bebbington, P., Foerster, A., Lewis, S. W., Murray, R. M., Russell, A., Sham, P. C., Toone, B. K. and Wilkins, S. (1993) 'Premorbid social under-achievement in schizophrenia. Results from the Camberwell Collaborative Psychosis Study', *The British Journal of Psychiatry*, Vol. 162, pp. 65–71.

Klippel, A., Viechtbauer, W., Reininghaus, U., Wigman, J., van Borkulo, C., Myin-Germeys, I. and Wichers, M. (2018) 'The Cascade of Stress: A Network Approach to Explore Differential Dynamics in Populations Varying in Risk for Psychosis', *Schizophrenia Bulletin*, Vol. 44, No. 2, pp. 328–337.

Kraan, T., Velthorst, E., Smit, F., de Haan, L. and van der Gaag, M. (2015) 'Trauma and recent life events in individuals at ultra high risk for psychosis: Review and meta-analysis', *Schizophrenia Research*, Vol. 161, pp. 143–149.

Lataster, J., Myin-Germeys, I., Lieb, R., Wittchen, H.-U. and van Os, J. (2012) 'Adversity and psychosis: a 10-year prospective study investigating synergism between early and recent adversity in psychosis', *Acta Psychiatrica Scandinavica*, Vol. 125, pp. 388–399.

Leff, J., Berkowitz, R., Shavit, N., Strachan, A., Glass, I. and Vaughn, C. (1990) 'A Trial of Family Therapy versus a Relatives' Group for Schizophrenia: Two-Year Follow-up', *British Journal of Psychiatry*, Vol. 157, pp. 571–577.

Miklowitz, D. J., George, E. L., Richards, J. A., Simoneau, T. L. and Suddath, R. L. (2003) 'A Randomized Study of Family-Focused Psychoeducation and Pharmacotherapy in the Outpatient Management of Bipolar Disorder', *Archives of General Psychiatry*, Vol. 60, pp, 904–912.

Mondelli, V., Dazzan, P., Hepgul, N., Di Forti, M., Aas, M., D'Albenzio, A., Di Nicola, M., Fisher, H., Handley, R., Reis Marques, T., Morgan, C., Navari, S., Taylor, H., Papadopoulos, A., Aitchison, K. J., Murray, R. M. and Pariante, C. M. (2010) 'Abnormal cortisol levels during the day and cortisol awakening response in first-episode psychosis: The role of stress and of antipsychotic treatment', *Schizophrenia Research*, Vol. 116, pp. 234–242.

Morgan, C., Fisher, H., Hutchinson, G., Kirkbride, J., Craig, T. K., Morgan, K., Dazzan, P., Boydell, J., Doody, G. A., Jones, P. B., Murray, R. M., Leff, J., Fearon, P. (2009) 'Ethnicity, social disadvantage and psychotic-like experiences in a healthy population based sample', *Acta Psychiatrica Scandinavica*, Vol. 119, pp. 226–235.

Morgan, C., Kirkbride, J., Hutchinson, G., Craig, T., Morgan, K., Dazzan, P., Boydell, J., Doody, G. A., Jones, P. B., Murray, R. M., Leff, J. and Fearon, P. (2008) 'Cumulative social disadvantage, ethnicity and first-episode psychosis: a case-control study', *Psychological Medicine*, Vol. 38, pp. 1701–1715.

Paykel, E. S. (1997) 'The Interview for Recent Life Events', *Psychological Medicine*, Vol. 27, pp. 301–310.

Paykel, E. S., Myers, J. K., Dienelt, M. N., Klerman, G. L., Lindenthal, J. J. and Pepper, M. P. (1969) 'Life Events and Depression: A Controlled Study', *Archives of General Psychiatry*, Vol. 21, No. 6, pp. 753–760.

Pignon, B., Lajnef, M., Kirkbride, J. B., Peyre, H., Ferchiou, A., Richard, J.-R., Baudin, G., Tosato, S., Jongsma, H., de Haan, L., Tarricone, H., Bernardo, M., Velthorst, E., Braca, M., Arango, C., Arrojo, M., Bobes, J., Del-Ben, C. M., Di Forti, M., Gayer-Anderson, C., Jones, P. B., La Cascia, C., Lasalvia, A., Rossi Menezes, P., Quattrone, D., Sanjuán, J., Selten, J.-P., Tortelli, A., Llorca, P.-M., van Os, J., Rutten, B. P. F., Murray, R. M., Morgan, C., Leboyer, M., Szöke, A. and Schürhoff, F. (2021) 'The Independent Effects of Psychosocial Stressors on Subclinical Psychosis: Findings From the Multinational EU-GEI Study', *Schizophrenia Bulletin*, Vol. 47, No. 6, pp. 1674–1684.

Rahe, R. H., Meyer, M., Smith. M., Kjaer, G. and Holmes, T. H. (1964) 'Social Stress and Illness Onset', *Journal of Psychosomatic Research*, Vol. 8, pp. 35–44.

Raune, D., Kuipers, E. and Bebbington, P. (2009) 'Stressful and intrusive life events preceding first episode psychosis', *Epidemiology and Psychiatric Sciences*, Vol. 18, No. 3, pp. 221–228.

Reininghaus, U. A., Morgan, C., Simpson, J., Dazzan, P., Morgan, K., Doody, G. A., Bhugra, D., Leff, J., Jones, P., Murray, R., Fearon, P and Craig, T. K.J . (2008) 'Unemployment, social isolation, achievement–expectation mismatch and psychosis: findings from the ÆSOP Study', *Social Psychiatry and Psychiatric Epidemiology*, Vol. 43, pp. 743–751.

Singh, G., Kaur, D. and Kaur, H. (1983) *Handbook for Presumptive Stressful Live Event Scale*. Agra: National Psychological Corporation.

Smyth, J. M. and Stone, A. A. (2003) 'Ecological Momentary Assessment Research in Behavioral Medicine', *Journal of Happiness Studies*, Vol. 4, pp. 35–52.

Spitzer, R., Endicott, J. and Robbins, E. (1975) *Research Diagnostic Criteria*. New York: New York State Psychiatric Institute.

Spitzer, R. L., Williams, J. B. W., Gibbon, M. and First, M. B. (1992) 'The Structured Clinical Interview for DSM-III-R (SCID): I: History, Rationale, and Description', *Archives of General Psychiatry*, Vol. 49, No. 8, pp. 624–629.

van Nierop, M., van Os, J., Gunther, N., Myin-Germeys, I., de Graaf, R., ten Have, M., van Dorsselaer, S., Bak, M. and van Winkel, R. (2012) 'Phenotypically Continuous With Clinical Psychosis, Discontinuous in Need for Care: Evidence for an Extended Psychosis Phenotype', *Schizophrenia Bulletin*, Vol. 38, No. 2, pp. 231–238.

Vinokur, A. and Selzer, M. L. (1975) 'Desirable Versus Undesirable Life Events: Their Relationship to Stress and Mental Distress', *Journal of Personality and Social Psychology*, Vol. 32, No. 2, pp. 329–337.

Wing, J. K., Cooper, J. E. and Sartorius, N. (1974) *The Measurement and Classification of Psychiatric Symptoms*. Cambridge: Cambridge University Press.

Wittchen, H-U., Essau, C.A., Hecht, H., Teder, W. and Pfister, H. (1989) 'Reliability of life event assessments: test-retest reliability and fall-off effects of the Munich Interview for the Assessment of Life Events and Conditions', *Journal of Affective Disorders*, Vol. 16, pp. 77–91.

Wittchen, H.-U., Lachner, G., Wunderlich, U. and Pfister, H. (1998) 'Test-retest reliability of the computerized DSM-IV version of the Munich-Composite International Diagnostic Interview (M-CIDI)', *Social Psychiatry and Psychiatric-Epidemiology*, Vol. 33, pp. 568–578.

8

JOINING THE DOTS …

How might all these epidemiological findings be drawn together? Is it realistic to try and join the dots? At one level, they might be considered to add very little to what is already generally felt. It is longstanding folklore that 'madness' runs in families, and difficult life circumstances are, in general, not conducive to well-being. It does not require large sums of money and an expert research team to establish that people with mental health difficulties are stigmatised and discriminated against, and it does not require large sums of money and an expert research team to establish that people fare better and are more likely to feel good about themselves when they experience those around them as caring and supportive. Nevertheless, all these facts and figures have been assembled at considerable cost. They are the result of meticulous scrutiny by highly trained and esteemed investigators, and they occupy many pages of scholarly books and journals.

The point, of course, is that all this work and related publications are testimony to the fact that associations between someone's social circumstances and their risk of troubling psychotic experiences have become the focus of active academic debate. This fuels more ideological debate about the nature and origins of psychotic experiences. For a host of reasons many clinicians and scholars take issue with the so-called biomedical approach to mental health difficulties, and research findings offering support for an alternative way to consider them are a welcome contribution to that debate. Recalling Popper (2002), the academic enterprise does not, of itself generate 'knowledge'. It generates opinions which, in contexts such as determining how to respond to a troublesome experience of psychosis, in their turn play various parts in influencing how it might be understood, what should be done about it, and by whom. Which opinions, and which interpretations of them exert what influence over these choices? How do those choices reflect the perceived authority of those holding them, and how is that authority received by those experiencing psychosis and their close associates? High quality research which has taken as many possible sources of error and misinterpretation into account leaves little scope for those who might challenge its findings, and thereby authorises and strengthens the influence of opinions based upon

DOI: 10.4324/9780429059094-9

them. It also widens debate. If, for example, it seems undeniable that adverse childhood experiences are associated with a substantially increased risk of psychosis in later life because the research testing that hypothesis is of high enough quality, then debate has to move on from whether or not that is the case, to what the practical implications of that might be.

Of course, there is always some uncertainty, but the quality and quantity of research that has now repeatedly identified associations between the likelihood of experiencing psychosis and: adverse childhood experiences, family background, migration, ethnicity, life events, accumulated distress, and city life, are such that its findings can be taken as the basis of further discussion, and the debate re-focused to consider their implications. New data may emerge. New ways of considering old data may develop, but this discussion concerns the implications of current findings rather than continuing any debate that might question them.

Associations between the risk of experiencing psychosis and adverse childhood experiences, family background, migration, ethnicity, life events, accumulated distress and city life are robust quantitative data that can each stand alone and function as separate fora within which their own cognoscenti debate their further details. On the other hand, they can also be thought of as markers on a wider landscape; dots to be joined in the hope of revealing a larger picture that might illuminate better understanding of the relationship between the social world and troublesome psychotic experiences. To a significant extent this is already happening. The data themselves reveal significant overlaps between, for instance, the effects of migration, urbanicity and living under disadvantaged circumstances, and between the effects of adverse childhood experiences, familial transmission and social support. Without supporting data, it has to be a speculative proposal to suggest that together and in their different ways these quantitative 'signals' reflect three influences upon the individual that might contribute to the risk of troubling psychotic experiences; namely, 'stress', 'social isolation', and the pattern of everyday human interactions, but it is a hypothesis worth considering. 'Stress' is where most debate about the consequences of adverse experiences winds up. 'Social isolation' is implicated in several of the various indicators, such as social fragmentation and social capital, which are prominent among the measures linking urbanicity to the likelihood of experiencing psychosis. The pattern of everyday human interactions reflects the geography and social composition of everyday life, measured, for instance in terms of ethnic density on the one hand, and neighbourhood composition and social cohesion on the other. The former is prominent among the links between migration and ethnicity, and troubling psychotic experiences, and the latter two play their parts in conceptualisations of urbanicity. Patterns of everyday human interaction also reflect personal qualities and propensities; 'Who am I comfortable with?', 'Can I do this?', 'Is this the sort of person others find attractive?', 'Do I enjoy solitary or convivial pursuits?', 'Where do I fit in?' all play their part in determining whom an individual might associate with, with what quality of relationship, and for how much of the time. It is not difficult to see how these can reflect, in one way or another and where relevant, the consequences of adverse childhood experiences, a toxic family environment, difficult living conditions, or migration. Before suggesting an approach which brings these together as potential contributors to the risk of experiencing psychosis, each needs to be considered in more detail.

'Stress'

When considering stress and responses to it, it is easy to fall down a biological, reductionist rabbit hole. Fight, flight, homeostasis and a host of other related phenomena have been variously conceptualised and investigated from physiological, humoral, neuroanatomical and neurochemical perspectives for decades. When threatened, mammals secrete more cortisol, shut down visceral blood flow, increase cardiac output, activate areas of the brain associated with vigilance, and display numerous other well documented responses. Humans are no different. If any sense is to be made of associations between the many documented sources of adversity and the risk of experiencing troublesome psychosis based upon this way of considering 'stress', then the experience of psychosis has to be framed in a similar way. Parallel decades of research have sought a full and sufficient biological, reductionist way of understanding psychosis and it has yet to emerge. For that reason, this discussion is predicated on the growing consensus that psychosis cannot be adequately understood in biomedical terms. If 'stressful' social conditions do indeed contribute to the risk of experiencing psychosis, then their contribution, also, has to be considered in other than biomedical terms. Another way of conceptualising 'stress' has to be recruited. Fortunately, there is one, and it has a long and respected history.

Lazarus and Folkman's (1984) *Stress, Appraisal, and Coping* is a re-working, with few changes in emphasis, of *Psychological Stress and the Coping Process* which was first published in 1966. At heart it is a detailed account of evidence and interpretations that establish the central role of appraisal in humans' and some other mammals' responses to 'stress'. Rather than passively reacting to a stressful situation with one or more biologically determined responses and reflexive or learned behaviours, the stressful situation elicits an appraisal of the threats and opportunities it represents, and this appraisal forms the basis of a bespoke, adaptive coping response. The emphasis is upon active and continual engagement with the environment, social or material, and the book as a whole offers a wealth of research findings which support this perspective, and many examples of how this process might proceed in differing circumstances. Lazarus' foregrounding of appraisal, interpretation and meaning as the primary determinants of human behaviour was a significant development in psychology and it played a part in the framing of cognitive behaviour therapy (Beck et al. 1979, p. 36).

In relation to difficult circumstances which are associated with an increased likelihood of troubling psychotic experiences Lazarus' perspective focuses upon what any one of them might imply to the individual in question, in the context in which they are operating. A particular life event, adverse living conditions, discrimination, or neighbourhood conflict will each be experienced in their own personal way, and their consequences will reflect how they are understood, what their implications are thought to be and what opportunities and resources are felt to be available. Rather than considering 'stress' as something that generates a particular set of physiological responses, 'stress' is a challenging state of affairs that demands some form of response, be it active and energetic engagement or withdrawal. What that response might be depends upon how the situation is understood, what resources are available or envisaged, and how personal capabilities are felt to match the tasks in hand. All of these are individual, and reflect details of the situation, how it is read, what choices there are and how they are appraised, who else is involved, and so on. From this perspective life events, adverse living conditions, urbanicity and other measurable vicissitudes might better be thought of as circumstances in which some people's understanding of them and resulting coping responses are more likely to include voice-hearing, odd beliefs, persecution or a need to withdraw. What might inform this further, then, is not more detailed information about the psychophysiology of 'stress', but a more detailed understanding of how and why some people experience such circumstances in these ways and respond with what is generally regarded as a troubling experience of psychosis, and some do not.

'Social isolation'

Several of the measures subsumed under urbanicity, such as social fragmentation, poor social capital, and social coherence, are conceived as indicators of poor social support. More specifically, social networks are smaller among young people experiencing psychosis for the first time (e.g. Gayer-Anderson and Morgan 2013) and larger among those with better three-year outcomes (e.g. Norman et al. 2005). Broadly defined, social support is associated with improved health and well-being across a wide range of circumstances and conditions, but how that comes about, and how measures implying low levels of social support are associated with an increased risk of troublesome psychotic experiences is much less well understood.

One frequently cited review (Barrera 1986) establishes distinctions between social embeddedness, perceived support and enacted support. Social embeddedness refers to the connections an individual has with significant others of their community. It is reflected in the size of measurable social networks and it confers a sense of 'being part of a community'. Perceived social support is characterised by the appraisal of how well connected one is to others. It resonates with Lazarus' considerations of how available resources are appraised and recruited into a coping response in terms of whether or not there are capable and reliable others to hand. Enacted support refers to clearly identifiable interventions which might mitigate the effects of hardship such as a food parcel or offers of child-care.

Another commonly encountered distinction is that between the 'buffering' effects of social support, and its more general and direct effects. The former refers to the buffering of difficulties by significant others, and is usually detected in terms of relationships between social contacts and the relief of hardship. The latter refers to a broader experience of social connectedness, similar to social embeddedness, and is usually measured as a reflection of the size and/or quality of social networks (Cohen and Wills 1985). Other concepts include social comparison, social exchange, social competence, emotional support, informational support, support with self-appraisal and social climate (Langford et al. 1997). Barrera discourages the use of concepts, measures and theorising that employ a mono-focal approach to social support (Barrera 1986, p. 440), and the same must apply to its obverse, social isolation and measures that impute it. Understanding what associations between the likelihood of troubling psychotic experiences, and measures that imply 'social isolation' actually represent, is going to require a much more detailed scrutiny of people's social interactions and how they are understood than we have to date, but the strength and reproducibility of those associations provides good reason for investigating them.

Patterns of everyday human interaction

The presence or otherwise of social support; what it means, and provides, for any one person in any one situation, is both bespoke to those circumstances and determined by the human interactions it embodies. People's interactions with one another are patterned. They live in a particular neighbourhood, they do or do not go to work and associate with others in a relatively predictable way, mostly they live with one another, they belong to clubs, go to church, mosque, temple or synagogue, socialise and so on. These patterns are inevitably related to the social variables associated with the risk of experiencing psychosis. A relatively privileged person will have an entirely different pattern of human interactions from someone who is unemployed and living off benefits in a rented room. Among those with significant experiences of psychosis their patterns of everyday human interaction may or may not be dominated by interactions with health-care professionals. A migrant or someone of an ethnic minority may be in a situation where they can choose, if they wish, to interact with others of a similar background. They may be in a situation where that is more difficult. It is arguably of central importance, that the socio-demographic measures which associate with the likelihood of troublesome psychotic experiences can also be viewed as measures reflecting circumstances associated with identifiably distinct patterns of human interaction.

Choices of company and how social interactions proceed also reflect personal characteristics. A shy and retiring person will have an entirely different pattern of everyday interactions from someone who is gregarious and outgoing. Someone who finds it difficult to trust others, who has perhaps been abused or feels themselves to be 'different' will find it difficult to associate with more than a very few others. The list of exemplars could run on. The point is that personal characteristics; personality, or habits of association, play a powerful part in determining patterns of everyday human interactions. Such personal characteristics are strongly influenced by childhood. One of the sequalae of adverse childhood experiences or an otherwise unhelpful family background is that they play a significant part in shaping subsequent habits of association.

In other words ...

Insofar as social phenomena associated with a heightened risk of troublesome psychotic experiences are considered to be sources of 'stress', then part of what they do is generate or provoke coping responses. These are bespoke; peculiar to the individual and the situation they are addressing, and reflect how the situation and available resources are understood. Insofar as social phenomena associated with a heightened risk of troublesome psychotic experiences are considered to reflect limited social support, then their consequences reflect the specifics of that person's social network; what it is, how well which participants can be trusted, what they offer, how well it is received, and so on. Both of these hinge upon subjective experiences; of 'stress' and how the situation generating it might be understood and addressed, and of other people and whether they are perceived to be available, supportive and offering something of value. The same social phenomena associated with a heightened risk of troubling psychotic experiences also predict patterns of everyday human interaction; who is frequently encountered and in what context, whether or not they are respected or threatening, what views they hold, do I agree with them, and more. If the personal meaning of difficult circumstances and how to respond to them, and the personal understanding of others' availability to support are the outcome of human interactions and exchanges, however personal, distant or even virtual, then who those interactions are with will influence the outcome. Thus, the whole can be considered through the lens of symbolic interactionism. How the situation is understood by the participant determines their response to it, but that understanding is the result of interactions with others and through such interactions, others' understandings. There is no assumption or prerequisite that one person's assessment of a situation has to conform to others', but it will be shaped by those of any they interact with. How these proceed and what outcomes result will be influenced by who those 'others' are, and the nature of the participant's relationships with them.

A mixed economy of opinions concerning the experience of psychosis

As outlined in Chapter 2, the Network Episode Model (Pescosolido 2011) provides a framework that organises the human interactions associated with 'illness' around three tiers. There might be other ways of doing this but the Network Episode Model is well established, comprehensive and has yet to be seriously challenged. The three tiers are: immediate associates; healthcare organisations, their staff, and other advisors; and the wider historical and socio-political context in which all of these are embedded. The social phenomena now robustly associated with the likelihood of troubling psychotic experiences can be considered in terms of the differing patterns of human interaction they imply, and therefore differing patterns of opinion and individuals' receptivity to them. Opinions contributing to interactions concerning psychosis are likely to differ from one social setting to another, and so there are likely to be differing meanings attached to psychotic experiences that also reflect the social settings in which they are generated. Up to a point that is already acknowledged in terms of differing cultures' approaches to psychotic experiences, but those debates are generally conducted in specialised circles (see for instance Cox 1991). The robust epidemiology reviewed in Chapters 3–7 suggests that this might be a more widely applicable way of considering variations in how psychotic experiences are understood and responded to across the board. At the 'immediate associates' level it is not difficult to envisage differences in opinions concerning what it means to be experiencing psychosis that match on to differences in socio-economic status, ethnicity, migrant status and population density, insofar as these reflect relevant education and experience, wealth and privilege. It is equally reasonable to argue that the same social features have effects upon whom someone experiencing psychosis might associate with. The nature and content of human interactions determining how someone might understand psychotic experiences are, up to a point, likely to reflect a number of socio-demographic variables.

The same is true at the level of 'healthcare organisations and their staff and other advisors'. People differ in how they perceive the authority and integrity of healthcare professionals and how they might be approached and negotiated with, and these differences will be reflected in the nature, content and outcomes of such interactions. Healthcare professionals or other advisors are unlikely to have been approached unless the experience of psychosis has come to be seen as a problem meriting external advice and intervention, either by the 'patient' or by their associates. Whether or not that happens, who is consulted with what questions and by what route will reflect how the problem has come to be understood, what other sources of support have been explored, and perceptions of how the external advisor might respond. It is a coping response in Lazarus' (1984) terms, and as such it will be the outcome of preceding human interactions that have generated a view of such

156

problems that includes 'this sort of thing merits professional intervention'. What determines that is going to be influenced by the perceived competence and availability of other sources of support, the readiness with which experiences of psychosis are understood as a medical condition, trust in authority and earlier experiences of comparable difficulties. These might include media representations, folklore, or representations drawn from family history.

As already noted, healthcare professionals and other external advisors are usually paid employees or self-employed experts. In part, they are doing this for a living and as a result, whatever their personal opinions might be, they are obliged to conform to certain views and expectations. It is conventional to consider employing organisations and other enduring features of the social world 'institutions' or 'structures', within or indeed despite which, individuals exert agency with varying degrees of success, Crossley makes the interesting point that institutions are but relatively stable, tight and enduring networks of mutually dependent human interactions (Crossley 2022). This is pertinent. If, for example, how the experience of psychosis is understood by the Royal College of Psychiatrists is recognised, not as an immutable, authoritative position, but the outcome of a particular set of human interactions, then it becomes more legitimate to question it. A similar argument can, of course, be mounted in relation to mental health nursing, social work and clinical psychology, but of course all of these professions and others related to them are perceived to be authoritative. They do embody experience; few people have encountered more instances of disturbing psychosis than a seasoned mental health nurse, and they do control access to relevant social and healthcare resources. For these reasons interactions with them are likely to elicit an opinion which is consistent with their peers', which is likely to be received as authoritative, and which promises assistance. That is particularly so when the opinion is a 'diagnosis'. Uncertainty is resolved, and there appears to be a clear way forward explaining what is going on in terms of a medical condition. This relieves all participants from responsibility for the problem, or attempting to resolve it. It is usually only later that the toxic effects of 'diagnosis'; possibly harmful medication, stigma and discrimination, damaged identity and reduced esteem become apparent.

The 'wider historical and socio-political context' refers to influences that reflect the broader setting. These are largely experienced unconsciously, as features of 'how the world is', but they find expression in human interactions that affirm shared values and understandings that can be difficult to challenge. How many young people (of all nationalities) have lost their lives, because the interactions they have had with friends, family and recruiting sergeants have all made it shameful and diminishing to resist joining up and going to war?

Sebastian Faulks paints a vivid picture of life in a late nineteenth-century asylum early in his remarkable novel, *Human Traces* (Faulks 2006). One notable portrayal is that of the admissions process, whereby an assortment of distressed, confused and unwanted people are brought to the asylum to be certified and accommodated. Assessments are brief. There are many to complete in a short time, and the purpose of the assessment is not to challenge the decision to admit or to explore why this is happening in any detail. It is simply to determine which ward each should be assigned to. Thereafter fates would be sealed. Discussion, debate and the interactions embodying them that determined the need for entry into the asylum had already been concluded, and not on the basis of careful and detailed professional assessment, but simply around questions of competence, means and desirability. Once condemned in this way, the certified would likely spend years incarcerated in overcrowded and very limiting conditions. Numbers continued to grow during the first half of the twentieth century until, by the 1950s, in the UK, some 150,000 people were corralled together in this way (Shorter 1997). It was how things were done and few questioned it until Goffman (1961) and others began to consider the consequences of institutionalisation, and parallels with Nazi brutality began to be recognised. Drug treatments followed, but with them also came the view that something is still needed to attenuate 'madness'.

'This is how things are, and this is how they are dealt with' is a powerful way of shutting down debate, and leaving questions unasked, never mind unanswered. It applied, for instance, to the slave trade and to public execution. Until the 1960s it applied to male homosexuality. Each of these has proved otherwise. Sugar, cotton and tobacco can be profitably produced without relying on slave labour. Criminals can be deterred without the occasional brutal spectacle, and no harm comes to others as a result of people openly expressing their sexuality. How psychotic experiences are understood and responded to are, hopefully, changing, but the process is a slow and tortuous one. Media representations, tabloid journalism and other resonances of unquestioned assumptions about psychotic experiences continue to find voice and maintain them. As a result, they influence discussion and debate among 'immediate associates' in ways that probably reflect variations in individuals' receptivity and attention to such portrayals and related populist opinion. They may, therefore, be reflected in associations between social circumstances and the likelihood of experiencing psychosis as a troubling phenomenon. Furthermore, as these influences continue to encourage an understanding of psychotic experiences as evidence of a serious illness meriting professional intervention, they also inhibit change among those same professionals, whose interests understandably lie with maintaining networks of interaction and related 'expert' debate that encourage dependency upon them.

From a symbolic interactionist perspective (Blumer 1969), how someone might come to understand the puzzling experience of hearing voices, odd beliefs, or feeling that others are hostile, is a reflection of the human interactions they are involved in. Those interactions will vary in the extent to which they influence that understanding and how receptive that person is to them. They might be exposed to others who readily interpret such experiences as signs of a serious illness that requires professional input or they might be exposed to others who prefer to dismiss them as less threatening. In either case, the influence of others' opinions about such experiences will vary in ways that reflect the relationships between that person and those they are interacting with. Those others might be experienced as informed, authoritative and trustworthy. They might be experienced as biased, ill-informed and manipulative, and as a result, how particular opinions are incorporated into that person's understanding of their experience will vary accordingly.

Contributing interactions are not restricted to family, friends and other close associates, although these are arguably the most influential. There could well be interactions with a healthcare professional or other advisors, such as a social worker, a priest, a rabbi or an imam. These may have been approached because of their perceived authority, their personal qualities, or because close associates have encouraged the consultation. Their opinion may well reflect specifics of the situation but it only carries authoritative weight if it also reflects the party line; 'this is how healthcare professionals understand this problem', 'this is how social workers understand this problem', 'this is how Christians understand this problem', 'this is how Jews understand this problem', 'this is how Moslems understand this problem', and so on. Whatever those views might be, they are likely to have an effect upon close associates' views. 'So, the doctor thinks you must have schizophrenia.' is going to have a powerful effect upon family discussions concerning what the voices, odd beliefs or suspiciousness represent. Furthermore, the extent to which the doctor's, or another advisor's opinion is assimilated into how the person in question and/or their close associates understand those experiences will be influenced by how readily they respect the authority of whoever provided it.

Finally, all of this is set within a broader landscape of time and place. As far as is known, what we currently refer to as troublesome psychotic experiences have occurred in all cultures and throughout recorded time. How they have been understood has changed across time and from setting to setting; in some as a divine gift, in some as evil demonic possession, in some as evidence of degeneracy, in some as the result of bad breeding, and of course, in the currently prevailing setting of a culture dominated by an attachment to empirical science and to risk management, as signs of a serious illness that threatens violence and is best contained by a commitment to sedating medication. Although that view is no longer any more credible than its antecedents, in many quarters it is still as influential as demonisation was when witches were burned at the stake, or eugenics was when asylum inmates were murdered by the Nazi regime. It is the current 'this is how these things are understood and this is how we deal with them'. As a result, it influences how experiences of psychosis are portrayed, and it influences how they are understood by many. It also influences the opinions and actions of authoritative contributors such as healthcare professionals, whose understandable interests are commonly served by conforming to it. Although it generally acts at an unconscious level, assumed and usually unquestioned, it plays a significant part in determining opinions across the board. Significantly, that is likely to include close associates of someone wondering what to make of puzzling experiences such as intrusive voices, odd beliefs or a sense of being threatened.

Psychotic experiences do not mean that someone having them is necessarily unreliable or dangerous, any more than they mean that the person in question is possessed by a demon, or that they are degenerate and culpable. How they are understood, in the same way that anything is understood, reflects the human interactions that have shaped that understanding. Although the debate is changing in some quarters, it is slow to change in others. This contribution to that process is to emphasise the central part everyday human interactions play in the construction of understanding anything, including the experience of voice hearing, strange beliefs or a sense of being under threat. Which human interactions play what parts in shaping any one person's understanding, again, of anything, will reflect where they live, whom they associate with and how receptive they are to the opinions they encounter in the course of this. This is no less true for how an understanding of psychotic experiences might be shaped, but it does offer a way of interpreting the considerable body of evidence that has established associations between certain social circumstances and an enhanced likelihood of understanding psychotic experiences as something dangerous, damaging and debilitating. It is a way of joining the array of dots recent, respected and reproducible psychiatric epidemiology offers. How experiences of voice hearing, strange beliefs, a sense of being under threat or other 'psychotic' experiences are understood determines responses to them, and how the person experiencing them is viewed by others and by themselves. Such understandings, or derived meanings, are the outcome of the human interactions those particular circumstances generate and contain. That pattern of human of human interactions is in part, at least, a reflection of the social circumstances in which they are operating, and of participants' interacting levels of trust and conviviality. Thus, adverse childhood experiences, family background, migration, ethnicity, life events, accumulated distress and city life all have the potential to influence the pattern of human interactions an individual 'patient' and their associates might experience, and as a result, in their own and various ways, influence how psychotic experiences might be understood and responded to.

This offers a way of accounting for the epidemiological findings but in doing so it demands a shift in how knowledge concerning psychosis is generally construed. Conventional approaches to psychosis have focused upon attempting to define it as an empirically fixed entity. The 1990 symposium (Flack et al. 1991) revealed how difficult it was to support that approach when a fuller range of viewpoints is taken into account. More general considerations of what knowledge is and how it is generated (Kuhn 2012; Popper 2002, Michel Foucault *via* Mambrol 2017, for instance) are substantive support of a more constructivist approach. Certainly, in relation to psychosis, it seems to be more productive to focus upon how it is understood and responded to in any given situation, than it is to attempt a full and sufficient definition that can helpfully apply under all circumstances. As outlined in Chapter 1, stigmatisation and discrimination are among the most debilitating consequences of being identified as someone with mental health difficulties, and these are not intrinsic features of mental health difficulties in themselves. They reflect others' understandings of them. Symbolic interaction offers a way of understanding how such understandings and responses to them come about. People act in response to the meaning they apply to a particular phenomenon or situation, and that meaning is the outcome of human interactions related to it (Blumer 1969). As outlined in Chapter 2, this approach to understanding mental health difficulties also has a long and respected background (Cooley, Mead, Goffman, Scheff, for instance).

Some suggestions

There is nothing especially new or entirely unfounded about the proposal that recent, respected and reproducible psychiatric epidemiology might reflect differing patterns of human interaction that of themselves generate differing understandings of what psychotic experiences represent and how they might be best responded to. What these more recent data do offer is some pointers towards testable hypotheses. Do social networks differ in ways that reflect the social variables that are associated with the risk of psychosis? Do opinions about the experience of psychosis vary in a similar way? Do people who have suffered adverse childhood experiences associate with others in a particular way? Do they have particular approaches to authority? What are the linkages between media portrayals of psychosis, professional opinions and how psychotic experiences are understood by those who have them? Effectively addressing many of these questions will perhaps require less quantitative methodologies than have tended to dominate social and psychiatric research in recent years. Nevertheless, a focus upon the construction of meaning in the course of human interactions offers some structure. Human interactions are identifiable events. Meanings can be abstracted from individual accounts, and patterns of interaction with individuals holding different opinions and differing levels of perceived or experienced authority can be mapped.

It is also worth considering what information is emerging as a result of psychotherapeutic approaches to the experience of psychosis. Reduced to their most simplistic, psychological therapies can be considered exercises in attempting to alter how things are understood, whether these be how dangerous spiders are, what it means to be feeling sad, frightened or elated, 'who I am' in relation to other people and, what it means to be hearing voices, feeling persecuted, or to be holding views and beliefs others don't seem to understand. As far as psychotherapeutic approaches to psychosis are concerned, recent years have seen shifts from giving advice to family and friends about how to 'live with' someone having such experiences, through cognitive behavioural techniques intended to mitigate the impact of voices, odd beliefs or a sense of being persecuted, to dialogic engagement that interacts with 'patients' and their close associates' understandings of 'psychosis', and in so doing, enables the development of less disabling ways of understanding what is happening. The next chapter explores this, with a view to unearthing what experiences of these approaches might reveal about the difficulties they are designed to mitigate.

References

BarreraJr., M. (1986) 'Distinctions Between Social Support Concepts, Measures, and Models', *American Journal of Community Psychology*, Vol. 14, No. 4, pp. 413–445.

Beck, A. T., Rush, J., Shaw, B. F. and Emery, G. (1979) *Cognitive Therapy of Depression*. New York: Guilford Press.

Blumer, H. (1969) *Symbolic Interactionism: Perspective and Method*. Berkeley and Los Angeles: University of California Press.

Cohen, S. and Wills, T. A. (1985) 'Stress, Social Support, and the Buffering Hypothesis', *Psychological Bulletin*, Vol. 98, No. 2, pp. 310–357.

Cox, J. L. (1991) 'Reading About... Transcultural Psychiatry', *British Journal of Psychiatry*, Vol. 158, pp. 579–582.

Crossley, N. (2022) 'A Dependent Structure of Interdependence: Structure and Agency in Relational Perspective', *Sociology*, Vol. 56, No. 1, pp. 166–182.

Faulks, S. (2006) *Human Traces*. London: Vintage.

FlackJr., W. F., Miller, D. R. and Wiener, M. (1991) *What Is Schizophrenia?* New York: Springer-Verlag.

Gayer-Anderson, C. and Morgan, C. (2013) 'Social networks, support and early psychosis: a systematic review', *Epidemiology and Psychiatric Sciences*, Vol. 22, pp. 131–146.

Goffman, E. (1961) *Asylums: Essays on the Condition of the Social Situation of Mental Patients and Other Inmates*. Garden City NY: Anchor Books.

Kuhn, T. S. (2012) *The Structure of Scientific Revolutions*. Fourth Edition. Chicago: University of Chicago Press.

Langford, C. P. H., Bowsher, J., Maloney, J. P. and Lillis, P. P. (1997) 'Social support: a conceptual analysis', *Journal of Advanced Nursing*, Vol. 25, pp. 95–100.

Lazarus, R. and Folkman, S. (1984) *Stress, Appraisal, and Coping*. New York: Springer.

Mambrol, N. (2017) 'Key Theories of Michel Foucault'. https://literariness.org/2017/03/28/key-theories-of-michel-foucault/ (accessed October 2022).

Norman, R. M. G., Malla, A. K., Manchanda, R., Harricharan, R., Takhar, J. and Northcott, S. (2005) 'Social support and three-year symptom and admission outcomes for first episode psychosis', *Schizophrenia Research*, Vol. 80, pp. 227–234.

Pescosolido, B. A. (2011) 'Organising the Sociological Landscape for the next decades of health and health care research: The Network Episode Model III-R as Cartographic Subfield Guide'. In B. A. Pescosolido, J. K. Martin, J. D. McLeod and A. Rogers (Eds.) *Handbook of the Sociology of Health, Illness and Healing*. New York: Springer, pp. 39–66.

Popper, K. R. (2002) *Conjectures and Refutations. The Growth of Scientific Knowledge*. London: Routledge and Kegan Paul.

Shorter, E. (1997) *A History of Psychiatry: From the Era of the Asylum to the Age of Prozac*. New York: John Wiley & Sons, Inc.

9

WHAT CAN BE LEARNED FROM 'WHAT HELPS'?

It is only since the closing years of the twentieth century that disabling experiences of psychosis have been widely considered something amenable to psychological 'therapy'. Freud and other earlier psychoanalytic and psycho-dynamically oriented theorists and practitioners tended to steer away from such clients. Investment in and attachment to biomedical explanations during the 1970s and 1980s (Kendler and Schaffner 2011) strengthened the professional view of psychosis as something beyond the reach of psychotherapy. It was only with the emergence of evidence that the emotional tenor of family life (Expressed Emotion) influenced the risk of intensified psychotic experiences and the likelihood of hospital admission (reviewed by Butzlaff and Hooley 1998), that psycho-social interventions began to be considered of value in their treatment, and began to be taken seriously. By 2014, formal British recommendations (National Institute for Clinical and Healthcare Excellence 2014) were explicitly encouraging psychological therapy in the form of either cognitive behaviour therapy, or a family intervention. This appears to reflect two parallel developments. On the one hand further research exploring the effects of expressed emotion in the social environment of susceptible individuals on the intensity of their experiences of psychosis encouraged trials of family therapy designed to reduce it, and on the other hand, the growth of enthusiasm for cognitive behaviour therapy (CBT) as an evaluable and therefore potentially evidence-based approach to psychological therapy in a wide range of contexts encouraged the development of individual therapies based upon that model. This enthusiasm extended into provision for people with troubling experiences of psychosis, and the result was the development of cognitive behaviour therapy for psychosis (CBTp). Cognitive behaviour therapy and family interventions are entirely different approaches, based on entirely different conceptual frameworks, and so although there is little doubt that interventions very broadly described as 'psychological therapy' can be of value to those experiencing psychosis, it remains very unclear how and why certain people obtain value from them; what the most useful approaches might be, and why it is that they are helpful when they are. These are real-world questions that justify closer scrutiny of the evidence that raises them.

DOI: 10.4324/9780429059094-10

Family Interventions and Cognitive Behaviour Therapy

In 2002 Pilling and colleagues (2002a) published a meta-analysis of relevant findings concerning family interventions and cognitive behaviour therapy for psychosis (CBTp) that were available at the time, and which most probably contributed to their inclusion in formal guidelines. They identified eighteen studies of a sufficient standard and where the value of family therapy had been explored. These involved 1,467 individuals experiencing psychosis. For the 'treatment' to be considered 'family therapy' it had to include family sessions with a specific supportive and treatment intention, and at least one of: psycho-education, problem solving/crisis management, or specific interventions with the identified patient. In addition, the 'treatment' had to be for at least six weeks. Some of the interventions were specifically focused on the 'identified patient's' family, and some were more broadly educational sessions involving more than one family at the same time. There were wide ranges of outcome measure and comparisons across the included studies. Single family but not group family interventions were associated with lower rates of recurring psychotic experiences when compared with standard treatments, but not when compared with other forms of active treatment such as an individual, personal programme of support and 'counselling'. Single family interventions were reliably associated with lower rates of readmission, and both forms of family intervention were associated with higher rates of medicines compliance.

In order to qualify as a trial of CBTp the study had to include a component which focused upon establishing links between clients' thoughts, feelings or actions in relation to identified psychotic experiences, and challenges to apparent misperceptions, irrational beliefs or reasoning biases related to them. An admissible study also had to include evidence of participants' self-monitoring of their thoughts, feelings and behaviours in relation to the identified psychotic experiences, and the promotion of alternative ways of responding to them. Eight trials of CBTp fulfilling these criteria were identified and considered. They involved 393 individuals who were experiencing psychosis. When compared with other less narrowly specified treatments, such as problem-solving, befriending or supportive counselling, there was no evidence that CBTp showed any advantage in reducing the intensity of psychotic experiences or the risk of admission over them. There was evidence of an association between CBTp and improvements in mental state, as measured by scores on clinically assessed symptom rating scales. CBTp offered no other advantage over other approaches to the experience of psychosis, and as with the family interventions, there was no evidence that particular personal characteristics such as the intensity of experiences or age of onset influenced the outcome of therapy. Further subsequent meta-analyses have come to very much the same conclusion (Zimmerman et al. 2005; Pfammatter et al. 2006; Wykes et al. 2008; Sarin et al. 2011), as did a multi-centre trial of CBTp for acutely disturbed individuals recently 'diagnosed' with Schizophrenia that was conducted across three centres in the UK (the SoCRATES trial, Tarrier et al. 2004). Here, CBTp and supportive counselling were compared with one another and with treatment as usual. 309 subjects were randomly allocated into one or another of the three treatment programmes. Neither CBTp or supportive counselling was associated with lower rates of recurring psychotic experiences or admission to hospital on that account than those receiving treatment as usual. Both the CBTp and supportive counselling subjects experienced greater reductions in their clinician-rated intensity of psychotic experiences than the treatment as usual subjects, and this effect was modestly greater following CBTp than it was following supportive counselling.

Bird and colleagues (2010) considered the contribution CBTp had made to services specifically identified as early interventions for psychosis and again, there was evidence of a helpful effect of CBTp upon the intensity of psychotic experiences in the short term, but not upon rates of relapse or of admission to hospital. Combining data from the three studies of early interventions for psychosis where they found specific mention of family intervention, family intervention had an effect upon relapse rates and the risk of admission to hospital, but not upon the intensity of psychotic experiences. Morrison and colleagues (2014) conducted a small (thirty-seven CBTp plus treatment as usual subjects, and thirty-seven just treatment as usual subjects) single-blind, randomised controlled trial among subjects experiencing psychosis who had chosen not to take antipsychotic medication. CBTp reduced the intensity of clinician-rated psychotic experiences and some aspects of improved personal and social functioning, but it did not affect the amount of distress associated with troublesome beliefs or voice hearing, or levels of depression, social anxiety, and self-rated recovery. In 2014 Burns and colleagues published a meta-analysis of trials where CBTp had been used to relieve psychotic experiences in subjects who were deemed to be medically 'treatment resistant'. Again, there was evidence of an effect upon the intensity of so-called positive symptoms and upon 'general symptoms', but no evidence of useful effects upon other measures of difficulty or distress.

Thus, Family Interventions and Cognitive Behaviour Therapy have both crossed evidential thresholds that admit them to the world of formally endorsed 'treatments' for troublesome experiences of psychosis. As specified by their proponents, they are quite different. The former involves psychoeducation, problem solving/crisis management and tailored interventions with the identified patient, and aims to influence how family and other close associates co-exist with the distressed person. The latter establishes links between recipients' thoughts, feelings or actions in relation to identified psychotic experiences, and challenges apparent misperceptions, irrational beliefs or reasoning biases related to them, with the aim of 'straightening out' distorted thinking. Neither offers a silver bullet that will immediately make the difficulty go away, or significantly alter its consequences. Other formalised psychological approaches have proved even less successful.

Social skills training and cognitive remediation

Pilling and colleagues also conducted a meta-analysis of trials where social skills training and cognitive remediation were explored (Pilling et al. 2002b). In this context social skills training referred to a structured group or an individual psychosocial intervention that was intended to enhance social performance and reduce distress and difficulty in social situations. For the purposes of evaluation, the intervention had to include assessments of social and interpersonal skills, especially; verbal and non-verbal communication, the subject's ability to recognise and respond to relevant social cues, and their ability to recognise and respond to appropriate social reinforcement. Nine studies fulfilling these criteria and of a sufficient methodological quality were identified. They involved 471 subjects. When brought together in a meta-analysis these studies were unable to demonstrate an effect of social skills training upon the rate of relapse or intensified experiences of psychosis, social functioning or measures of general adjustment and quality of life.

To be included as a trial of cognitive remediation, the study had to be of an intervention focused on improving one or more of the cognitive functions deemed to be impaired amongst those experiencing psychosis, such as verbal memory, visual memory, attention or executive function. Experimental investigations have suggested that these might be implicated in the experience of psychosis. Five such studies were identified. They involved 170 participants. Methods of assessment and intervention varied widely, and there were individual instances of productive change, but when the studies were brought together, they provided no evidence of improvement in either the specific cognitive functions nominally addressed by the therapy, or wider measures such as the intensity of psychotic experiences, the risk of admission to hospital or overall well-being.

Metacognitive training

An approach which attempts to blend cognitive remediation with CBTp and 'psychoeducation' is metacognitive training (MCT) (Moritz et al. 2010). MCT aims to address so-called cognitive biases such as a tendency to jump to conclusions, difficulties with taking others' perspectives and deficits in 'social cognition'. A meta-analysis of published trials in which MCT had been evaluated as a 'treatment' for psychotic experiences was published in 2016 (Eichner & Berna 2016). Fifteen studies meeting their inclusion criteria were identified. Eleven provided data concerning effects upon 'positive symptoms' which revealed a small to medium sized effect, eleven provided data concerning effects upon 'delusions' and also revealed a small to medium sized effect. Five provided data concerning the acceptability of MCT, which was high. A subsequent evaluation of MCT (Ochoa et al.. 2017) which compared MCT with 'psychoeducation' found no difference between them in their effects upon the intensity of psychotic experiences, though MCT was associated with greater changes in targeted phenomena such as a tendency to jump to conclusions, tolerance of frustration and the ability to understand others' points of view (theory of mind). These approaches, too, have failed to offer a psychotherapeutic 'silver bullet' to the problem of the experience of psychosis.

The Dodo bird, again?

Investigating formally defined psychological therapies intended to relieve or prevent troubling psychotic experiences draws attention to wider questions about psychological therapies. What is it that actually makes a difference? This has been debated for decades, beginning, perhaps, with Rosenzweig's reflections (Rosenzweig 1936). Specified psychotherapeutic 'techniques' seem to share the ability to make useful differences, but the extent to which that happens appears to be common across them, irrespective of the techniques involved or their underpinning conceptual framework. As Lewis Carroll's fictional Dodo Bird in *Alice's Adventures in Wonderland* famously declared, '*Everybody* has won, and *all* must have prizes'. For years, many have contended that one widely accepted explanation for this is that it is the quality of relationship between client and therapist that primarily determines outcome, irrespective of the techniques and underpinning theoretical framework the therapist has chosen to adopt (Middleton 2015, pp. 93–126). How does this play out in relation to psychological approaches to alleviating or even preventing the experience of psychosis?

Summarised, the evidence seems to be that family interventions can reduce rates of relapse, the frequency of intensified episodes of psychosis, and the risk of hospital admission; that CBTp can, to a modest degree, reduce the intensity of psychotic experiences though not reliably more so than less precisely defined psychological interventions, and that MCT has similar effects and has been shown to affect other related phenomena. These barely add up to substantially better ways of explaining the experience of psychosis, how it might have come about and how it might be relieved, but they do indicate that the experience of psychosis should not be considered entirely beyond the reach of psychosocial interventions, or that it is sufficiently explained or understood as a purely biomedical phenomenon. These pointers also open up the value of considering psychosocial approaches to the experience of psychosis in much the same way that psychosocial approaches to other forms of psychological or mental distress are considered. Central to these is the question of whether psychotherapeutic relief from such distress is the result of something specific and particular to the form of the approach, or whether the experienced relief and recovery reflect other processes inherent in, but not defined by, that particular approach. It is barely controversial that the quality and nature of relationships between mental health service users and the clinicians they encounter have a part to play in determining outcome, but there is debate and controversy over how that might be conceptualised. In particular, in relation to specific models of therapy such as CBTp, it is of central importance that the relative contributions of the specific approach and procedures, and those of a helping relationship are clarified. As Tarrier and Wykes summarise, '... not one study [of CBTp] has shown clear and significant overall differences between CBT and the non-specific control groups' (Tarrier & Wykes 2004, p. 1384). In this context 'non-specific control groups' refers to 'dummy' treatments, such as supportive counselling, befriending or problem solving, which do not include the specific framework, processes and procedures considered to characterise CBTp. A treatment arm comprising 'dummy' treatment is included in such trials because it is widely accepted that the provision of a therapeutic relationship offering warmth, supportive and empathic listening, and some expectation of efficacy is helpful in its own right. The purpose of a formal clinical trial of psychological therapy is to establish how a particular therapeutic approach such as CBTp might improve upon that. The failure of practically all trials of CBTp to demonstrate an advantage over 'dummy' treatments raises some interesting questions and adds weight to arguments which suggest it naïve to believe that 'dummy' or 'control' treatments are truly inert (Turner 2012), especially in the context of psychological treatment trials. If they are not inert, as it seems, then perhaps they embody something of therapeutic value which in the case of CBTp may be as helpful as the cognitive behaviour therapy itself.

Goldsmith and colleagues (Goldsmith et al. 2015) attempted to tease this out quantitatively by using data from the SoCRATES trial. It was well conducted from a methodological point of view. There were clear and explicit inclusion criteria, an adequate number of subjects, good 'blinding' of assessors and a 'control' treatment arm (supportive counselling). Assessments of the extent to which sessions providing CBTp and those providing supportive counselling confirmed that they differed, the former conforming to a CBT model and the latter not doing so. There were significant reductions in the intensity of psychotic experiences among those receiving CBTp and among those receiving supportive counselling when compared with those receiving neither, but in this respect, there was no difference between the two treated groups.

Aware of the possibility that it might prove to be relevant, the trialists also made assessments of the quality of relationship between clients and their therapists, termed here as the therapeutic alliance (TA). TA was assessed four weeks into therapy, when it was estimated that sufficient time would have elapsed for a relationship to have developed, but before any changes in the experience of psychosis might influence it. A therapist-rated measure (the

Psychotherapy Status Report (PSR; Frank & Gunderson 1990)) and a client-rated measure (the self-report version of the California Therapeutic Alliance Scales (CALPAS; Marmar et al. 1989)) were used to assess TA. In this analysis they used the CALPAS data, because client-rated measures of therapeutic alliance are considered to be more closely associated with outcome than therapist-rated measures.

Structural equation modelling was used to parcel out the influences of pre- and post-randomisation effects upon outcome. The former included scores on the Positive and Negative Symptom Scale (PANSS), years in education, the duration of untreated psychotic experiences, and the research centre (Manchester, Liverpool, or Nottinghamshire). The latter included interactions between these pre-randomisation measures and treatment allocation, the number of sessions attended, and CALPAS score. This allowed for the separate effects upon outcome (post-treatment PANSS score) of the number of sessions attended and the quality of relationship (CALPAS score) to be estimated, and this in turn allowed estimates to be made of the effects upon outcome of differing numbers of sessions at different levels of relational quality, namely the interaction between the number of sessions attended and the quality of the therapeutic relationship. This was significant, suggesting that in the presence of a good relationship, additional sessions resulted in better outcomes, whereas in the presence of a poorer quality relationship, additional sessions resulted in poorer outcomes and in some cases deterioration. These findings were independent of treatment allocation; whether treatment was with CBTp or with supportive counselling. Given that there was no opportunity for it to develop, therapeutic alliance (TA) was neither assessed nor included in analyses among subjects allocated to treatment as usual.

These findings can be interpreted as evidence of a dose-response relationship between the quality of the therapeutic relationship and the number of sessions. Within the limits of the trial, more sessions of a better-quality relationship resulted in better outcomes and more sessions of a lower quality relationship resulted in poorer outcomes or even deterioration. In other words, the quality of the therapeutic relationship appears to have directly influenced outcome, rather than it being a passive association with an otherwise successful treatment such as CBTp. The Dodo-Bird verdict appears to be far from extinct, even in the context of psychological approaches to the experience of psychosis.

Wider implications

Most settings where people with troubling experiences of psychosis are provided for do not include formally organised psychotherapy. Nevertheless, they are settings where clients and clinicians interact, where therapeutic relationships or alliances develop, and where any effects of their quality might become apparent. Howgego and colleagues (2003) reported on five studies in which clinical outcome and the quality of therapeutic relationship with community mental health team personnel had both been measured among individuals with 'diagnoses' of Schizophrenia or Schizoaffective Disorder and high rates of hospitalisation or heavy reliance on mental health services. There was evidence of an association between the quality of relationship and improved outcomes such as reduced symptom severity, improved global functioning and higher community living skills, improved quality of life, medication compliance and client satisfaction with treatment. McCabe and Priebe (2004) subsequently reviewed the English language literature that involved the treatment of 'severe mental illness' and reported on the quality of client-professional interpersonal relationships. The expression 'severe mental illness' was acknowledged as an arbitrary term, but one which would capture reports of individuals who had past or ongoing troublesome experiences of psychosis, and who were being provided for by mental health services. A number of different scales were used to 'measure' the quality of relationship, and some used clients', some therapists' and some both sets of responses across a variety of dimensions. Despite this heterogeneity, there was consensus supporting general agreement between the several scales, and that in this context it was safe to assume that they were effectively measuring a common underlying construct, apart perhaps from some differences between clients' and professionals' emphasis upon the importance of agreement over tasks and goals. There were twenty-two studies providing information about one or another form of therapeutic outcome and the quality of relationship. Outcome measures included; symptom severity, quality of life, social functioning and time spent in hospital over a twenty-month follow-up period. These variations in the way in which outcome was assessed made it difficult to make any quantitative estimate of the association between relationship quality and outcome but in virtually all instances it was clearly present.

In 2005 Priebe and colleagues published the findings of a qualitative investigation into factors influencing clients' readiness to engage with London Assertive Outreach (AO) teams. AO teams are intended to provide for clients who have shown reluctance to engage with mental health services and yet remain troubled by mental health difficulties, in particular and most commonly, by experiences of psychosis. This investigation involved forty people who all had past or present experiences of psychosis and who had shown a reluctance to engage with community mental health services. All but two had past experience of hospitalisation and in more than half of them, this had been on an involuntary (formal, legally sanctioned) basis. All were interviewed in an exploratory way, with particular attention to episodes of engagement and disengagement, the circumstances surrounding them and clients' understandings of why and how they engaged and disengaged. Disengagement; a reluctance to accept input from the AO team, was associated with a desire to view themselves as an independent and able person, with disappointment in the quality or nature of the therapeutic relationship and with a sense of losing control as a result of medication and its effects. Engagement; a readiness to accept input from the AO teams, was associated with an appreciation of the additional time and commitment the team invested in each client, the experience of receiving support and encouragement independently of a focus on medication, and a sense of being in partnership with their professional contacts. Specifically in relation to the therapeutic relationship, engagement and recovery were enabled when there was an experience of professionals having the time and flexibility to be available when sought and as a result, build mutually trusting and consistent relationships that respected clients' felt needs, and which were experienced as collaborative rather than coercive and contingent upon conforming to institutional expectations. Disengagement and poor progress towards recovery were associated with a sense of being defined by and contained within the role of 'patient', and in a relationship that focused upon institutional expectations (commonly pressure to accept medication against their wishes), rather than one which accommodated them as an autonomous person.

This focus upon the value of respecting the client's position and perspective was taken up in the form of a multi-centre clinical trial which assessed the effects of a structured approach to identifying and responding to clients' orientations (Priebe et al. 2007). It was a computer mediated procedure designed to draw practitioners' attention to clients' satisfaction with eight aspects of their everyday life; mental health, physical health, accommodation, job situation, leisure activities, friendships, safety, and relationships with family or partner, and three aspects of their treatment; practical help, psychological help and medication. Each item was rated on a scale of 1–7, from 'couldn't be worse' to 'couldn't be better', and was followed by a question exploring whether or not the client wanted any additional or different help in that domain. If the answer to this was 'yes', the nature of requested support was recorded. This procedure was applied every 2 months in the course of routine case review meetings. Clearly it was designed as an algorithm that would reliably introduce clients' needs and concerns into routine case reviews, and offer a structured way of auditing progress towards that. 134 clinicians representing 507 clients from across sites in Spain, The Netherlands, Sweden, Germany, Switzerland and the UK were recruited and randomly allocated to an intervention group that was to use the algorithm (sixty-four clinicians; 256 clients) and a treatment as usual group (seventy clinicians; 235 clients). All clients had received a 'diagnosis' of Schizophrenia, Delusional Disorder or Other non-organic psychotic disorder. In other words, all had either past or ongoing troublesome experiences of psychosis. After twelve months 451 (89%) clients were available for a follow up assessment which involved quantitative measures of their subjective quality of life (the Manchester Short Assessment of Quality of Life Schedule), unmet needs for care (the Camberwell Assessment of Need Short Appraisal

Schedule), satisfaction with treatment (the Client Satisfaction Questionnaire) and the intensity of psychotic experiences (the 30-item Positive and Negative Syndrome Scale). Clients whose treatment had included use of the structured algorithm reported significantly higher quality of life scores, fewer unmet needs and higher rates of satisfaction with treatment. There was no difference in the experiences of psychosis between the groups. It would seem that introducing a structured way of drawing attention to clients' perspectives improves outcomes.

Similar findings emerged from a related study which explored differences between clients' and clinicians' ratings of clients' needs (Junghan et al. 2007). Client-rated unmet need was associated with poorer client and clinician ratings of the therapeutic relationship. Clinician-rated unmet need was associated with better client ratings of the relationship. As client-rated unmet need fell across time, client but not clinician ratings of the relationship improved. In other words, unsurprisingly, the perceived quality of relationship was related to the extent to which clients felt that their needs were being addressed. Bjørngaard and colleagues (2007) considered data from 969 patients being provided for by forty mental health teams in Norway. Here, client satisfaction with the therapeutic relationship was assessed using a six-item scale that considered; the time available for contact or dialogue, clinicians' ability to listen and understand, continuity in the form of following up planned interventions, respect for clients' views and opinions, cooperation among clinicians, and readiness to incorporate clients' views into treatment decisions. Treatment outcome and well-being were quantified using the Health of the Nation Outcome Scales (HoNOS) and Global Assessment of Functioning (GAF) scales. Once again, client satisfaction with the therapeutic relationship was associated with better treatment outcomes and better overall well-being.

Considerations of 'recovery'

For many, evaluations of mental health services and/or therapy that focus upon clinical ratings of psychotic symptoms or 'levels of function' are unsatisfactory because they are rarely derived from, or reflect, service users' perspectives of what really matters or makes a meaningful difference. In recent decades the notion of 'recovery' has developed as a more meaningful way of understanding relief from psychosis and other forms of 'mental illness', and of reflecting improved ability and well-being. Following Deegan (1988), Slade and colleagues (2012) established the parameters of a state of affairs characterised by experiences of connectedness, hope, a positive sense of identity, meaningfulness and empowerment. Notionally this offers a summary of relevant clients' experiences that might define them as more or less 'recovered' from a period of mental health difficulties.

Bjornestad and colleagues (2018) provide an example of how, from this perspective, psychological therapy can contribute to 'recovery'. The explicit objective of their study was to explore what fully recovered service users found to have been the most appreciated ingredients of psychological interventions provided during the recovery process, following a first troubling experience of psychosis. The investigation was conducted within the context of following up individuals who had experienced a distressing first episode of psychosis in southern Norway (Helgestad et al. 2012). A qualitative approach was adopted. Ten male and ten female subjects were recruited for interview from among some 400 who had been followed up after a first experience of psychosis which had occurred between 1997 and 2014. At the time of the interview all twenty were living independently and were in full time employment or education. In other words, by these criteria, they could be considered to have 'recovered'. 'Diagnoses' at the time of first contact included; Affective Disorder with mood incongruent delusions, Psychosis not otherwise specified, Delusional Disorder, Schizoaffective Disorder and Brief Psychotic Disorder. They were relatively young (mean age 25.8 years) and had experienced a relatively short period of untreated psychosis (mean duration 26.5 weeks). Initially all had been advised to use antipsychotic medication, though seven did not follow this advice. All received psychological therapy from a range of traditions (mainly CBTp) with psychologists, psychiatrists, psychiatric nurses or social workers. On average, subjects participated in 76.3 forty-five-minute sessions over a period of 2.74 years, though these durations varied quite widely.

In order to explore subjectively useful therapeutic components of their treatment, the interviews followed a semi-structured format enquiring into person-specific factors, environmental factors and treatment-related factors. Each of these was introduced with an open-ended question, for example, 'How would you describe the treatment you have received, from the day you got into difficulties until today?' which was then followed up with further probes. Participants were encouraged to relate their experiences of different contexts, asking questions such as, 'Can you please elaborate on how the psychological therapy helped you in the acute phase?' or 'Can you tell me a bit more about if and how therapy helped you in your social life?'. The interview schedule was co-designed and honed with input from service user researchers. Most interviews were conducted in an institutional setting, and their durations ranged from thirty-seven to seventy-six minutes.

Three of the investigating team independently conducted a thematic analysis of interview transcripts, and then compared their interpretations to arrive at a consensus. There were few radical disagreements. The analysis resulted in five interrelated themes.

Help with the basics

During the acute phase of their distress, participants appreciated acknowledgement of their difficulties and vulnerability. It was essential for them to feel that their therapist had a warm and respectful style, and that he or she had specific suggestions and advice about how to handle specific issues such as others' expectations. Presenting such suggestions in direct and everyday language, and in relation to practical matters such as a daily routine were particularly helpful. Acknowledgement of their clients' difficulties and communication of the ability to contain and address them inculcated a sense of being understood, of safety and of hope. This played an important part in engaging, and an appetite for further sessions. Subjects also appreciated being offered effective strategies for dealing with distressing voices that involved an acknowledgement of their reality, to whom they were attributed, and what did or did not alleviate them. This component introduced a sense of mastery and control over otherwise distressing and disturbing experiences.

Having a companion when moving through chaotic turf

All participants emphasised that liking their therapist on a personal level, was central to the success of therapy in helping them towards recovery. They recognised and valued it when the therapist showed unconditional acceptance and genuine closeness. This built trust, made it easier to address what was difficult and contributed to the development of a relationship within which the therapist was seen as a companion: a person in whom they could trust and confide their deepest secrets, including potentially shameful psychotic and traumatic experiences. Participants also valued the part therapists could play in maintaining continuity of their life story and identity through episodes of on-going psychosis, and thus provide an antidote to associated periods of mental chaos and disorganisation.

Creating a common language

Many participants reflected upon the isolation associated with psychotic experiences and the value of opportunities to share them in a non-judgemental way. Several described this as a language-creating process whereby frightening thoughts, experiences and emotions could be named and described in ways that made them more acceptable, and therefore less distressing. 'Delusional' thinking could be addressed and understood in a context that did not engender defensiveness, and therefore allowed gentle and constructive challenges.

Putting psychotic experiences in brackets, and cultivating all that is healthy

This referred to the application of firm but considered pressure which reinforced progress and adaptive behaviours. A prerequisite was the development of a strong alliance based upon an acknowledgment of difficulties, but within which expectations of change could be made. This was described as a balancing act wherein the therapist would know when to push; to encourage, for instance, social contact; when to hold, and when to step back.

Building a bridge from psychotic experiences to the outside world

For most participants, experiencing psychosis was incompatible with regarding themselves a full citizen, and along with this came a sense of hopelessness and passivity. Recovery involved breaking out from this and no longer feeling themselves excluded from the community. Here, the therapist was felt to be a source of support and advice, but also someone with professional expertise who was in the background, and available to be consulted when needed. Again, participants appreciated their therapist applying sensitive pressure in order to maintain progress, and thereby taking an active role in finding the right challenges and areas to focus on.

Perhaps three things emerge from this description of individuals' experiences of psychological therapy in the course of 'recovery' from experiences of psychosis. What is appreciated and appears to contribute to success is the acknowledgement of difficulties and distress early in the engagement. This enables the development of a relationship in which mutual respect, personal closeness, and an experience of being unconditionally supported are key features. Once established, that relationship then forms a crucible within which the therapist can exert carefully considered pressure to change social practices, re-appraise or contextualise disturbing interpretations or better manage disturbing psychotic experiences. It appears to be the establishment of that relationship that lies at the heart of successful therapy. Kathleen Anthony had come to similar conclusions in a similar way (Anthony 2008). She interviewed ten subjects with a view to establishing how helping partnerships with others had enabled people with 'serious mental illness' to arrive at a 'recovered' state. Subjects from a range of ages, degrees of recovery, educational background and 'diagnosis' were engaged with. This was through interview and supported by artefacts such as artwork, poetry, prose and photographs which were considered to have made a significant contribution to the process of 'recovery'. Background questions driving the investigation were: 'What are people's experiences of "recovery" from "serious mental illness"?', 'How do people describe the experience of helping partnerships that facilitate "recovery"?', 'What are the underlying themes and contexts that account for the experience of partnerships that facilitate "recovery"?' and 'Where in the "recovery" process do these partnerships form?'. Five characteristics of successfully helpful partnerships were identified; caring and respectful communication, resourcefulness, patience and an orientation towards recovery, knowledgeable teacher and interdependence. Underpinning these were experiences of relational authenticity, and of the knowledge and authority to assist with institutional barriers and make

176

connections with others. This was identified as a particularly important feature of such partnerships. All participants needed financial, medical, housing, social and vocational rehabilitation links to establish stability in their lives, which appropriately authorised and empowered professionals were able to provide. The role of helping partners in supporting patience and persistence in the face of setbacks was also emphasised. Seven participants developed intense helping partnerships with peers/friends, or groups of peers, which for some were the most important feature of their 'recovery' journey. There was evidence from some of a redemptive dimension in helping others in a comparable situation, and this contributed to the development of supportive and helping social networks through and within which there could be steady growth in 'normalisation'.

A similar finding arose from a critical interpretive synthesis of findings from thirteen reports considering the therapeutic relationship between individuals experiencing psychosis and their clinicians in community case management settings that were identified by Farrelly and Lester (2014). One of the additional findings from this synthesis was that in such settings, helpful relationships between clients and professionals engendering mutual trust, respect and shared decision making were difficult to achieve. The main barrier appeared to be a lack of clarity concerning the purpose of their interactions. The institutional setting is one in which service users and professionals often have differing priorities; service users might be seeking a supportive relationship but institutional pressures are often such that community case managers and other community mental health care staff feel obliged to prioritise interactions that protect service users and themselves in the event of a relapse. A reason for this is that the part played by the development of a trusting, respectful and balanced relationship in supporting stability and recovery has not been considered anything more than a facilitating background to mental health service provision. In fact, there is considerable evidence to argue that it is much more than that, and that it could be regarded as it's central feature.

Relationship *as* therapy

As already noted, Rosenzweig adopted Lewis Carroll's fictional Dodo Bird's 'Everybody has won, and all must have prizes' in 1936. He raised the possibility that the outcome of psychological therapy might reflect influences common to all forms of therapy rather than effects directly attributable to the particular technique or theoretical position taken by the therapist in question. This has come to be recognised as the most appropriate way of understanding similarities and differences between psychotherapies when considered as such, rather than as mental health service provision in general. A series of reviews and meta-analyses of outcome data over the last half century all broadly agree. The first was published in the 1970s (Luborsky et al. 1975), and others have followed (Wampold et al. 1997; Stiles et al. 2008;

Budd and Hughes 2009). Unsurprisingly there have been criticisms of this conclusion, for instance Klein 2002, and Clark et al. 2008, but the 'Dodo Bird Verdict' has an established place in the language of psychotherapy research and its implications are profound. Broad analyses of currently available data conclude that there is no detectable difference in efficacy between differing psychotherapeutic approaches, and that what does appear to influence outcome is the operation of several so-called common factors. These have been variously articulated, most famously by Jerome D. Frank, namely; an intense, emotionally charged, confiding relationship with a help-ing person, often with the participation of a group, a rationale, or myth, which includes an explanation of the cause of the person's distress and a method for relieving it, provision of new information concerning the nature and sources of the person's problems and possible alternative ways of dealing with them, strengthening the patient's expectations of help through the per-sonal qualities of the therapist enhanced by their status in society and the setting in which they work, and provision of success experiences which fur-ther heighten the person's hopes and enhance their sense of mastery, inter-personal competence or capability (Frank 1971). It is not difficult to see how any form of helping relationship, particularly but not necessarily one arising in a 'clinical' context might embody some or all of these qualities. They resonate well with what has been variously described in clinical contexts as a good quality therapeutic relationship, working alliance, helping alliance or therapeutic alliance. Ways in which 'ordinary' helping relationships might incorporate them are reflected in expressions such as: 'A shoulder to cry on', 'Reliable and trustworthy', 'They know what they are talking about', 'Helped to put things in perspective', 'Challenging', 'Insightful' and so on.

It seems irrefutable that troublesome experiences of psychosis can be alle-viated by psychological means, and the research data suggest that a major if not central contributor to such processes is the development of a helping relationship, in which mutual respect, personal closeness, and an experience of being unconditionally supported are key features. If we move from think-ing of these 'non-specific' factors as merely the background to well con-ducted therapeutic interventions, to thinking of them as core features of what really helps alleviate distress and enables 'recovery', then the part played in causing them to be at the heart of what should happen when assisting people with the experience of psychosis can become clearer. The research evidence points towards the need to recognise that entering into relationship with the client and *their* relationships is the core feature of any attempt to alleviate the effects of psychotic experiences, if not a wider range of mental health difficulties. In symbolic interactionist terms, a successful therapeutic relationship can become a human interaction, with profound and helpful effects upon how psychotic experiences might be understood, and what their implications might be.

Open Dialogue

That is precisely what Open Dialogue sets out to achieve. This is not the place to go into the approach in much detail. Open Dialogue is currently offering considerable promise as a way of providing for people who are experiencing psychosis and, indeed, a wider range of mental health difficulties. As a result, it is generating a growing literature, perhaps the most definitive to date being Putman and Martindale's (2022) edited collection.

In brief, Open Dialogue originated in Western Lapland in the 1980s, and it has two distinctive features. The first is that it offers care at the social network level by staff trained in family, systems and related approaches. In this respect it accommodates research findings already noted. From the 1970s onwards it has become clear that the emotional tenor of family life (Expressed Emotion) influences the risk of recurring psychotic experiences onwards, and it has become clear that approaches which acknowledge and address the part families and other intimate social networks play in generating such effects are effective interventions. As a result, family interventions have been an evidence-based contribution to the 'treatment' of people experiencing psychosis for many years. The second is that Open Dialogue recognises the central importance of relationship in all forms of psychotherapeutic endeavour, again something thoroughly endorsed by the evidence.

Open Dialogue, therefore, has two fundamental characteristics. It is a community-based, integrated treatment system that engages families and social networks from the very beginning of their seeking help, and it employs a distinct form of therapeutic conversation within the treatment meeting. The treatment meeting constitutes the key therapeutic context of Open Dialogue. It is an encounter that brings together contributing professionals, the identified 'patient', and their relational network into a collaborative enterprise. The distinctive form of therapeutic conversation is one that encourages authentic dialogue. 'Professionals' resist exercising authority, except where it might be directly productive, as in the course of arranging housing, financial, or other forms of practical support. Uncertainties are embraced, and rather than framing the occurrence of psychotic experiences as 'another case of ...', it is framed as a unique set of circumstances requiring bespoke solutions that the network as a whole has to generate. Thus, all concerned work together on an even footing, and in so doing generate, shape and refresh relationships.

Open Dialogue is currently generating very promising results. In non-randomised trials conducted in Finland, more than 70% of people treated with an Open Dialogue approach following a first experience of psychosis returned to study, work or work-seeking within two years, despite lower rates of medication and hospital admission compared with treatment as usual. Longer term follow-up studies suggest these to be enduring effects (Seikkula et al. 2006, 2011; Bergstrom et al. 2018). Formal evaluation is now underway elsewhere. If this promise from Finland is replicated, then it will provide powerful evidence in support of a relational or interactional approach to the experience of psychosis. Troublesome experiences of psychosis can be ameliorated, and their effects mitigated by recognising the part human interactions play in intensifying and maintaining them, and that such interactions can be influenced, mended, healed or improved by practitioners modelling alternative and non-judgemental interpretations of what is happening.

Stigma and 'recovery'

'Getting better' after the experience of 'mental illness' is as much a matter of acquiring a sense of comfortable association with others and related self-worth, as it is the business of overcoming identifiable symptoms. There is a considerable and growing academic literature that attempts to define full recovery, but most agree that it centres upon developing resilience, a commendable identity and associated self-esteem, and with them the ability to set and achieve new goals and take part in healthy relationships and meaningful activities. This has become the explicit aim of many statutory mental health services, informal organisations and research endeavour.

There is related evidence that the journey to recovery centres upon overcoming the consequences of others' stigmatising and frequently authoritarian and paternalizing attitudes and behaviours. In the context of 'recovery communities' in Washington DC, participants did not report stigma and discrimination as commonly experienced problems, instead they reported stigma and discrimination as omnipresent *potential* problems against which they were continuously vigilant, and against which they took preventive measures such as paying direct attention to their dress, appearance, conduct and demeanour (Whitley and Campbell 2014). Participants expressed awareness of a hostile external environment and a need to consciously present in ways that would mitigate that hostility. These are characteristics of an oppressed minority and although good relationships, satisfying work, personal growth and an acceptable living environment are all uncontroversial aims, achieving them is less than straightforward.

A central feature of such endeavours has to be the part played by those with relevant experiences to share. Llewellyn-Beardsley and colleagues (2019) were able to identify forty-five studies which together report upon 629 recovery narratives, or stories, and synthesise them. Altogether these stories paint a rich picture of varying experiences, strategies and outcomes. They speak of 'escape', 'enlightenment', 'endeavour' and 'endurance'. Outcomes range from 'recovered' through 'living well' and 'making progress' to 'surviving from day to day', and of challenges at personal, socio-political and systemic levels. Rather than an identifiable path, 'recovery', in these terms, emerges as a highly personal process incorporating shifting perspectives, changing relationships and varying forms of negotiation with a commonly adverse social context (Hui et al. 2021). A challenge for the future is going to be the need to balance interest in enabling 'recovery' with these historical adversities. The concept of recovery emerged from the so-called survivor movement, which has focused upon the strengthening and emancipation of individuals traumatized by their experience of mental health services and other manifestations of stigma and discrimination. Much of this has been achieved by the sharing of such stories, individually and collectively. Making this part of an institutionalised endeavour risks authenticity. Although 'recovery' has been taken up as a guiding principle in mental health systems internationally, the implementation of 'recovery' as an explicit feature of formal mental health services has been criticized; that it is a professional co-optation which occludes issues of social justice, that it commodifies experiences in systems that sustain subjugation, and that it is a cover for neoliberalism (Recovery in the Bin 2015; Perkins and Repper 2017; McCabe et al. 2018). These have to be acknowledged as genuine reservations, especially as they come from those who have experienced the social exclusion generated by stigma and discrimination, themselves a reflection of not only antiquated notions of what 'mental illness' is, but also a consequence of contemporary social structures such as those constructed around the sick role.

When viewed through the eyes of those subjected to the discrimination that accompanies a 'diagnosis' of psychotic illness, it is not difficult to see how social structures and the discourses they embody result in interactions that are highly toxic and rarely justified. It is revealing that the most helpful interventions appear to be those which achieve a dismantling of this stigmatised identity, rather than those which continue to pursue it under the guise of 'treating an illness', whether that be by medical or psychotherapeutic means.

References

Anthony, K. H. (2008) 'Helping Partnerships that Facilitate Recovery from Severe Mental Illness', *Journal of Psychosocial Nursing*, Vol. 46, No. 7, pp. 24–33.

Bergström, T., Seikkula, J., Alakare, B., Maki, P., Kdnˈas-Saviaro, P., Taskila, J.T., Tolvanen, A. and Aaltonen, J. (2018) 'The family-oriented open dialogue approach in the treatment of first-episode psychosis: Nineteen-year outcomes', *Psychiatry Research*, Vol. 270, pp. 18–175.

Bird, V., Premkumar, P., Kendall, T., Whittington, C., Mitchell, J. and Kuipers, E. (2010) 'Early intervention services, cognitive–behavioural therapy and family intervention in early psychosis: systematic review', *The British Journal of Psychiatry*, Vol. 197, pp. 350–356.

Bjørngaard, J. H., Ruud, T. and Friis, S. (2007) 'The impact of mental illness on patient satisfaction with the therapeutic relationship: A multilevel analysis', *Social Psychiatry and Psychiatric Epidemiology*, Vol. 42, pp. 803–809.

Bjornestad, J., Veseth, M., Davidson, L., Joa, I., Johannessen, J. O., Larsen, T. K., Melle, I. and Hegelstad, W. T. V. (2018) 'Psychotherapy in Psychosis: Experiences of Fully Recovered Service Users', *Frontiers in Psychology*, Vol. 9. doi:10.3389/fpsyg.2018.01675..

Budd, R. and Hughes, I. (2009) 'The Dodo Bird Verdict – Controversial, Inevitable and Important: A Commentary on 30 Years of Meta-Analyses', *Clinical Psychology and Psychotherapy*, Vol. 16, pp. 510–522.

Burns, A. M. N., Erickson, D. H. and Brenner, C. A. (2014) 'Cognitive-Behavioral Therapy for Medication-Resistant Psychosis: A Meta-Analytic Review', *Psychiatric Services*, Vol. 65, No. 7, pp. 874–880.

Butzlaff, R. L. and Hooley, J. M. (1998) 'Expressed Emotion and Psychiatric Relapse: A Meta-analysis', *Archives of General Psychiatry*, Vol. 55, pp. 547–552.

Clark, D. M., Fairburn, C. G. and Wessely, S. (2008) 'Psychological treatment outcomes in routine NHS services: a commentary on Stiles *et al.* (2007) ', *Psychological Medicine*, Vol. 38, pp. 629–634.

Deegan, P. E. (1988) 'Recovery: The lived experience of rehabilitation', *Psychosocial Rehabilitation Journal*, Vol. 11, No. 4, pp. 11–19.

Eichner, C. and Berna, F. (2016) 'Acceptance and Efficacy of Metacognitive Training (MCT) on Positive Symptoms and Delusions in Patients With Schizophrenia: A Meta-analysis Taking Into Account Important Moderators', *Schizophrenia Bulletin*, Vol. 42, No. 4, pp. 952–962.

Farrelly, S. and Lester, H. (2014) 'Therapeutic relationships between mental health service users with psychotic disorders and their clinicians: a critical interpretive synthesis', *Health and Social Care in the Community*, Vol. 22, No. 5, pp. 449–460.

Frank, A. F. and Gunderson, J. G. (1990) 'The Role of the Therapeutic Alliance in the Treatment of Schizophrenia: Relationship to Course and Outcome', *Archives of General Psychiatry*, Vol. 47, No. 3, pp. 228–236.

Frank, J. (1971) 'Therapeutic factors in psychotherapy: Eleventh Emil A Guthell Memorial Lecture of the Association for the Advancement of Psychotherapy, New York City, November 1 1970', *American Journal of Psychotherapy*, Vol. 25, pp. 350–361.

Goldsmith, L. P., Lewis, S. W., Dunn, G. and Bentall, R. P. (2015) 'Psychological treatments for early psychosis can be beneficial or harmful, depending on the therapeutic alliance: an instrumental variable analysis', *Psychological Medicine*. doi:10.1017/S003329171500032X.

Hegelstad, W. T. V., Larsen, T. K., Auestad, B., Evensen, J., Haahr, U., Joa, I., Johannesen, J. O., Langeveld, J., Melle, I., Opjordsmoen, S., Rossberg, J. I. and Rund, B. R. (2012) 'Long-Term Follow-Up of the TIPS Early Detection in Psychosis Study: Effects on 10-Year Outcome', *American Journal of Psychiatry*, Vol. 169, No. 4, pp. 374–380.

Howgego, I. M., Yellowlees, P., Owen, C., Meldrum, L. and Dark, F. (2003) 'The Therapeutic Alliance: The Key to Effective Patient Outcome? A Descriptive Review of the Evidence in Community Mental Health Case Management', *Australian & New Zealand Journal of Psychiatry*, Vol. 37, No. 2, pp. 169–183.

Hui, A., Rennick-Egglestone, S., Franklin, D., Walcott, R., Llewellyn-Beardsley, J., Ng, F., Roe, J., Yeo, C., Deakin, E., Brydges, S., Moran, P. P., McGranahan, R., Pollock, K., Thornicorft, G. and Slade, M. (2021) 'Institutional injustice: Implications for system transformation emerging from the mental health recovery narratives of people experiencing marginalisation', *PLoS ONE*, Vol. 16, No. 4. doi:10.1371/journal.pone.0250367.

Junghan, U. M., Leese, M., Priebe, S. and Slade, M. (2007) 'Staff and patient perspectives on unmet need and therapeutic alliance in community mental and therapeutic alliance in community mental health services', *British Journal of Psychiatry*, Vol. 191, pp. 543–547.

Kendler, K. S. and Schaffner, K. F. (2011) 'The Dopamine Hypothesis of Schizophrenia: An Historical and Philosophical Analysis', *Philosophy, Psychiatry, & Psychology*, Vol. 18, No. 1, pp. 41–63.

Klein, D. F. (2002) 'Dodo Deliberations', *American Psychological Association*, Vol. D12, pp. 28–29.

Llewellyn-Beardsley, J., Rennick-Egglestone, S., Callard, F., Crawford, P., Farkas, M., Hui, A., Manley, D., McGranahan, R., Pollock, K., Ramsay, A., Sælør, K. T., Wright, N. and Slade, M. (2019) 'Characteristics of mental health recovery narratives: Systematic review and narrative synthesis', *PLoS ONE*, Vol. 14, No. 3. doi:10.1371/journal.pone.0214678.

Luborsky, L., Singer, B. and Luborsky, L. (1975) 'Comparative studies of psychotherapies: Is it true that "everyone has won and all must have prizes"?', *Archives of General Psychiatry*, Vol. 32, pp. 995–1008.

Marmar, C. R., Weiss, D. S. and Gaston, L. (1989) 'Toward the Validation of the California Therapeutic Alliance Rating System', *Journal of Consulting and Clinical Psychology*, Vol. 1, No. 1, pp. 46–52.

McCabe, R. and Priebe, S. (2004) 'The Therapeutic Relationship in the Treatment of Severe Mental Illness: A Review of Methods and Findings', *International Journal of Social Psychiatry*, Vol. 50, No. 2, pp. 115–128.

McCabe, R., Whittington, R., Cramond, L. and Perkins, E. (2018) 'Contested understandings of recovery in mental health', *Journal of Mental Health*, Vol. 27, No. 5, pp. 475–481.

Middleton, H. (2015) *Psychiatry Reconsidered. From Medical Treatment to Supportive Understanding*. Basingstoke: Palgrave Macmillan, pp. 93–126.

Moritz, S., Vitzthum, F., Randjbar, S., Veckenstedt, R. and Woodward, T. (2010) 'Detecting and defusing cognitive traps: metacognitive intervention in schizophrenia', *Current Opinion in Psychiatry*, Vol. 23, pp. 561–569.

Morrison, A. P., Turkington, D., Pyle, M., Spencer, H., Brabban, A., Dunn, G., Christodoulides, T., Dudley, R., Chapman, N., Callcott, P., Grace, T., Lumley, V., Drage, L., Tully, S., Irving, K., Cummings, A., Byrne, R., Davies, L. M. and Hutton, P. (2014) 'Cognitive therapy for people with schizophrenia spectrum disorders not taking antipsychotic drugs: a single-blind randomised controlled trial', *Lancet*, Vol. 383, pp. 1395–1403.

National Institute for Clinical and Healthcare Excellence (2014) *Psychosis and schizophrenia in adults: prevention and management: Clinical guideline*. London: NICE.

Ochoa, S., López-Carrilero, R., Barrigón, M. L., Pousa, E., Barajas, A., Lorente-Rovira, E., González-Higueras, F., Grasa, E., Ruiz-Delgado, I., Cid, J., Birulés, I., Esteban-Pinos, I., Casañas, R., Luengo, A., Torres-Hernández, P., Corripio, I., Montes-Gámez, M., Beltran, M., De Apraiz, A., Domínguez-Sánchez, L., Sánchez, E., Llacer, B., Pélaez, T., Bogas, J. L., Moritz, S. and the Spanish Metacognition Study Group (2017) 'Randomized control trial to assess the efficacy of metacognitive training compared with a psychoeducational group in people with a recent-onset psychosis', *Psychological Medicine*, Vol. 47, pp. 1573–1584.

Perkins, R. and Repper, J. (2017) 'When is a "recovery college" not a "recovery college"?', *Mental Health and Social Inclusion*, Vol. 21, No. 2, pp. 65–72.

Pfammatter, M., Junghan, U. M. and Brenner, H. D. (2006) 'Efficacy of Psychological Therapy in Schizophrenia: Conclusions From Meta-analyses', *Schizophrenia Bulletin*, Vol. 32, No. S1, pp. s64–s80.

Pilling, S., Bebbington, P., Kuipers, E., Garety, P., Geddes, J., Orbach, G. and Morgan, C. (2002a) 'Psychological treatments in schizophrenia: I. Meta-analysis of family intervention and cognitive behaviour therapy', *Psychological Medicine*, Vol. 32, pp. 763–782.

Pilling, S., Bebbington, P., Kuipers, E., Garety, P., Geddes, J., Martindale, B., Orbach, G. and Morgan, C. (2002b) 'Psychological treatments in schizophrenia: II. Meta-analyses of randomized controlled trials of social skills training and cognitive remediation', *Psychological Medicine*, Vol. 32, pp. 783–791.

Priebe, S., McCabe, R., Bullenkamp, J., Hansson, L., Lauber, C., Martinez-Leal, R., Rösseler, W., Salize, H., Svensson, B., Torres-Gonzales, F., van Den Brink, R., Wiersma, D. and Wright, D. J. (2007) 'Structured patient-clinician communication and 1-year outcome in community mental healthcare: Cluster randomised controlled trial', *British Journal of Psychiatry*, Vol. 191, pp. 420–426.

Priebe, S., Watts, J., Chase, M. and Matanov, A. (2005) 'Processes of disengagement and engagement Processes of disengagement and engagement in assertive outreach patients: qualitative study', *British Journal of Psychiatry*, Vol. 187, pp. 438–443.

Putman, N. and Martindale, B. (2022) *Open Dialogue for Psychosis. Organising Mental Health Services to Prioritise Dialogue, Relationship and Meaning*. Abingdon: Routledge.

Recovery in the Bin (2015) 'Recovery in the Bin: Key principles agreed and adopted by group members', *Asylum Magazine*, Vol. 2, pp. 21–22.

Rosenzweig, S. (1936) 'Some implicit common factors in diverse methods of psychotherapy', *American Journal of Orthopsychiatry*, Vol. 6, pp. 412–415.

Sarin, F., Wallin, L. and Widerlöv, B. (2011) 'Cognitive behavior therapy for schizophrenia: A meta-analytical review of randomized controlled trials', *Nordic Journal of Psychiatry*, Vol. 65, No. 3, pp. 162–174.

Seikkula, J., Aaltonen, J., Alakare, B., Haarakangas, K., Keränen, J. and Lehtinen, K. (2006) 'Five-year experience of first-episode nonaffective psychosis in open-dialogue approach: Treatment principles, follow-up outcomes, and two case studies', *Psychotherapy Research*, Vol. 16, No. 2, pp. 214–228.

Seikkula, J., Alakare, B. and Aaltonen, J. (2011) 'The Comprehensive Open-Dialogue Approach in Western Lapland: II. Long-term stability of acute psychosis outcomes in advanced community care', *Psychosis*, Vol. 3, No. 3, pp. 192–204.

Slade, M., Leamy, M., Bacon, F., Janosik, M., Le Boutillier, C., Williams, J. and Bird, V. (2012) 'International differences in understanding recovery: systematic review', *Epidemiology and Psychiatric Sciences*, Vol. 21, pp. 353–364.

Stiles, W. B., Barkham, M., Mellor-Clark, J. and Connell, J. (2008) 'Effectiveness of cognitive-behavioural, person-centred, and psychodynamic therapies in UK primary-care routine practice: replication in a larger sample', *Psychological Medicine*, Vol. 38, pp. 677–688.

Tarrier, N., Lewis, S., Haddock, G., Bentall, R., Drake, R., Kinderman, P., Kingdon, D., Siddle, R., Everitt, J., Leadley, K., Benn, A., Grazebrook, K., Haley, C., Akhtar, S., Davies, L., Palmer, S. and Dunn, G. (2004) 'Cognitive-behavioural therapy in first-episode and early schizophrenia', *British Journal of Psychiatry*, Vol. 184, pp. 231–239.

Tarrier, N. and Wykes, T. (2004) 'Is there evidence that cognitive behaviour therapy is an effective treatment for schizophrenia? A cautious or cautionary tale? ', *Behaviour Research and Therapy*, Vol. 42, pp. 1377–1401.

Turner, A. (2012) '"Placebos" and the logic of placebo comparison', *Biology & Philosophy*, Vol. 27, pp. 419–432.

Wampold, B. E., Mondin, G. W., Moody, M., Stich, F., Benson, K. and Hyun-nie, A. (1997) 'A Meta-analysis of Outcome Studies Comparing Bona Fide Psychotherapies: Empirically, "All Must Have Prizes"', *Psychological Bulletin*, Vol. 112, pp. 203–215.

Whitley, R. and Campbell, R. D. (2014) 'Stigma, agency and recovery amongst people with severe mental illness', *Social Science & Medicine*, Vol. 107, pp. 1–8.

Wykes, T., Steel, C., Everitt, B. and Tarrier, N. (2008) 'Cognitive Behavior Therapy for Schizophrenia: Effect Sizes, Clinical Models, and Methodological Rigor', *Schizophrenia Bulletin*, Vol. 34, No. 3, pp. 523–537.

Zimmermann, G., Favrod, J., Trieu, V. H. and Pomini, V. (2005) 'The effect of cognitive behavioral treatment on the positive symptoms of schizophrenia spectrum disorders: A meta-analysis', *Schizophrenia Research*, Vol. 77, pp. 1–9.

INDEX

Indexer: Dr Laurence Errington